W9-AZI-538

Radford's
Artistic Bungalows

The Complete 1908 Catalog

Radford Architectural Company

DOVER PUBLICATIONS, INC.
Mineola, New York

Published in Canada by General Publishing Company, Ltd., 30 Lesmill Road, Don Mills, Toronto, Ontario.
Published in the United Kingdom by Constable and Company, Ltd., 3 The Lanchesters, 162–164 Fulham Palace Road, London W6 9ER.

Bibliographical Note

This Dover edition, first published in 1997, is an unabridged republication of the work originally published by The Radford Architectural Company, Chicago, in 1908.

Library of Congress Cataloging-in-Publication Data

Radford's artistic bungalows : the complete 1908 catalog / Radford Architectural Company.
p. cm.
Originally published: Chicago, Ill : Radford Architectural Company, 1908.
Includes index.
ISBN 0-486-29678-4 (pbk.)
1. Bungalows—Designs and plans—Catalogs. 2. Radford Architectural Company—Catalogs. I. Radford Architectural Company.
NA7571.R34 1997
728'.373'0973—dc21 96-53259
CIP

Manufactured in the United States of America
Dover Publications, Inc., 31 East 2nd Street, Mineola, N.Y. 11501

Radford's Artistic Bungalows

The bungalow age is here. It is the renewal in artistic form of the primitive "love in a cottage" sentiment that lives in some degree in every human heart. Architecturally, it is the result of the effort to bring about harmony between the house and its surroundings, to get as close as possible to nature.

So we see the bungalow nestling in the woods, inviting with its hospitality on the plains and roosting serenely on the crags by the sea. In every case its appearance bespeaks a blithesome geniality and an informal hospitality. There is nothing formal about it, and this very restfulness of appearance refreshes the city tired dweller who is the slave of conventionalities.

The bungalow is a tangible protest of modern life against the limitations and severities of humdrum existence. It is "homey," and comes near to that ideal you have seen in the dreamy shadows of night when lying restless on your couch you have yearned for a haven of rest. Maybe it has a wide, low, spreading roof, which sweeps down and forms a covering for the porch. It has a large healthy chimney, patios, with fountains, large verandas, good sized living and dining rooms, so arranged possibly that by the use of portable wood screens they may be partitioned off or thrown into one apartment.

And while primarily intended for the wilds, this form or style of home has been seized upon eagerly by home builders in every hamlet of the land, in every town and every city. So that out of this general demand for homes of this character all sections of the country are being beautified with little structures that delight the eye.

The bungalow originated in India where many types of them are seen. Frequently there the structure is built on stilts from eight to twelve feet high, to protect the occupants from wild animals and serpents. In America, however, the bungalow cannot be built too close to the ground, and, indeed, the purpose always should be to make the bungalow a harmonious part of the grounds surrounding it. Wide cemented porches are frequently laid flat on the surface, so that the indoors and outdoors might be said to join hands. Rustic baskets frequently ornament porch walls built of cobble-stones or clinker brick. There really is no limit to the ornamentation of the bungalow that will be in keeping with its character. Fountains may be placed, or even miniature waterfalls, that will add to the effect. In every case the artistic sense of the builder must be expressed in accord with the immediate location. The beauty and restfulness of little sun parlors caress tired nerves and make new men out of old. A riotous, untrimmed garden of ferns may be added to the lawn decorations, or clambering roses, vines and wide-spreading trees.

It is on account of the great attractiveness of the bungalow and the great demand for buildings of that construction by home builders that this volume is offered to the public. In its preparation a vast amount of deep study of the subject, and tireless energy, have been given by the most eminent architects of the country. So that in this volume is condensed the best thought on bungalow construction that it is possible to secure. The home builder will find here every style of bungalow that has proved itself worthy of being classed with that form of construction, so that any taste may be suited.

If the reader intends to build a bungalow he may be assured of a number of facts that commend themselves to him about the houses shown in this book.

Every design shown is intended for the man of moderate means.

Most of them can be built at an outlay no greater than that for a severe, old-style unornamented house.

There are designs for small families and others for large ones.

Each design is original.

If any person is intending to build a home and is limited in his means, he cannot do better than to build a bungalow. It matters not whether it be in the city or in the country, for a bungalow built after any design in this book will be an ornament anywhere.

Remember this: It is always possible and easy to sell a bungalow when the plain house of the same cost would find no sale. This is the most important factor, financially, concerning the subject of home building. Too often home builders construct houses that lack style, and when a rainy day comes and they want to sell the house, there is no buyer, because the house is "like thousands of others."

The reason why a house will not sell in nine cases out of ten is because it has no individuality.

A bungalow has individuality. It has that something that makes passersby turn after they have passed the house and say, "How cozy."

It is the "cozy" house that it pays to build.

It is the "cozy" house that your wife wants to live in.

It is the "cozy" house that always sells.

Now, if you have decided to build a bungalow, the next step will be to select the design from this book. In selecting the design consider well the needs of the family, as to room, and also the natural surroundings and lay of the lot you are going to build on. That will have much to do with the design. And in placing the location of the building on the lot, do not build exactly in the center of the lot as so many do, but place the structure at one side or well back, so that the grounds will be ample for trees and shrubbery, making the bungalow and the grounds one harmonious whole.

Having selected your design, the next step is to order your plans. Never build without plans. You probably will not have to go out of your own neighborhood to find unfortunates who have tried to build without plans, thinking they could watch the construction and save the price of the plans. You know how they worried their lives nearly out, how they saw the materials going to waste that were cut up haphazard and by guess, and how there was no style to the house or it was, and is, an eyesore in the neighborhood.

A man who builds a house owes a duty not alone to himself but to the neighborhood as well. He really has no moral right to construct a home that will be a blight on the landscape. The other home owners in the neighborhood have some rights. The kind of house built without plans is the kind that lacks all the style and makeup that help beautify any neighborhood. It is the most expensive house to build, too. There is loss in materials, loss in time—ripping out work that has been incorrectly placed—loss in the time of workmen, and, worst of all, the loss in nervous energy because of sleepless nights due to trying to think out ways to correct mistakes due to the lack of well and correctly drawn plans.

The plans for every bungalow shown in this book were drawn by the best licensed architects, men who have made a life study of home construction, who know the economy of planning buildings that make possible the use of the standard sizes of lumber, who know the artistic requirements of a bungalow, and who in every detail of the plan have had in view the production of the greatest amount of room, solidity of construction and ornamentation with the least outlay. So we repeat—never build without plans.

As a rule the prospective home builder has determined on a fixed amount which he wants to spend on his house. This is wise and business-like. As to the cost of the houses built after the various designs in this book, a minimum and maximum price can be given, but the only way to get accurate figures is to go to your responsible building material dealer, who will give you an accurate estimate. He is the only man who can do so, because he knows the price of all the material in your neighborhood, the cost of freight, and the price of labor. All these factors vary in different parts of the country. For instance, cement may be $1.50 a barrel in one section and $2.25 in another. So that a bungalow which would be built for $1,200 in one section would cost $1,800 in another part of the country. So you can readily see that the local price of materials, freight and labor in your own immediate neighborhood are the determining factors. And the only man who knows all these figures is your responsible dealer. He will gladly give you the estimate, because he is the man who probably will supply you with the materials for your bungalow.

We Illustrate in this Book the perspective view and floor plans of over 250 low and medium-priced houses. In the preparation of this work great care has been exercised in the selection of original, practical and attractive house designs, such as seventy-five to ninety per cent of the people to-day wish to build. In drawing these plans special effort has been made to provide for the MOST ECONOMICAL CONSTRUCTION, thereby giving the home builder and contractor the benefit of the saving of many dollars; for in no case have we put any useless expense upon the building simply to carry out some pet idea. Every plan il lustrated will show, by the complete working plans and specifications, that we give you designs that will work out to the best advantage and will give you the most for your money; besides every bit of space has been utilized to the best advantage.

$100.00 Plans for only $10.00 This department has for its foundation the best equipped architectural establishment ever maintained for the purpose of furnishing the public with complete working plans and specifications at the remarkably low price of only $7.00 to $15.00 per set. Every plan we illustrate has been designed by a licensed architect, who stands at the head of his profession in this particular class of work and has made a specialty of low and medium-priced houses. The price usually charged for this work is from $75.00 to $100.00.

What We Give You The first question you will ask is, "What do we get in these complete working plans and specifications? Of what do they consist? Are they the cheap printed plans on tissue paper without details or specifications?" We do not blame you for wishing to know what you will get for your money.

Blue Printed Working Plans The plans we send out are the regular blue printed plans, drawn one-quarter inch scale to the foot, showing all the elevations, floor plans and necessary interior details. All of our plans are printed by electricity on an electric circular blue-printing machine, and we use the very best grade of electric blue-printing paper; every line and figure showing perfect and distinct.

Foundation and Cellar Plans This sheet shows the shape and size of all the walls, piers, footings, posts, etc., and of what materials they are constructed; shows the location of all windows, doors, chimneys, ash-pits, partitions, and the like. The different wall sections are given, showing their construction and measurements from all the different points.

Floor Plans These plans show the shape and size of all rooms, halls and closets; the location and size of all doors and windows; the position of all plumbing fixtures, gas lights, registers, pantry work, etc., and all the measurements that are necessary are given.

Elevations A front, right, left and rear elevation are furnished with all the plans. These drawings are complete and accurate in every respect. They show the shape, size and location of all doors, windows, porches, cornices, towers, bays, and the like; in fact, give you an exact scale picture of the house as it should be at completion. Full wall sections are given, showing the construction from foundation to roof, the height of stories between the joists, height of plates, pitch of roof, etc.

Roof Plan This plan is furnished where the roof construction is at all intricate. It shows the location of all hips, valleys, ridges, decks, etc. All the above drawings are made to scale one-quarter inch to the foot.

Details All necessary details of the interior work, such as door and window casings and trim, base, stools, picture moulding, doors, newel posts, balusters, rails, etc., accompany each set of plans. Part is shown in full size, while some of the larger work, such as stair construction, is drawn to a scale of one and one-half inch to the foot. These blue-prints are substantially and artistically bound in cloth and heavy water-proof paper, making a handsome and durable covering and protection for the plans.

Specifications The specifications are typewritten on Lakeside Bond Linen paper, and are bound in the same artistic manner as the plans, the same cloth and water-proof paper being used. They consist of twenty-two pages of closely typewritten matter, giving full instructions for carrying out the work. All necessary directions are given in the clearest and most explicit manner, so that there can be no possibility of a misunderstanding.

Basis of Contract The working plans and specifications we furnish can be made the basis of contract between the home builder and the contractor. This will prevent mistakes, which cost money, and they will prevent disputes which are unforeseen and never settled satisfactorily to both parties. When no plans are used the contractor is often obliged to do some work he did not figure on, and the home builder often does not get as much for his money as he expected, simply because there was no basis on which to work and upon which to base the contract.

No Misunderstanding Can Arise when a set of our plans and specifications is before the contractor and the home builder, showing the interior and exterior construction of the house as agreed upon in the contract. Many advantages may be claimed for the complete plans and specifications. They are time savers, and, therefore, money savers. Workmen will not have to wait for instructions when a set of plans is left on the job. They will prevent mistakes in cutting lumber, in placing door and window frames, and in many other places where the contractor is not on the work and the men have received only partial or indefinite instructions. They also give instructions for the working of all material to the best advantage.

Free Plans for Fire Insurance Adjustment You take every precaution to have your house covered by insurance; but do you make any provision for the adjustment of the loss, should you have a fire? There is not one man in ten thousand who will provide for this embarrassing situation. You can call to mind instances in your own locality where settlements have been delayed because the insurance companies wanted some proof which could not be furnished. They demand proof of loss before paying insurance money, and they are entitled to it. We have provided for this and have inaugurated the following plan, which cannot but meet with favor by whoever builds a house from our plans.

Immediately Upon Receipt of Information from you that your house has been destroyed by fire, either totally or partially, we will forward you, free of cost, a duplicate set of plans and specifications, and in addition we will furnish an affidavit giving the number of the design and the date when furnished, to be used for the adjustment of the insurance.

Without One Cent of Cost to You and without one particle of trouble. We keep a record of the number of the house design and the date it was furnished, so that, in time of loss, all it will be necessary for you to do is to drop us a line and we will furnish the only reliable method of getting a speedy and satisfactory adjustment. This may be the means of saving you hundreds of dollars, besides much time and worry.

Our Liberal Prices

Many have marveled at our ability to furnish such excellent and complete working plans and specification at such low prices. We do not wonder at this, because we charge but $7.00 to $15.00 for a more complete set of working plans and specifications than you would receive if ordered in the ordinary manner, and when drawn especially for you, at a cost of from seventy-five to one hundred dollars. On account of our large business and unusual equipment, and owing to the fact that WE DIVIDE THE COST of these plans among so many, it is possible for us to sell them at these low prices. The margin of profit is very close, but it enables us to sell thousands of sets of plans, which save many times their cost to both the owner and the contractor in erecting even the smallest dwelling.

Our Guarantee

Perhaps there are many who feel that they are running some risk in ordering plans at a distance. We wish to assure our customers that there is no risk whatever. If, upon receipt of these plans, you do not find them exactly as represented, if you do not find them complete and accurate in every respect, if you do not find them as well prepared as those furnished by any architect in the country, or any that you have ever seen, we will refund your money upon the return of the plans from you in perfect condition. All of our plans are prepared by architects standing at the head of their profession, and the standard of their work is the very highest. We could not afford to make this guarantee if we were not positive that we were furnishing the best plans put out in this country, even though our price is not more than one-seventh to one-tenth of the price usually charged.

Bill of Material

We do not furnish a bill of material. We state this here particularly, as some people have an idea that a bill of material should accompany each set of plans and specifications. In the first place, our plans are gotten up in a very comprehensive manner, so that any carpenter can easily take off the bill of material without any difficulty. We realize that there are hardly two sections of the country where exactly the same kinds of materials are used, and, moreover, a bill which we might furnish would not be applicable in all sections of the country. We furnish plans and specifications for houses which are built as far north as the Hudson Bay and as far south as the Gulf of Mexico. They are built upon the Atlantic and Pacific Coasts, and you can also find them in Australia and South Africa. Each country and section of a country has its peculiarities as to sizes and qualities; therefore, it would be useless for us to make a list that would not be universal. Our houses, when completed, may look the same whether they are built in Canada or Florida, but the same materials will not be used, for the reason that the customs of the people and the climatic conditions will dictate the kind and amount of materials to be used in their construction.

Estimated Cost

It is impossible for anyone to estimate the cost of a building and have the figures hold good in all sections of the country. We do not claim to be able to do it. The estimated cost of the houses we illustrate is based on the most favorable conditions in all respects, and includes everything but the plumbing and heating. We are not familiar with your local conditions, and, should we claim to know the exact cost of a building in your locality, a child would know that our statement was false. We leave this matter in the hands of the reliable contractors, for they, and they alone, know your local conditions.

We Wish to be Frank With You and therefore make no statement that we cannot substantiate in every respect. If a plan in this book pleases you; if the arrangement of the rooms is satisfactory, and if the exterior is pleasing and attractive, then we make this claim—that it can be built as cheaply as if any other architect designed it, and we believe cheaper.

We Have Studied Economy in construction, and our knowledge of all the material that goes into a house qualifies us to give you the best for your money. We give you a plan that pleases you, one that is attractive, and one where every foot of space is utilized at the least possible cost. Can any architect do more, even at seven to ten times the price we charge you for plans?

Reversing Plans We receive many requests from our patrons for plans exactly according to the designs illustrated, with the one exception of having them reversed or placed in the opposite direction. It is impossible for us to make this change and draw new plans, except at a cost of about eight times our regular price. We see no reason why our regular plans will not answer your purpose. Your carpenter can face the house exactly as you wish it, and the plans will work out as well facing in one direction as in another. We can, however, if you wish, and so instruct us, make you a reversed blue-print and furnish it at our regular price; but in that case all the figures and letters will be reversed, and, therefore, liable to cause as much confusion as if your carpenter reversed the plan himself while constructing the house.

We Would Advise however, in all cases where the plan is to be reversed, and there is the least doubt about the contractor not being able to work from the plans as we have them, that two sets of blue-prints be purchased, one regular and the other reversed, and in such cases we will furnish two sets of blue-prints and one set of specifications for only fifty per cent added to the regular cost, making the $10.00 plan cost only $15.00.

Immediate Delivery Guaranteed Our equipment and facilities are such that we can send out the same day we receive order the complete plans and specifications for any house we illustrate. Delivery is made by express whenever possible, otherwise plans and specifications are forwarded by mail.

PUBLISHED BY

The Radford Architectural Co.

1827-29-31-33 Prairie Ave., Chicago, Illinois

Design No. 5079

Size: Width, 32 feet 6 inches; Length, 25 feet

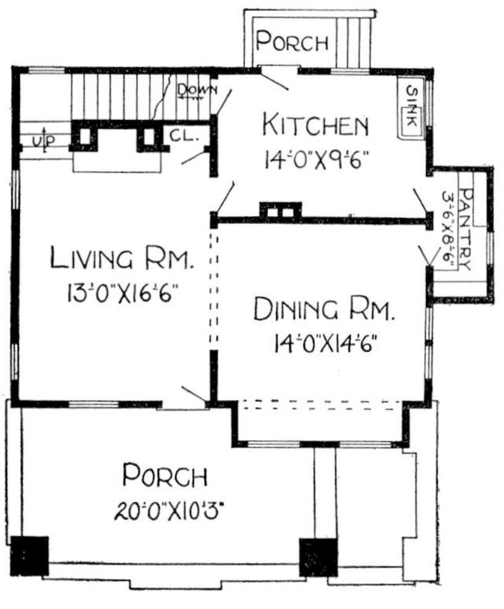

First Floor Plan

Blue prints consist of cellar and foundation plan; roof plan; first and second floor plans; front, two side elevations; wall sections and all necessary interior details. Specifications consist of twenty-two pages of typewritten matter.

PRICE

of Blue Prints, together with a complete set of typewritten specifications

ONLY

$12.00

We mail Plans and Specifications the same day order is received.

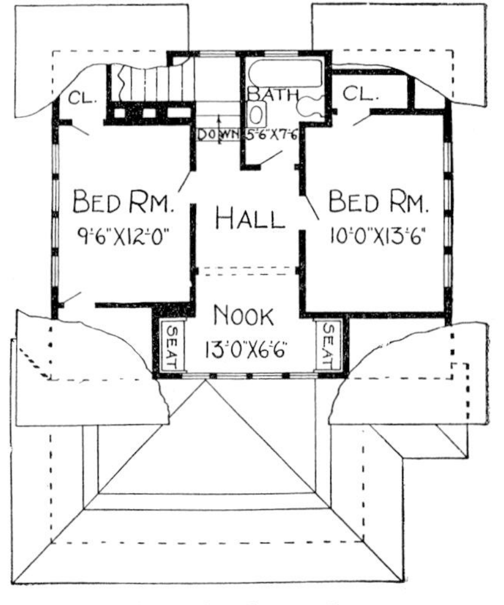

Second Floor Plan

Design No. 5026

Size: Width, 29 feet; Length, 35 feet

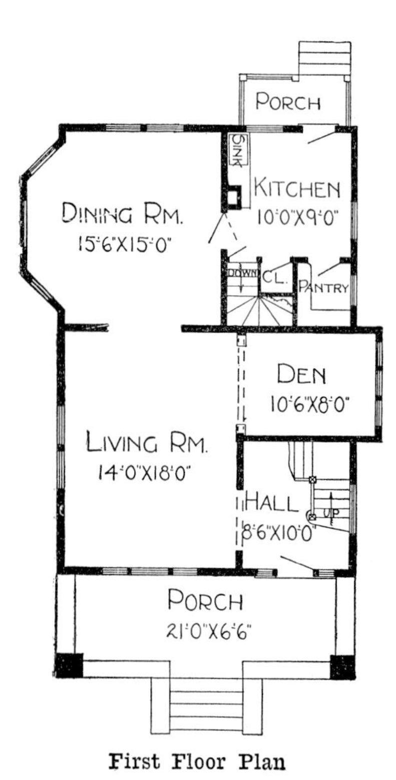

First Floor Plan

Blue prints consist of basement plan; roof plan; first and second floor plans; front, rear, two side elevations; wall sections and all necessary interior details. Specifications consist of twenty-two pages of typewritten matter.

PRICE

of Blue Prints, together with a complete set of typewritten specifications

ONLY

We mail Plans and Specifications the same day order is received.

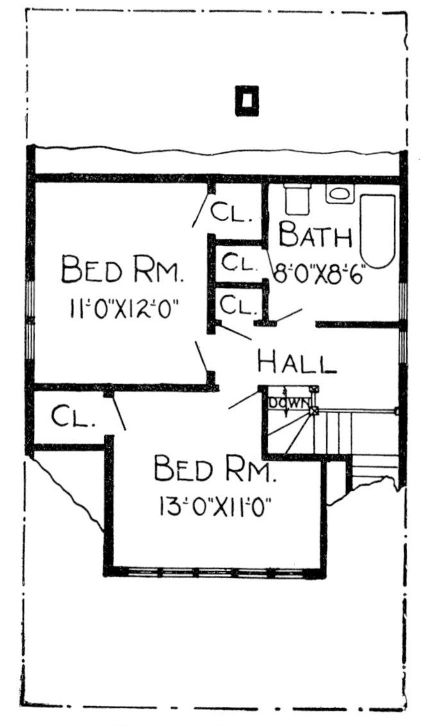

Second Floor Plan

Design No. 5044

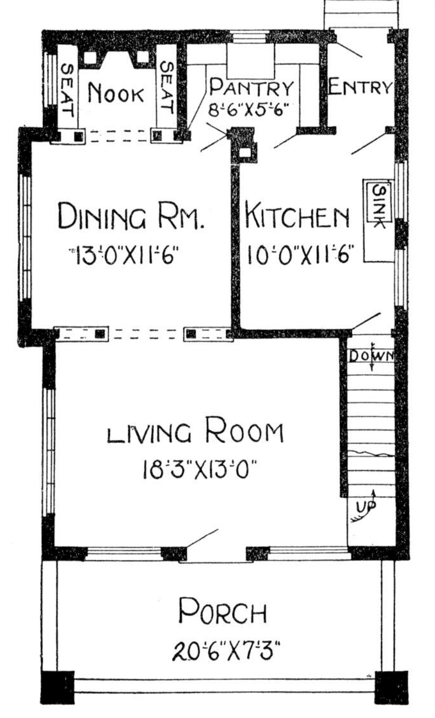

First Floor Plan

Size: Width 24 feet 8 inches; Length, 32 feet 8 inches

Blue prints consist of basement plan; roof plan; first and second floor plans; front, rear, two side elevations; wall sections and all necessary interior details. Specifications consist of twenty-two pages of typewritten matter.

PRICE

of Blue Prints together with a complete set of typewritten specifications

ONLY

We mail Plans and Specifications the same day order is received.

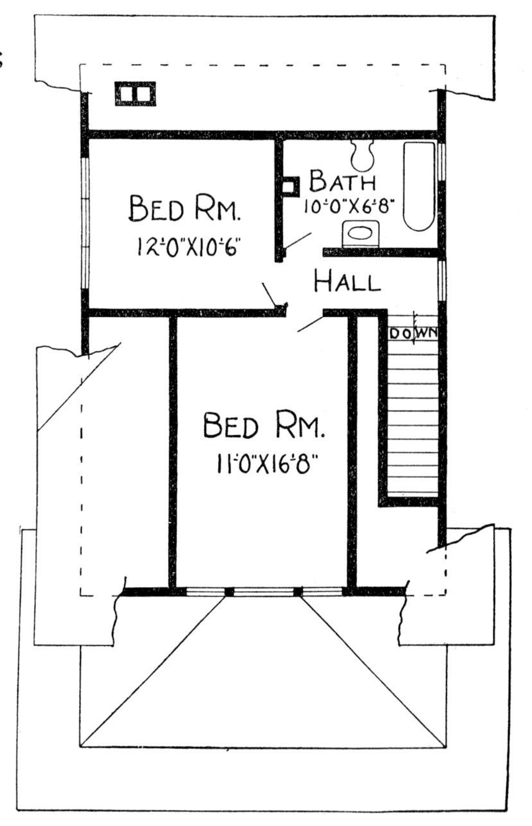

Second Floor Plan

Design No. 5024

Size: Width, 40 feet; Length, 29 feet 6 inches

PRICE

of Blue Prints, together with a complete set of typewritten specifications

ONLY

10.00

We mail Plans and Specifications the same day order is received.

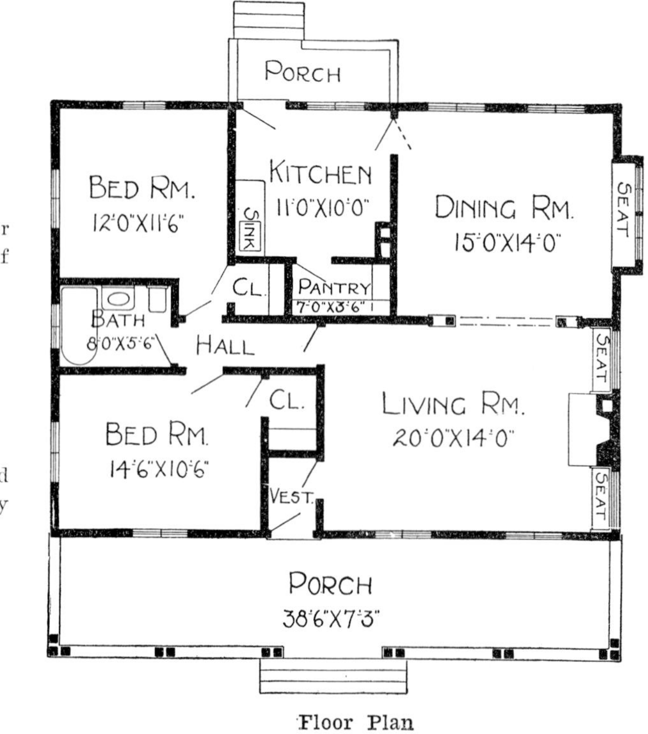

Floor Plan

Blue prints consist of basement plan; roof plan; floor plan; front, rear, two side elevations; wall sections and all necessary interior details. Specifications consist of twenty-two pages of typewritten matter.

Design No. 5037

Size: Width, 38 feet; Length, 35 feet

Blue prints consist of basement plan; roof plan; floor plan; front, rear, two side elevations; wall sections and all necessary interior details. Specifications consist of twenty-two pages of typewritten matter.

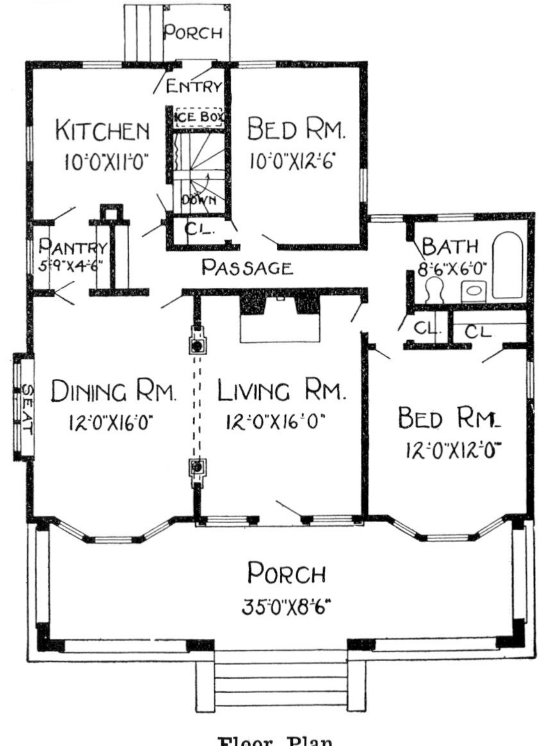

Floor Plan

PRICE

of Blue Prints, together with a complete set of typewritten specifications

ONLY

We mail Plans and Specifications the same day order is received.

Design No. 5096

Size: Width, 28 feet; Length, 26 feet

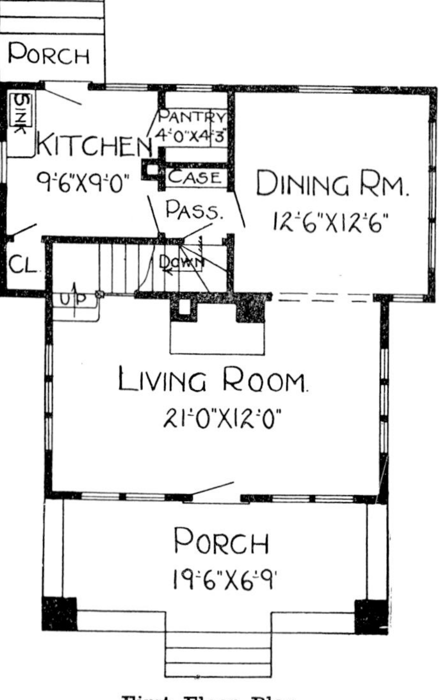

First Floor Plan

Blue prints consist of basement plan; roof plan; first and second floor plans; front, rear, two side elevations; wall sections and all necessary interior details. Specifications consist of twenty-two pages of typewritten matter.

PRICE

of Blue Prints, together with a complete set of typewritten specifications

ONLY

We mail Plans and Specifications the same day order is received

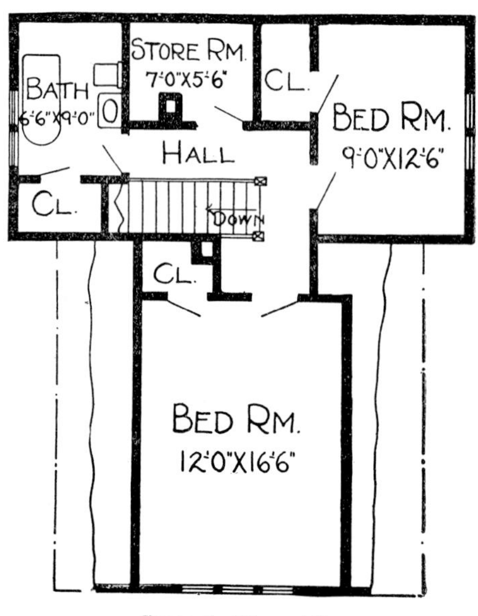

Second Floor Plan

Design No. 6001=B

Size: Width, 33 feet; Length, 40 feet

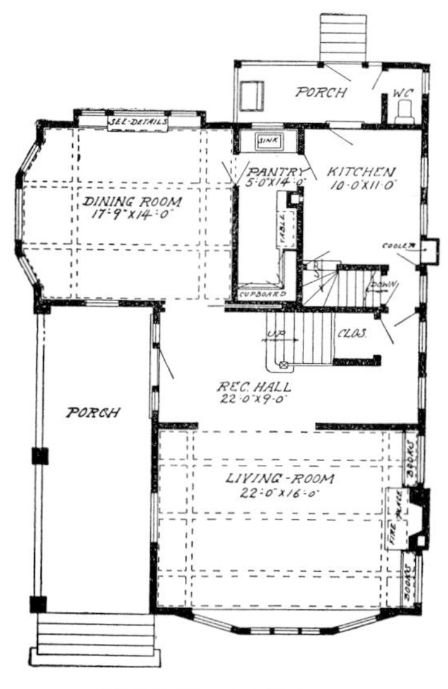

First Floor Plan

Blue prints consist of basement plan; roof plan; first and second floor plans; front, rear, two side elevations; wall sections and all necessary interior details. Specifications consist of twenty-two pages of typewritten matter.

PRICE

of Blue Prints, together with a complete set of typewritten specifications

ONLY

We mail Plans and Specifications the same day order is received.

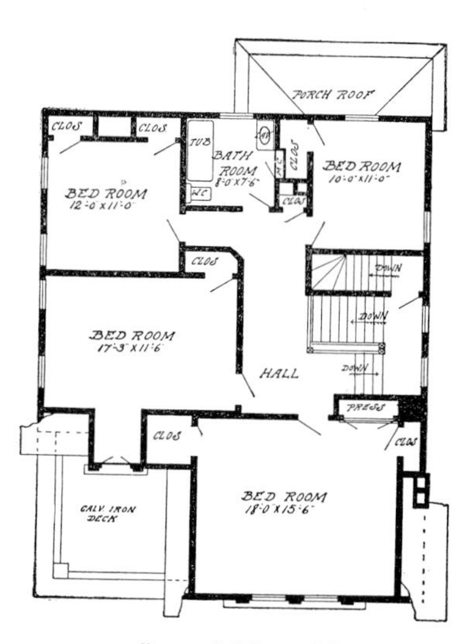

Second Floor Plan

Design No. 7019=B

Size: Width, 43 feet; Length, 36 feet 6 inches

PRICE

of Blue Prints, together with a complete set of typewritten specifications

ONLY

$12.00

We mail Plans and Specifications the same day order is received.

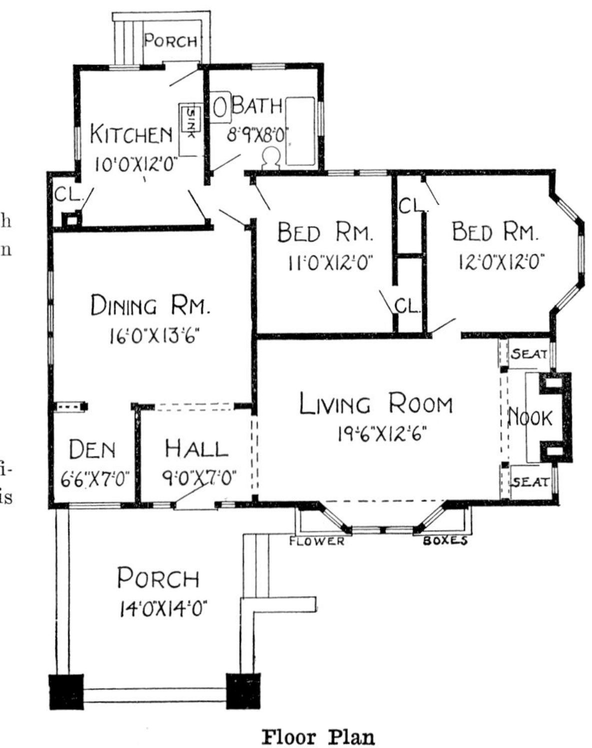

Floor Plan

Blue prints consist of foundation plan; roof plan; floor plan; front, rear, two side elevations; wall sections and all necessary interior details. Specifications consist of twenty-two pages of typewritten matter.

Design No. 5002

Size: Width, 38 feet; Length, 36 feet 6 inches

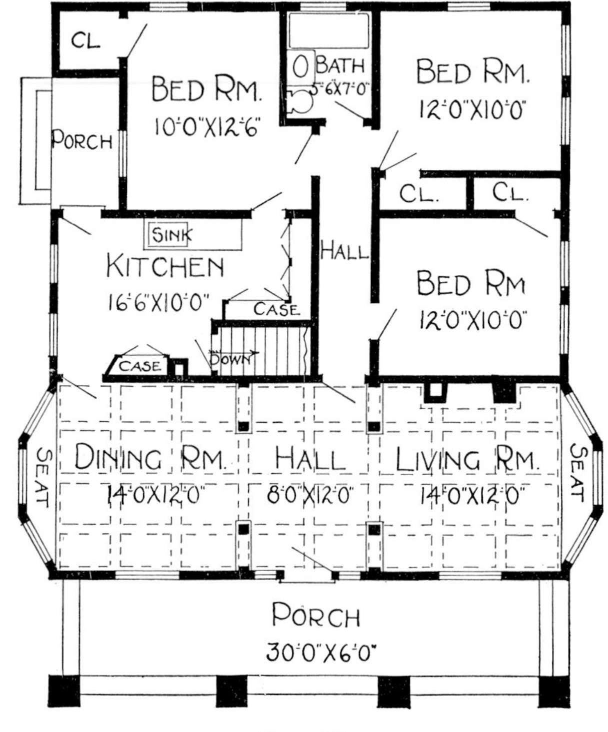

Floor Plan

Blue prints consist of basement plan; floor plan; front, rear, two side elevations; wall sections and all necessary interior details. Specifications consist of twenty-two pages of typewritten matter.

PRICE

of Blue Prints, together with a complete set of typewritten specifications

ONLY

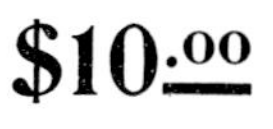

$10.00

We mail Plans and Specifications the same day order is received.

Design No. 5107

Size: Width, 36 feet; Length, 31 feet

PRICE

of Blue Prints, together with a complete set of typewritten specifications

ONLY

$10.00

We mail Plans and Specifications the same day order is received.

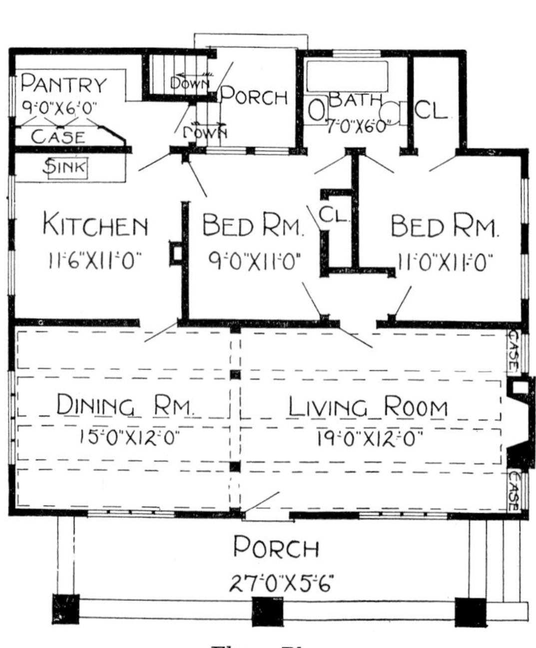

Floor Plan

Blue prints consist of basement plan; floor plan; front, rear, two side elevations; wall sections and all necessary interior details. Specifications consist of twenty-two pages of typewritten matter.

Design No. 8302-B

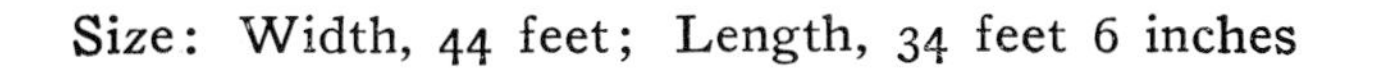

Size: Width, 44 feet; Length, 34 feet 6 inches

Blue prints consist of foundation plan; roof plan; floor plan; front, rear, two side elevations; wall sections and all necessary interior details. Specifications consist of twenty-two pages of typewritten matter.

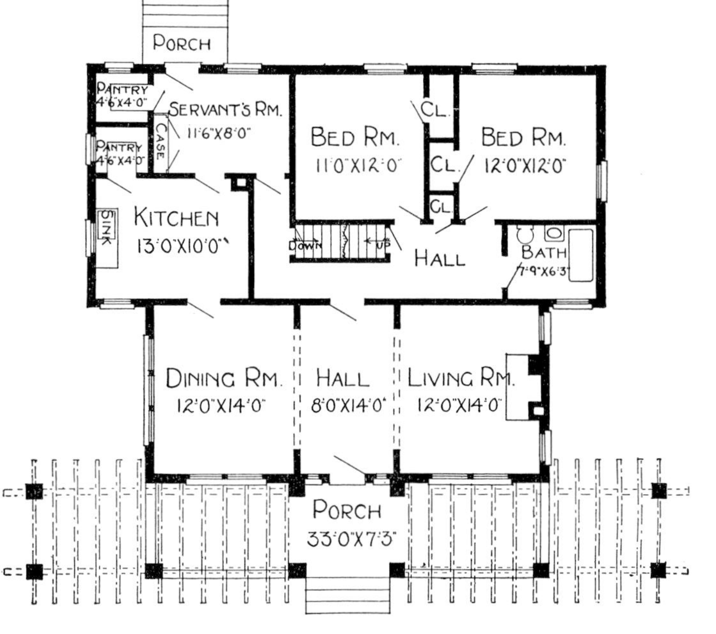

Floor Plan

PRICE

of Blue Prints, together with a complete set of typewritten specifications

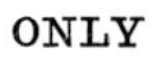

ONLY

$12.00

We mail Plans and Specifications same day order is received.

Design No. 5025

Size: Width, 31 feet; Length, 30 feet

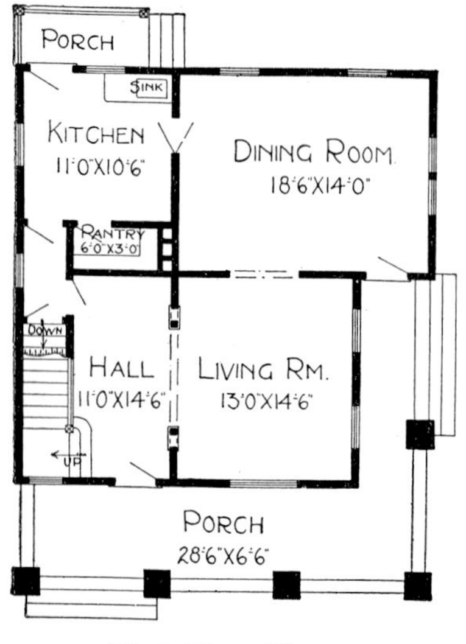

First Floor Plan

Blue prints consist of basement plan; roof plan; first and second floor plans; front, rear, two side elevations; wall sections and all necessary interior details. Specifications consist of twenty-two pages of typewritten matter.

PRICE

of Blue Prints, together with a complete set of typewritten specifications

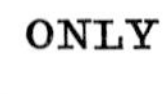

We mail Plans and Specifications the same day order is received.

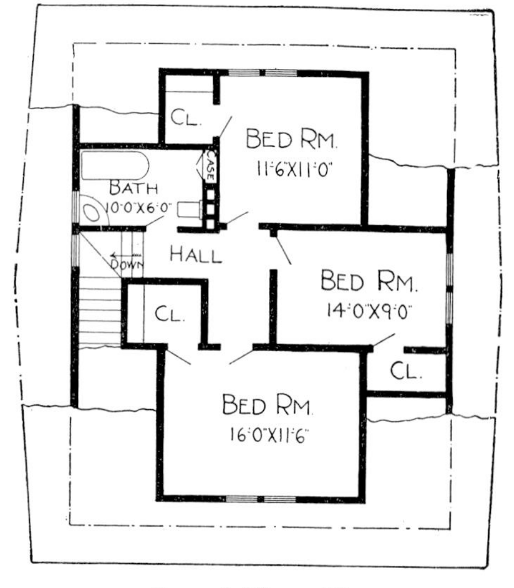

Second Floor Plan

Design No. 5078

Size: Width, 30 feet; Length, 40 feet 6 inches

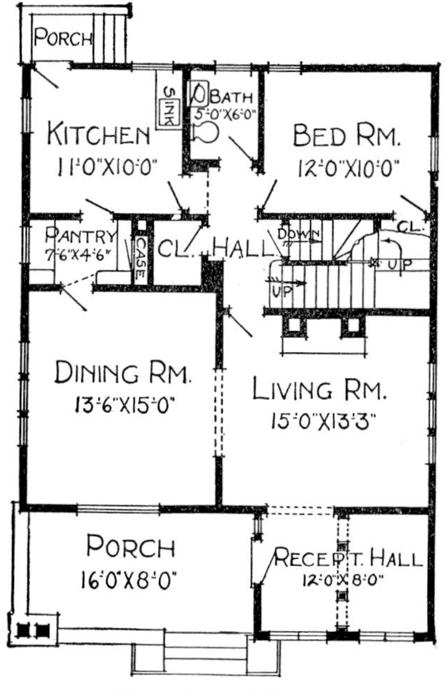

First Floor Plan

Blue prints consist of basement plan; roof plan; first and second floor plans; front, rear, two side elevations; wall sections and all necessary interior details. Specifications consist of twenty-two pages of typewritten matter.

PRICE

of Blue Prints, together with a complete set of typewritten specifications

ONLY

$12.00

We mail Plans and Specifications the same day order is received.

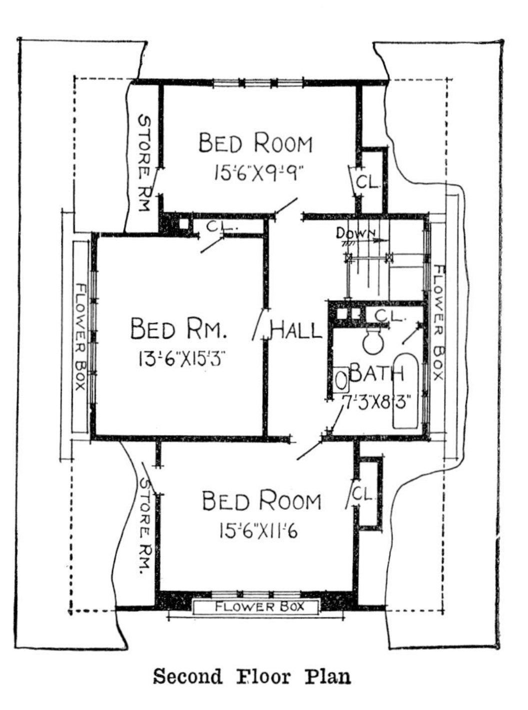

Second Floor Plan

Design No. 5031

Size: Width, 38 feet; Length, 33 feet

PRICE

of Blue Prints, together with a complete set of typewritten specifications

ONLY

$10.00

We mail Plans and Specifications the same day order is received.

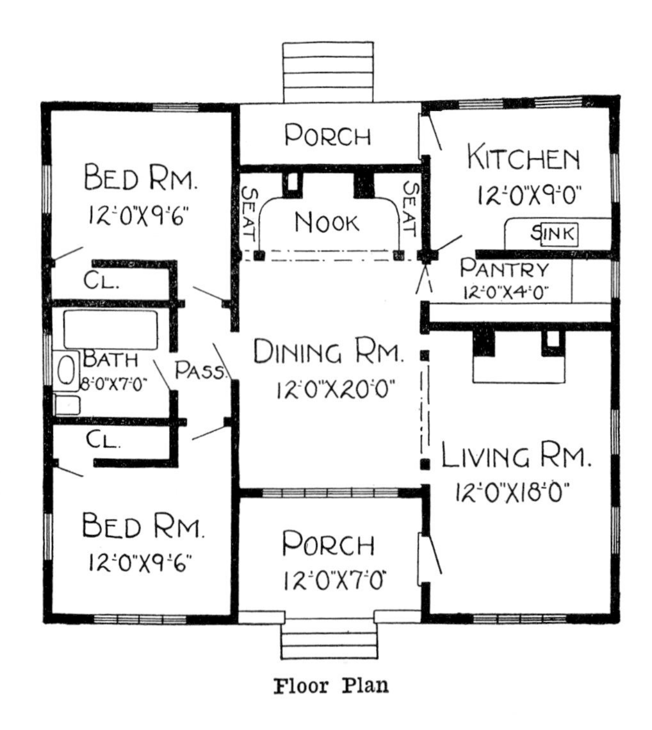

Floor Plan

Blue prints consist of foundation plan; floor plan; front, rear, two side elevations; wall sections and all necessary interior details. Specifications consist of twenty-two pages of typewritten matter.

Design No. 8334=B

Size: Width, 38 feet; Length, 33 feet 6 inches

Blue prints consist of basement plan; floor plan; front, rear, two side elevations; wall sections and all necessary interior details. Specifications consist of twenty-two pages of typewritten matter.

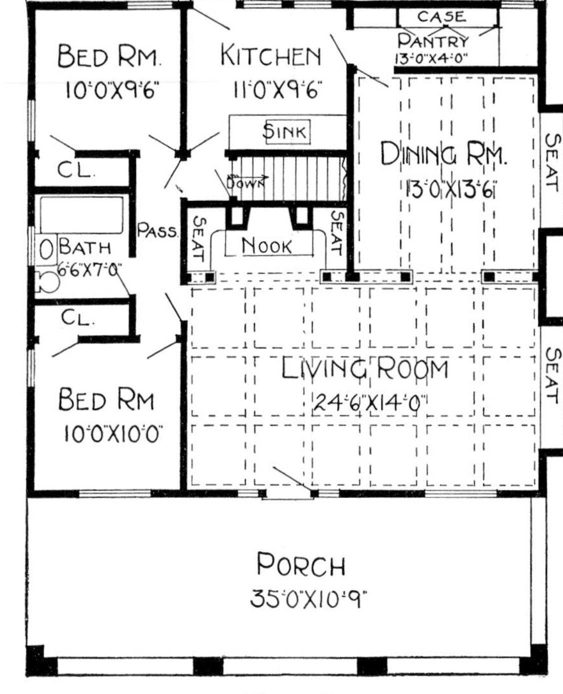

Floor Plan

PRICE

of Blue Prints, together with a complete set of typewritten specifications

ONLY

We mail Plans and Specifications the same day order is received.

Design No. 5038

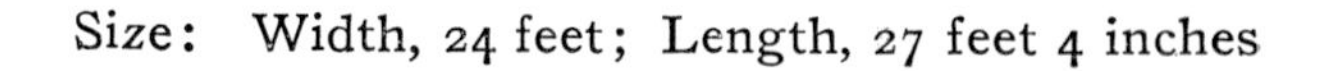

Size: Width, 24 feet; Length, 27 feet 4 inches

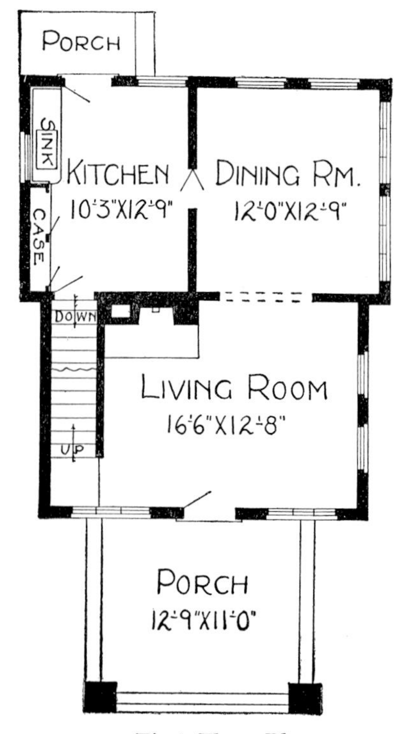

First Floor Plan

Blue prints consist of basement plan; roof plan; first and second floor plans; front, rear, two side elevations; wall sections and all necessary interior details. Specifications consist of twenty-two pages of typewritten matter.

PRICE

of Blue Prints, together with a complete set of typewritten specifications

ONLY

$12.00

We mail Plans and Specifications the same day order is received.

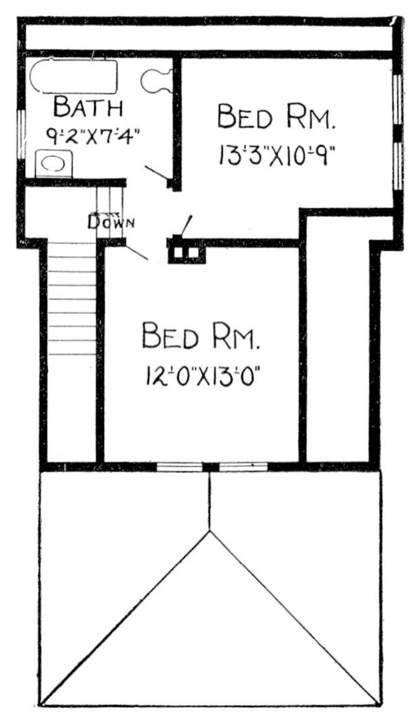

Second Floor Plan

Design No. 6039=B

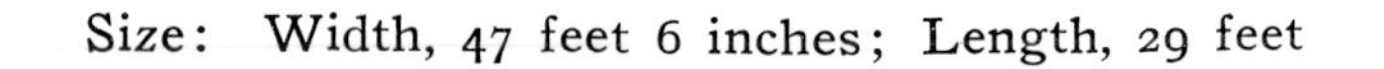

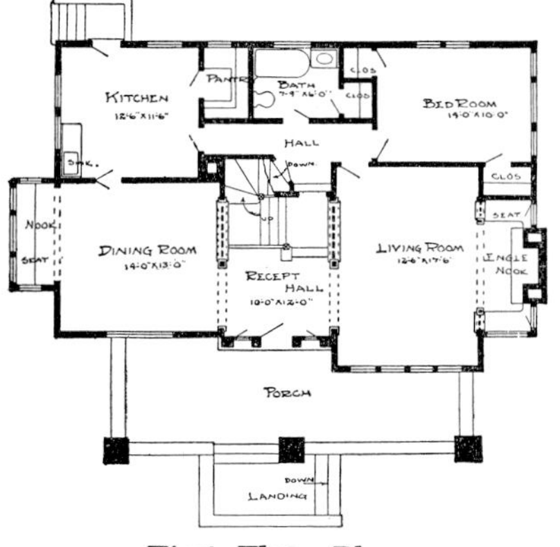

First Floor Plan

Blue prints consist of basement plan; roof plan; first and second floor plans; front, rear, two side elevations; wall sections and all necessary interior details. Specifications consist of twenty-two pages of typewritten matter.

PRICE

of Blue Prints, together with a complete set of typewritten specifications

ONLY

We mail Plans and Specifications the same day order is received.

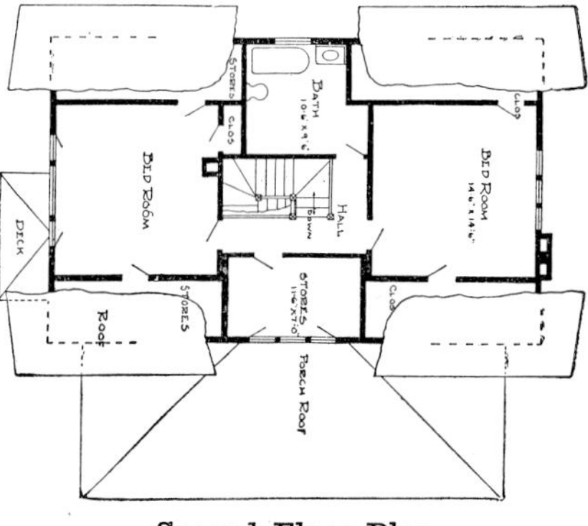

Second Floor Plan

Design No. 9090=B

Size: Width, 27 feet 4 inches; Length, 28 feet 4 inches

PRICE

of Blue Prints, together with a complete set of typewritten specifications

ONLY

$10.00

We mail Plans and Specifications the same day order is received.

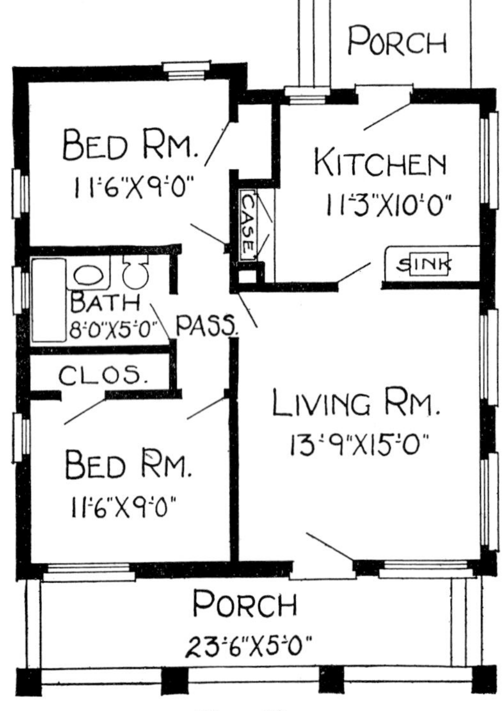

Floor Plan

Blue prints consist of foundation plan; floor plan; front, rear, two side elevations; wall sections and all necessary interior details. Specifications consist of twenty-two pages of typewritten matter.

Design No. 5085

Size: Width, 30 feet 6 inches; Length, 40 feet 6 inches

Blue prints consist of foundation plan; attic and roof plan; floor plan; front, rear, two side elevations; wall sections and all necessary interior details. Specifications consist of twenty-two pages of typewritten matter.

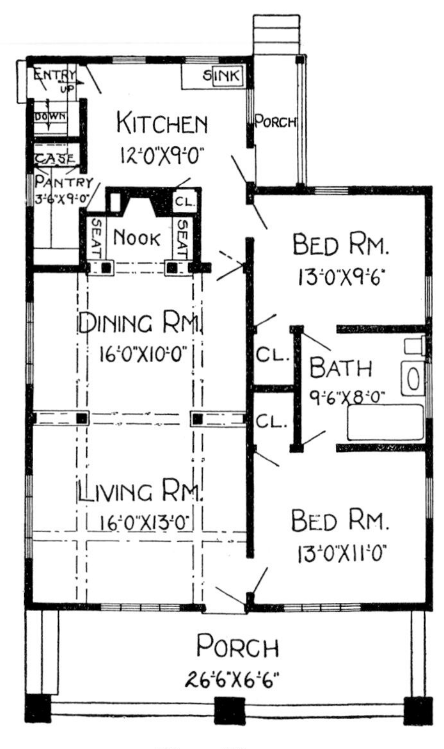

Floor Plan

PRICE

of Blue Prints, together with a complete set of typewritten specifications

ONLY

$10.00

We mail Plans and Specifications the same day order is received.

Design No. 8199=B

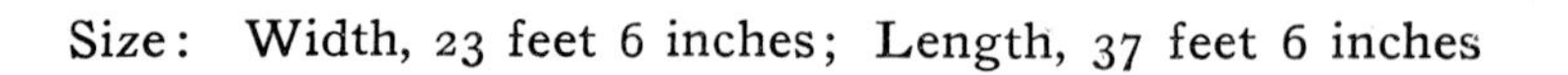

Size: Width, 23 feet 6 inches; Length, 37 feet 6 inches

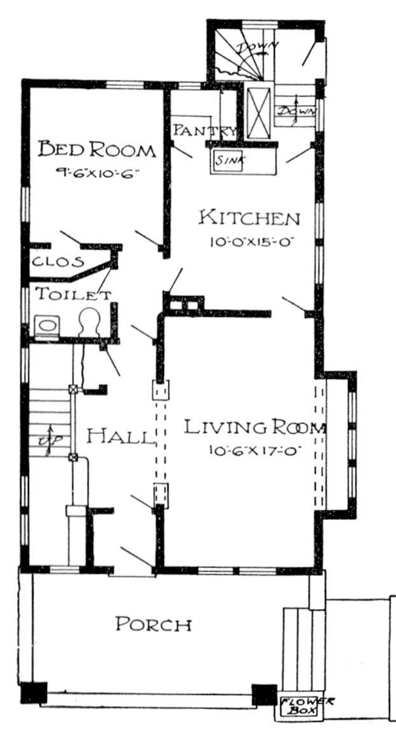

First Floor Plan

Blue prints consist of basement plan; roof plan; first and second floor plans; front, rear, two side elevations; wall sections and all necessary interior details. Specifications consist of twenty-two pages of typewritten matter.

PRICE

of Blue Prints, together with a complete set of typewritten specifications

ONLY

$15.00

We mail Plans and Specifications the same day order is received.

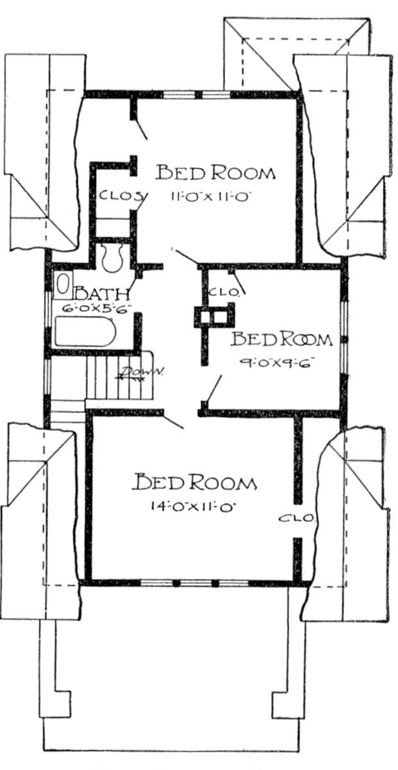

Second Floor Plan

Design No. 5109

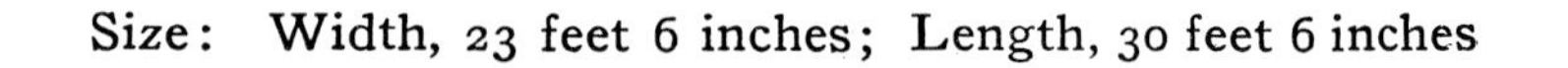

Size: Width, 23 feet 6 inches; Length, 30 feet 6 inches

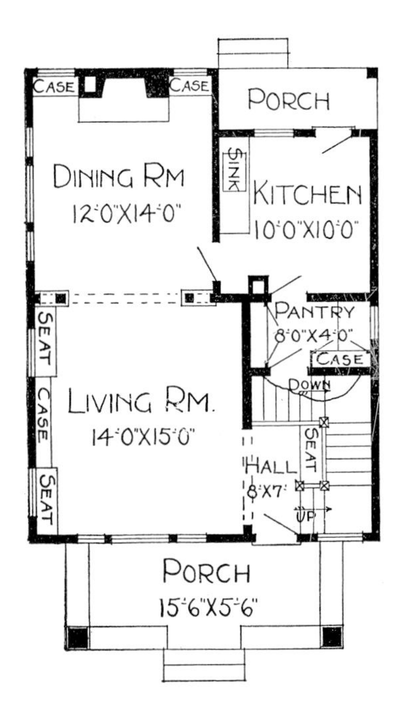

First Floor Plan

Blue prints consist of basement plan; roof plan; first and second floor plans; front, rear, two side elevations; wall sections and all necessary interior details. Specifications consist of twenty-two pages of typewritten matter.

PRICE

of Blue Prints, together with a complete set of typewritten specifications

ONLY

$12.00

We mail Plans and Specifications the same day order is received.

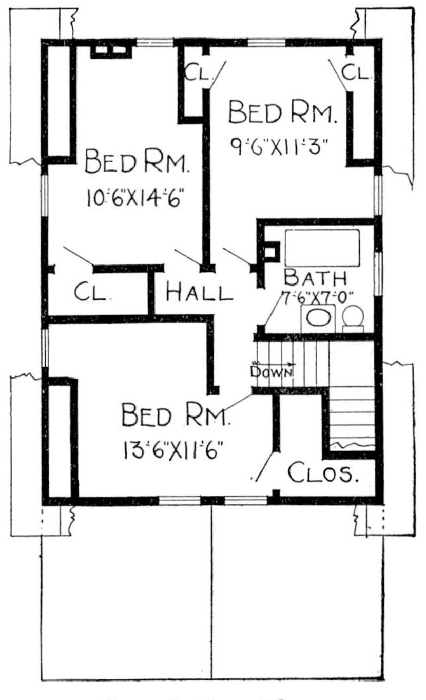

Second Floor Plan

Design No. 6061-B

Size: Width, 37 feet 6 inches; Length, 47 feet 6 inches

PRICE

of Blue Prints, together with a complete set of typewritten specifications

ONLY

$10.00

We mail Plans and Specifications the same day order is received.

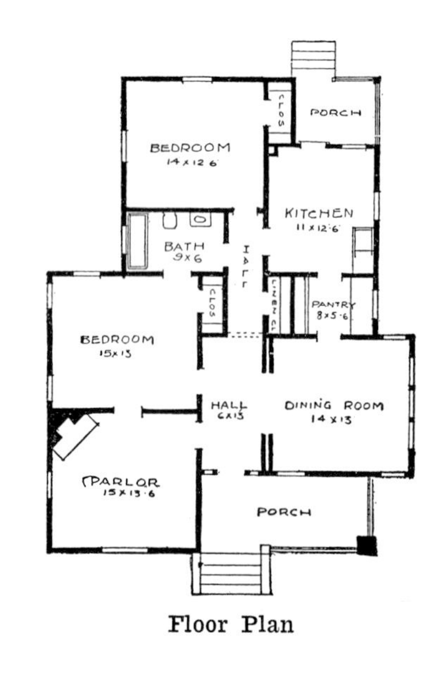

Floor Plan

Blue prints consist of foundation plan; roof plan; floor plan; front, rear, two side elevations; wall sections and all necessary interior details. Specifications consist of twenty-two pages of typewritten matter.

Design No. 6042-B

Size: Width, 31 feet; length, 40 feet

Blue prints consist of basement plan; attic and roof plan; floor plan; front, rear, two side elevations; wall sections and all necessary interior details. Specifications consist of twenty-two pages of typewritten matter.

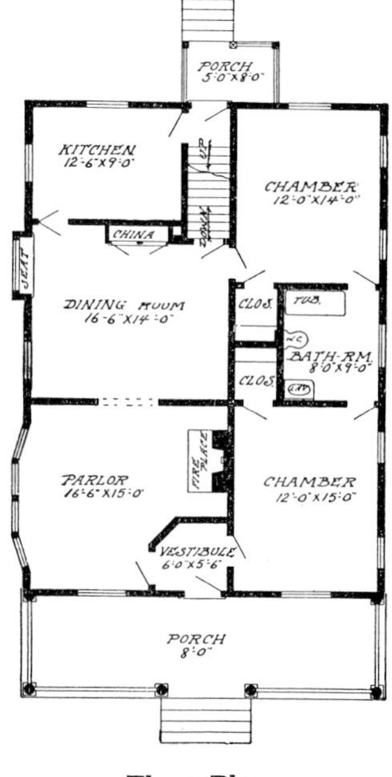

Floor Plan

PRICE

of Blue Prints, together with a complete set of typewritten specifications

ONLY

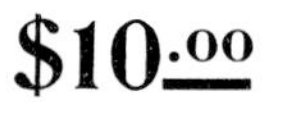

We mail Plans and Specifications the same day order is received.

Design No. 9058-B

Size: Width, 26 feet; Length, 36 feet

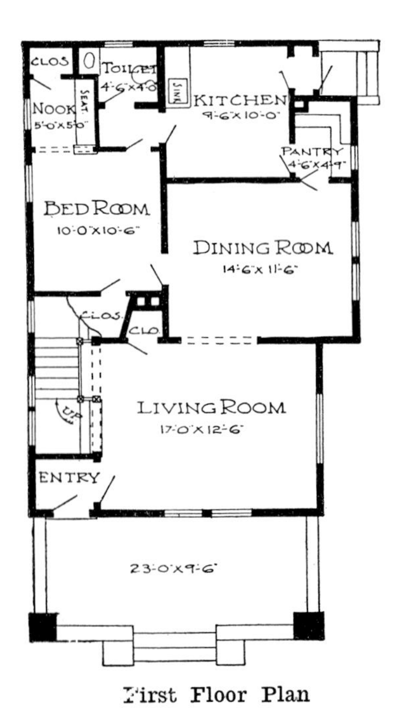

First Floor Plan

Blue prints consist of foundation plan; first and second floor plans; front, rear, two side elevations; wall sections and all necessary interior details. Specifications consist of twenty-two pages of typewritten matter.

PRICE

of Blue Prints, together with a complete set of typewritten specifications

ONLY

$12.00

We mail Plans and Specifications the same day order is received.

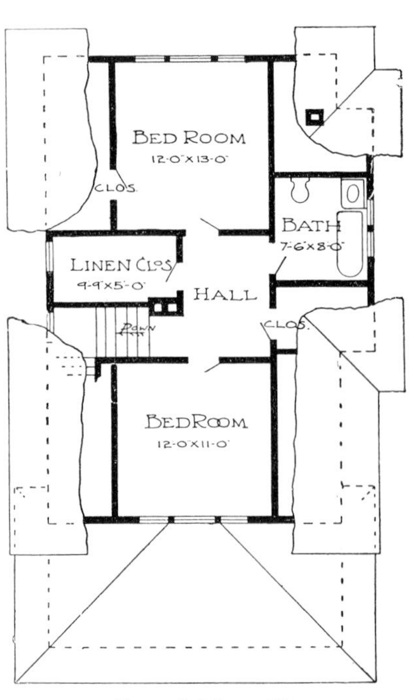

Second Floor Plan

Design No. 7098-B

Size: Width, 44 feet 6 inches; Length, 24 feet 6 inches

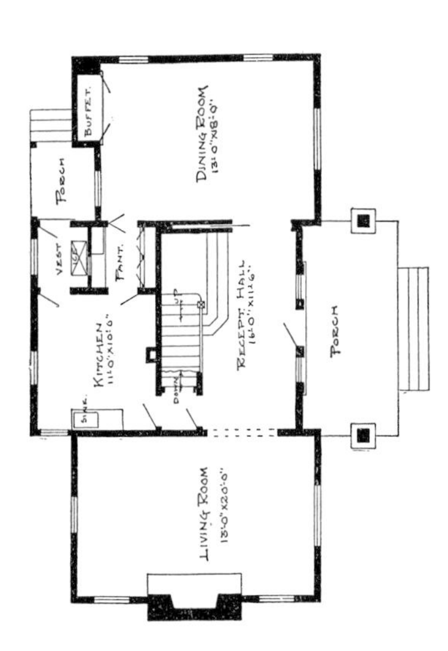

First Floor Plan

Blue prints consist of basement plan; roof plan; first and second floor plans; front, rear, two side elevations; wall sections and all necessary interior details. Specifications consist of twenty-two pages of typewritten matter.

PRICE

of Blue Prints, together with a complete set of typewritten specifications

ONLY

$12.00

We mail Plans and Specifications the same day order is received.

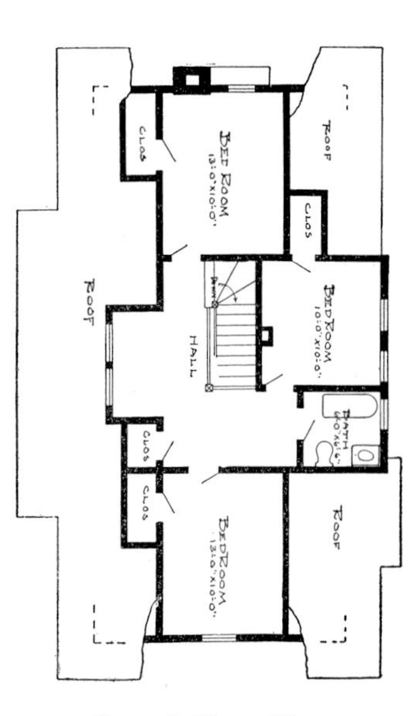

Second Floor Plan

Design No. 9046=B

Size: Width, 25 feet 6 inches; Length, 40 feet

PRICE

of Blue Prints, together with a complete set of typewritten specifications

ONLY

$12.00

We mail Plans and Specifications the same day order is received.

BED ROOM 11'-6"x9'-6"
CLOS
BATH 6'-6"x6'-2"
SINK
DINING ROOM 14'-0"x12'-6"
KITCHEN 9'-10"x11'-0"
PANTRY 4'-0"x6'-0"
SEAT
LIVING ROOM 12'-0"x16'-0"
SEAT
NOOK
SEAT
PORCH 15'-6"x9'-6"

Floor Plan

Blue prints consist of basement plan; roof plan; floor plan; front, rear, two side elevations; wall sections and all necessary interior details. Specifications consist of twenty-two pages of typewritten matter.

Design No. 5064

Size: Width, 24 feet; Length, 35 feet 6 inches

Blue prints consist of foundation plan; roof plan; floor plan; front, rear, two side elevations; wall sections and all necessary interior details. Specifications consist of twenty-two pages of typewritten matter.

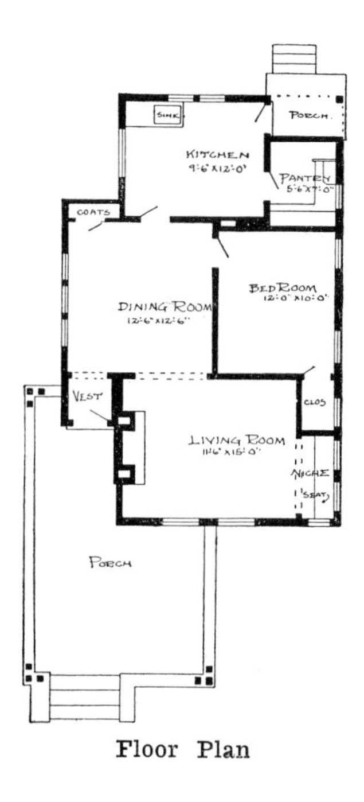

Floor Plan

PRICE

of Blue Prints, together with a complete set of typewritten specifications

ONLY

We mail Plans and Specifications the same day order is received.

Design No. 5113

Size: Width, 38 feet; Length, 33 feet

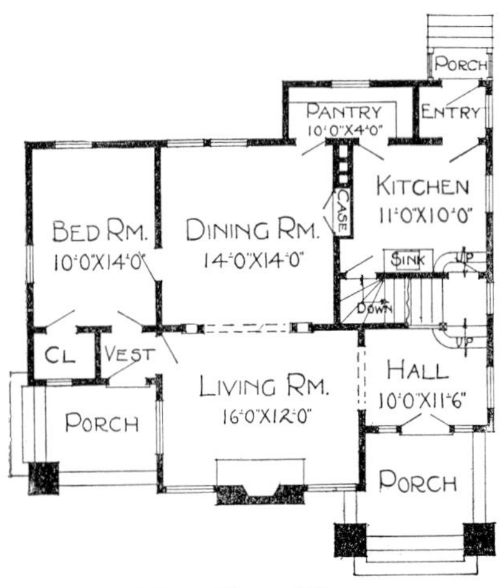

First Floor Plan

Blue prints consist of basement plan; roof plan; first and second floor plans; front, rear, two side elevations; wall sections and all necessary interior details. Specifications consist of twenty-two pages of typewritten watter.

PRICE

of Blue Prints, together with a complete set of typewritten specifications

ONLY

We mail Plans and Specifications the same day order is received.

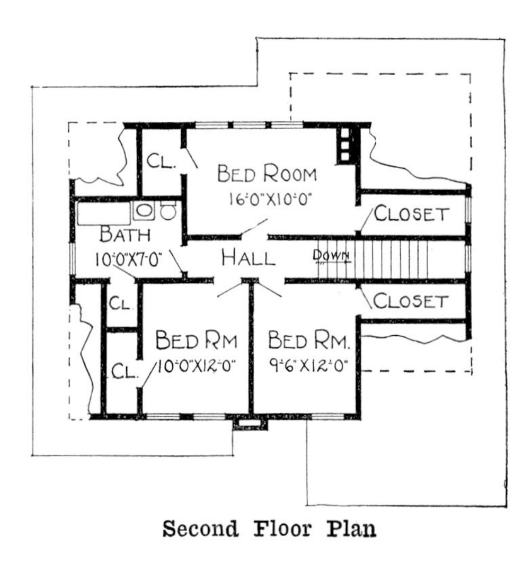

Second Floor Plan

Design No. 5055

Size: Width, 29 feet 6 inches; Length, 28 feet 6 inches

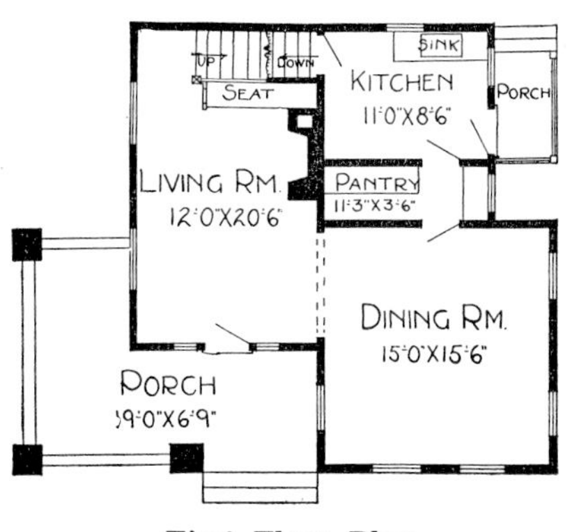

First Floor Plan

Blue prints consist of basement plan; roof plan; first and second floor plan; front, rear, two side elevations; wall sections and all necessary interior details. Specifications consist of twenty-two pages of typewritten matter.

PRICE

of Blue Prints together with a complete set of typewritten specifications

ONLY

$10.00

We mail Plans and Specifications the same day order is received.

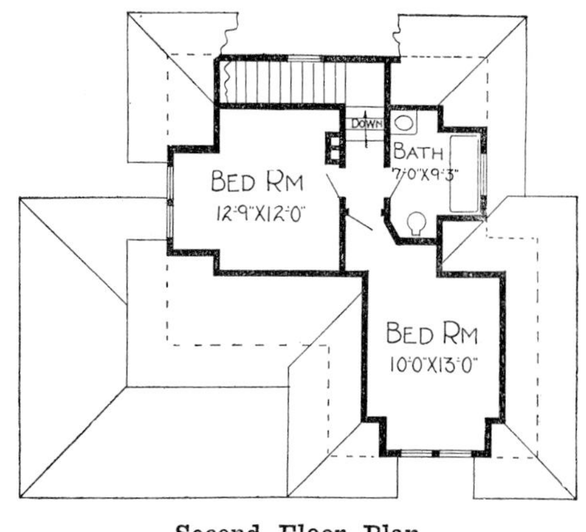

Second Floor Plan

Design No. 5111

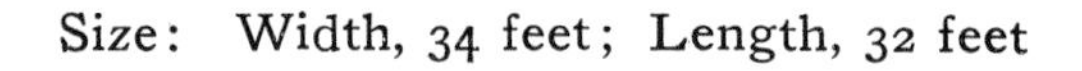

Size: Width, 34 feet; Length, 32 feet

PRICE

of Blue Prints, together with a complete set of typewritten specifications

ONLY

$8.00

We mail Plans and Specifications the same day order is received.

PORCH
KITCHEN 11'-0"X11'-6"
SINK
PANTRY 4'-9"X5'-3"
CASE
DOWN
CL.
DINING ROOM 16'-6"X14'-6"
BATH 6'-6"X5'-6"
HALL
BED RM. 10'-0"X12'-0"
LIVING RM. 12'-0"X16'-0"
BED RM. 10'-0"X13'-0"
CL.
CL.
PORCH 31'-0"X6'-6"

Floor Plan

Blue prints consist of basement plan; floor plan; front, rear, two side elevations; wall sections and all necessary interior details. Specifications consist of twenty-two pages of typewritten matter.

Design No. 5131

Size: Width, 30 feet; Length, 36 feet

Blue prints consist of basement plan; floor plan; front, rear, two side elevations; wall sections and all necessary interior details. Specifications consist of twenty-two pages of typewritten matter.

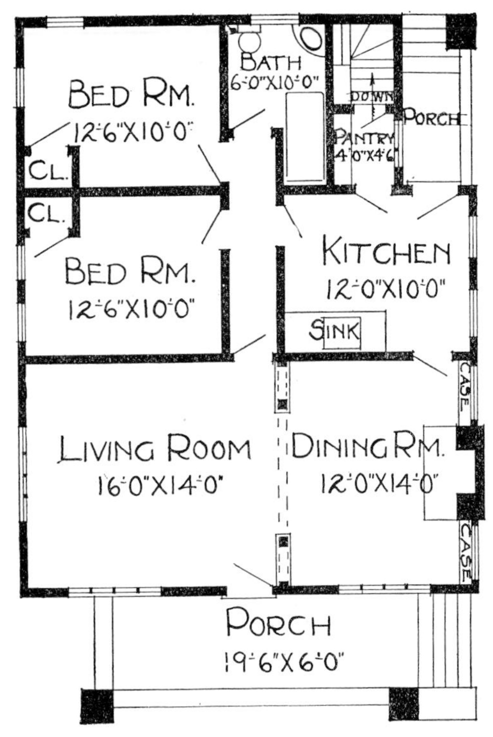

Floor Plan

PRICE

of Blue Prints, together with a complete set of typewritten specifications

ONLY

We mail Plans and Specifications the same day order is received.

Design No. 5094

Size: Width, 26 feet; Length, 35 feet

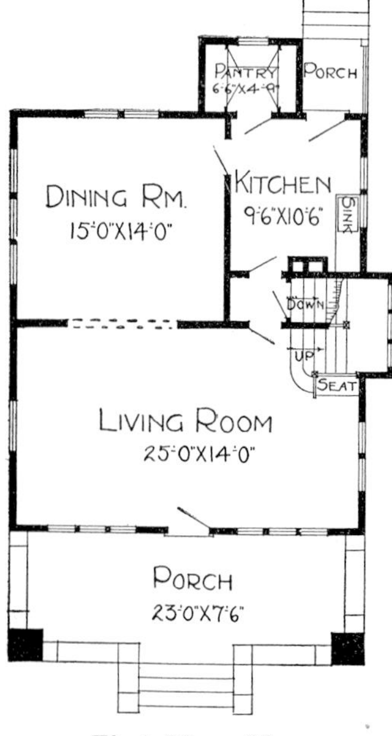

First Floor Plan

Blue prints consist of basement plan; roof plan; first and second floor plans; front, rear, two side elevations; wall sections and all necessary interior details. Specifications consist of twenty-two pages of typewritten matter.

PRICE

of Blue Prints, together with a complete set of typewritten specifications

ONLY

$12.00

We mail Plans and Specifications the same day order is received.

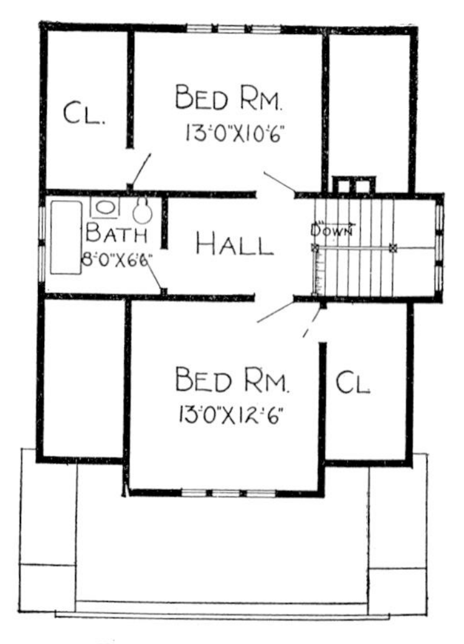

Second Floor Plan

Design No. 5028

Size: Width, 28 feet; Length, 25 feet 6 inches

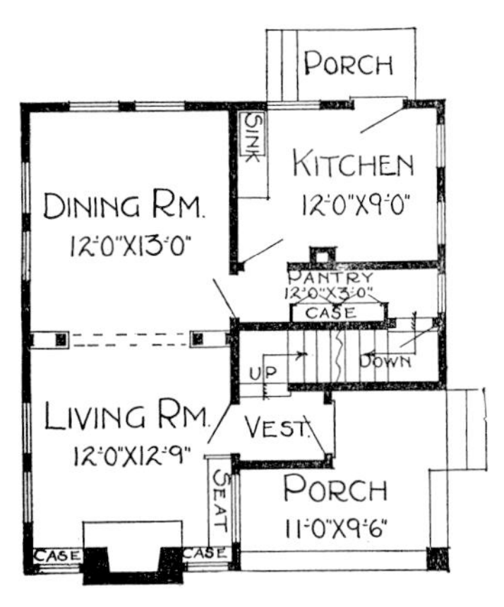

First Floor Plan

Blue prints consist of basement plan; roof plan; first and second floor plans; front, rear, two side elevations; wall sections and all necessary interior details. Specifications consist of twenty-two pages of typewritten matter.

PRICE

of Blue Prints, together with a complete set of typewritten specifications

ONLY

We mail Plans and Specifications the same day order is received.

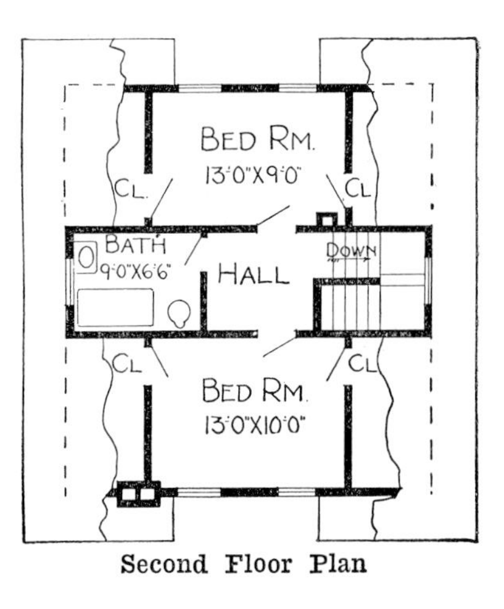

Second Floor Plan

Design No. 8301=B

Size: Width, 30 feet; Length, 34 feet 6 inches

PRICE

of Blue Prints, together with a complete set of typewritten specifications

ONLY

$10.00

We mail Plans and Specifications the same day order is received.

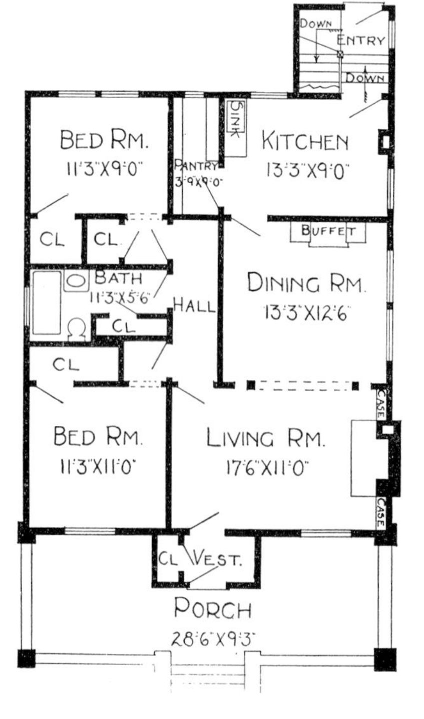

Floor Plan

Blue prints consist of basement plan; floor plan; front, rear, two side elevations; wall sections and all necessary interior details. Specifications consist of twenty-two pages of typewritten matter.

Design No. 5058

Size: Width, 32 feet; Length, 40 feet

Blue prints consist of basement plan; attic and roof plan; floor plan; front, rear, two side elevations; wall sections and all necessary interior details. Specifications consist of twenty-two pages of typewritten matter.

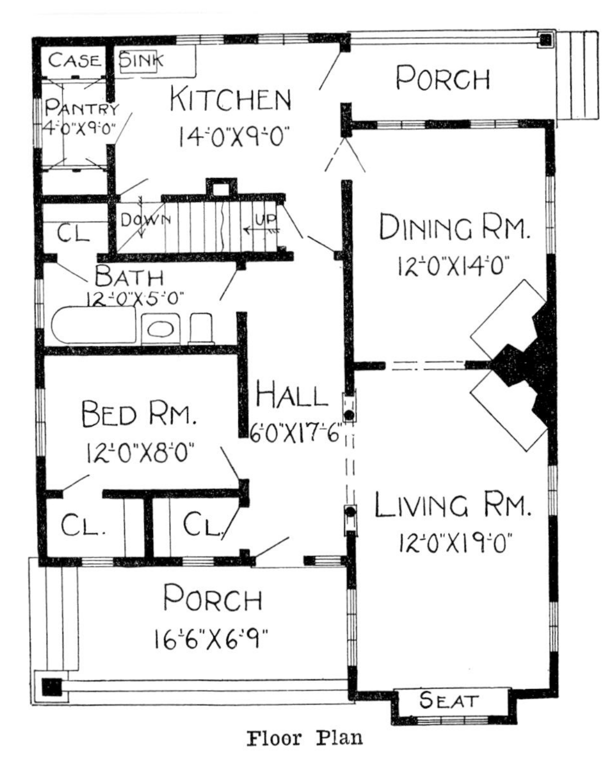

Floor Plan

PRICE

of Blue Prints, together with a complete set of typewritten specifications

ONLY

We mail Plans and Specifications the same day order is received.

Design No. 5087

Size: Width, 25 feet; Length, 28 feet

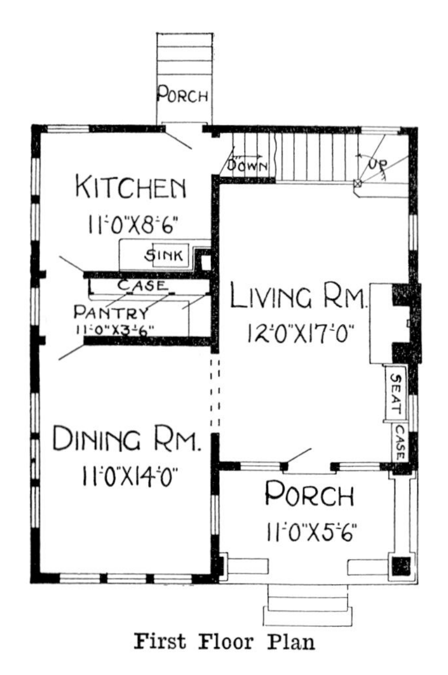

First Floor Plan

Blue prints consist of cellar and foundation plan; roof plan; first and second floor plans; front, two side elevations; wall sections and all necessary interior details. Specifications consist of twenty-two pagec of typewritten matter.

PRICE

of Blue Prints, together with a complete set of typewritten specifications

ONLY

We mail Plans and Specifications the same day order is received.

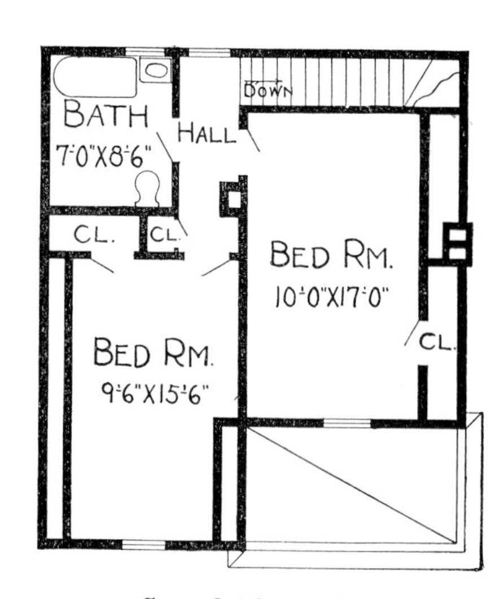

Second Floor Plan

Design No. 5100

Size: Width, 34 feet; Length, 24 feet 6 inches

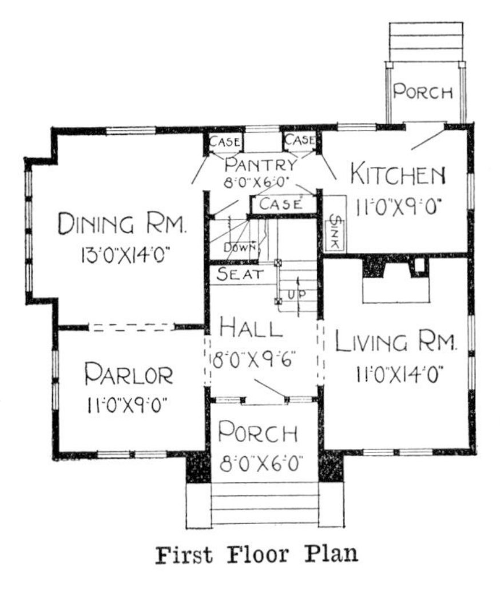

First Floor Plan

Blue prints consist of basement plan; roof plan; first and second floor plans; front, rear, two side elevations; wall sections and all necessary interior details. Specifications consist of twenty-two pages of typewritten matter.

PRICE

of Blue Prints, together with a complete set of typewritten specifications

ONLY

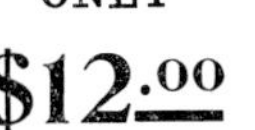

$12.00

We mail Plans and Specifications the same day order is received.

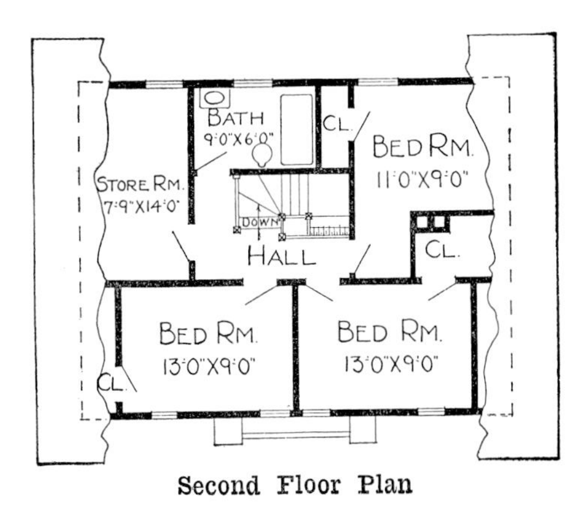

Second Floor Plan

Design No. 5105

Size: Width, 28 feet; Length, 28 feet

PRICE

of Blue Prints together with a complete set of typewritten specifications

ONLY

$8.00

We mail Plans and Specifications the same day order is received.

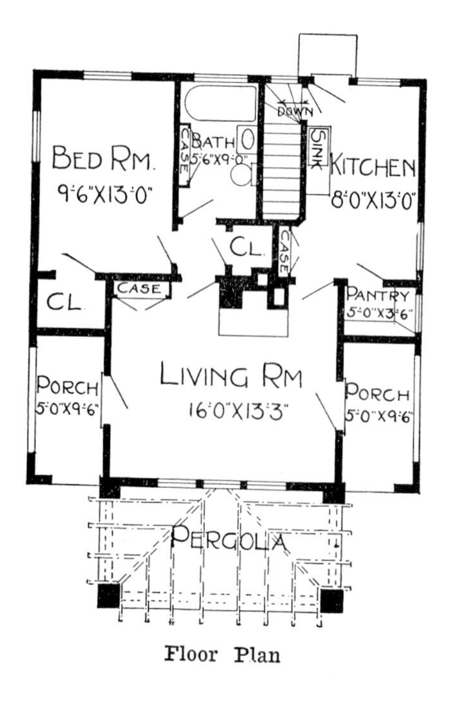

Floor Plan

Blue prints consist of basement plan; floor plan; front, rear, two side elevations; wall sections and all necessary interior details. Specifications consist of twenty-two pages of type written matter.

Design No. 5054

Size: Width, 24 feet; Length, 24 feet

Blue prints consist of foundation plan; roof plan; floor plan; front, rear, two side elevations; wall sections and all necessary interior details. Specifications consist of twenty-two pages of typewritten matter.

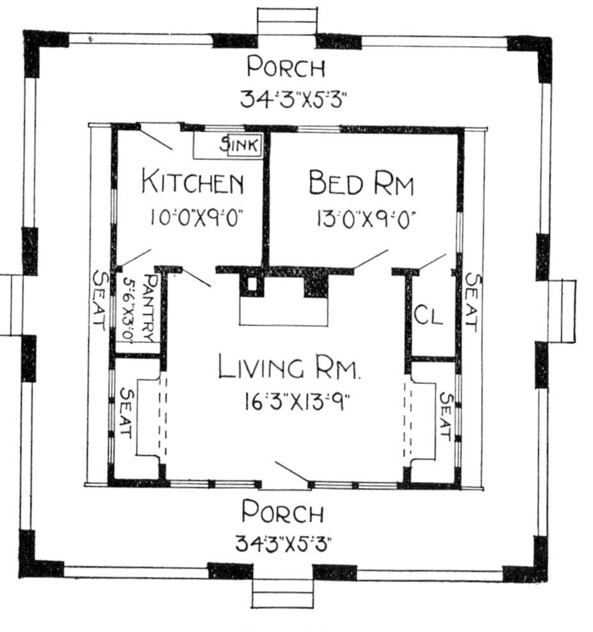

Floor Plan

PRICE

of Blue Prints, together with a complete set of typewritten specifications

ONLY

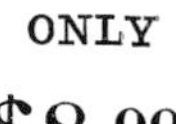

$8.00

We mail Plans and Specifications the same day order is received.

Design No. 5029

Size: Width, 28 feet 6 inches; Length, 29 feet 6 inches

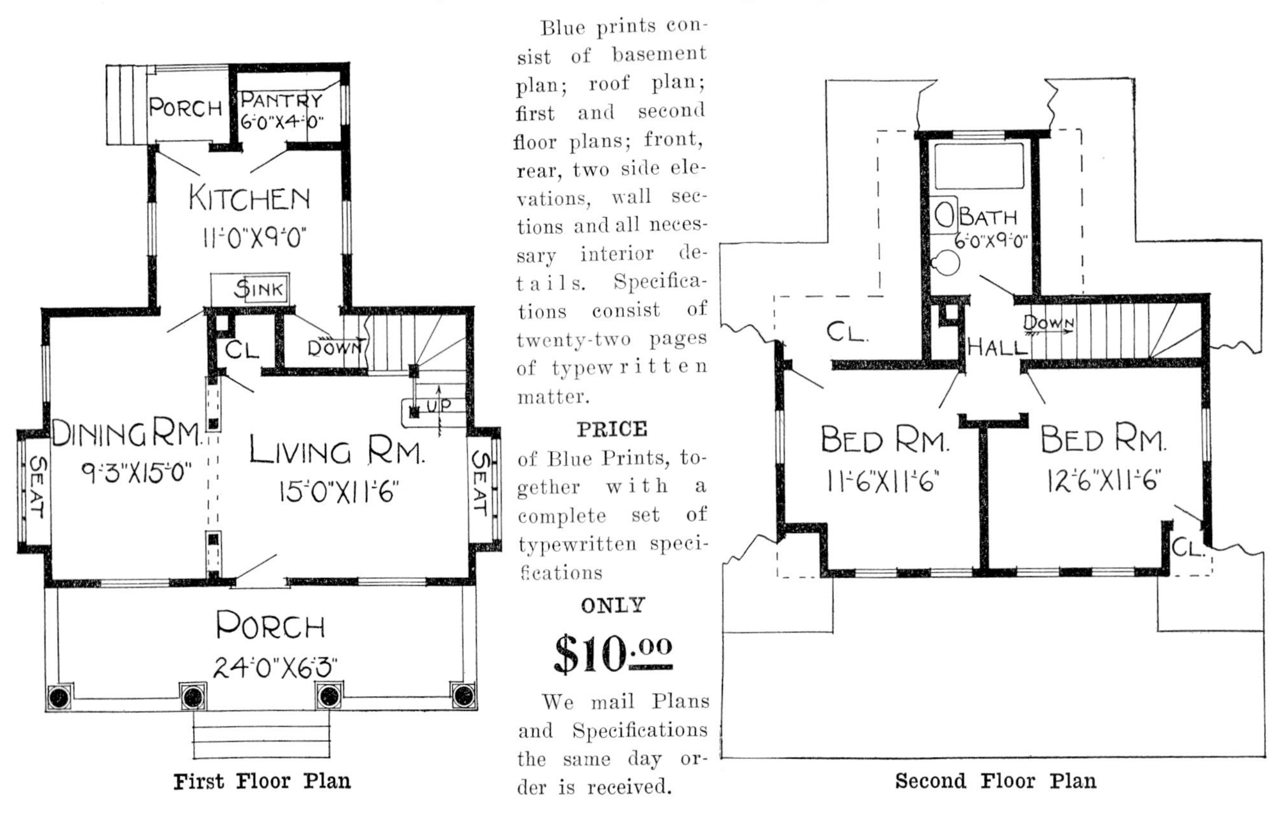

First Floor Plan

Second Floor Plan

Blue prints consist of basement plan; roof plan; first and second floor plans; front, rear, two side elevations, wall sections and all necessary interior details. Specifications consist of twenty-two pages of typewritten matter.

PRICE

of Blue Prints, together with a complete set of typewritten specifications

ONLY

$10.00

We mail Plans and Specifications the same day order is received.

Design No. 5063

Size: Width, 31 feet; Length, 35 feet

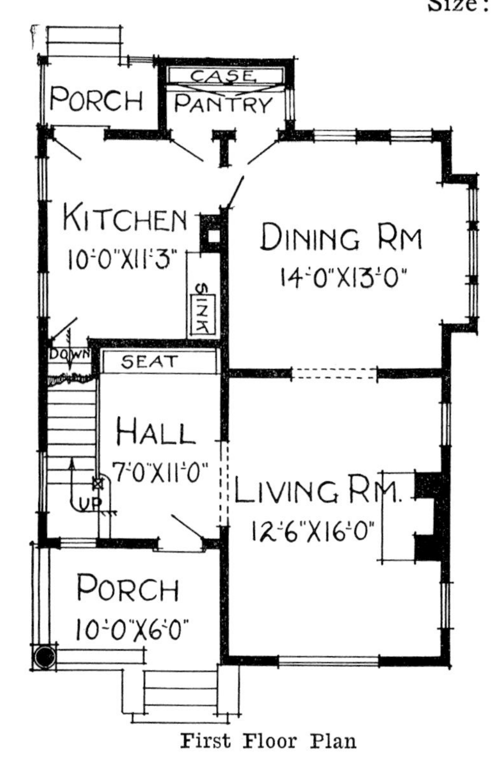

First Floor Plan

Blue prints consist of basement plan; roof plan; first and second floor plans; front, rear, two side elevations; wall sections and all necessary interior details. Specifications consist of twenty-two pages of typewritten matter.

PRICE

of Blue Prints, together with a complete set of typewritten specifications

ONLY

We mail Plans and Specifications the same day order is received.

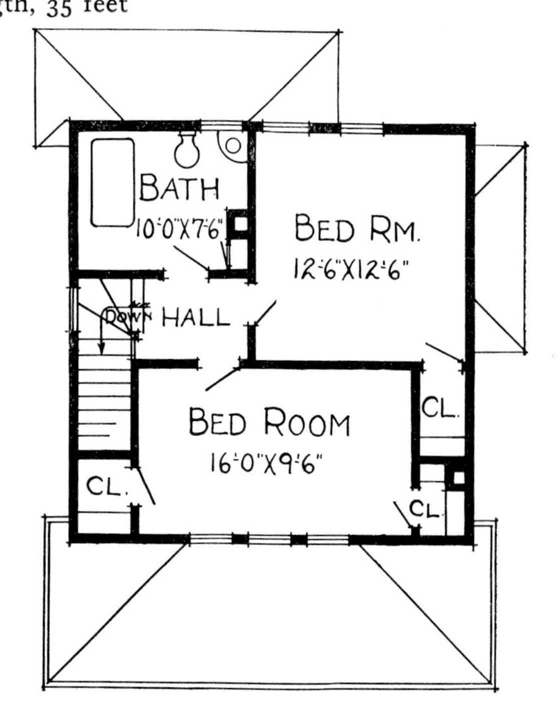

Second Floor Plan

Design No. 5001

Size: Width, 35 feet; Length, 35 feet

PRICE

of Blue Prints, together with a complete set of typewritten specifications

ONLY

$8.00

We mail Plans and Specifications the same day order is received.

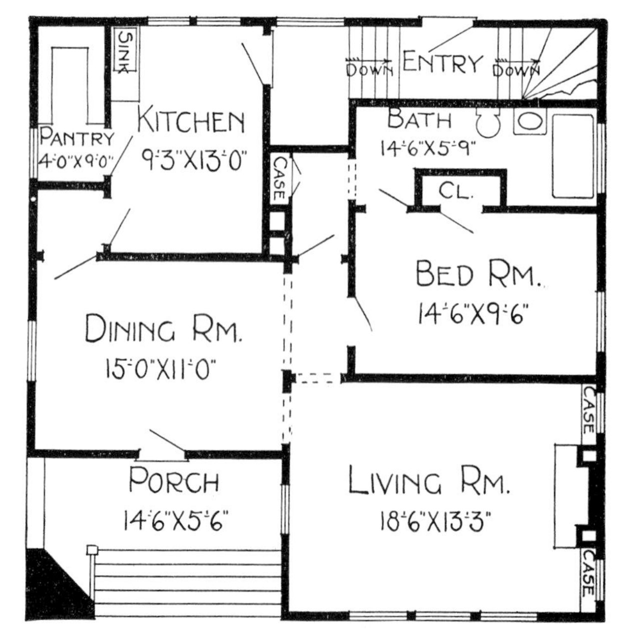

Floor Plan

Blue prints consist of basement plan; floor plan; front, rear, two side elevations; wall sections and all necessary interior details. Specifications consist of twenty-two pages of typewritten matter.

Design No. 5008

Size: Width, 30 feet; Length, 29 feet

Blue prints consist of basement plan; floor plan; front, rear, two side elevations; wall sections and all necessary interior details. Specifications consist of twenty-two pages of typewritten matter.

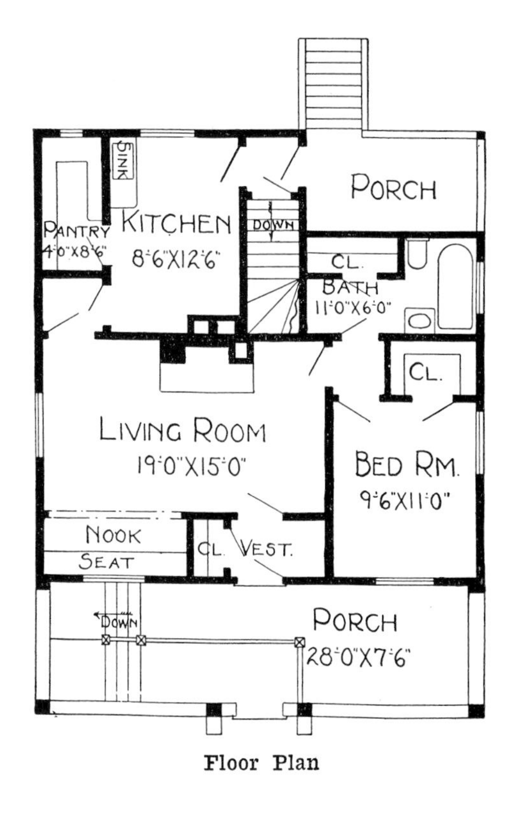

Floor Plan

PRICE

of Blue Prints, together with a complete set of typewritten specifications

ONLY

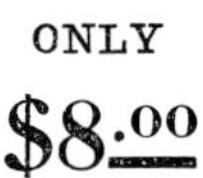

$8.00

We mail Plans and Specifications the same day order is received.

Design No. 5120

Size: Width, 36 feet; Length, 29 feet 6 inches

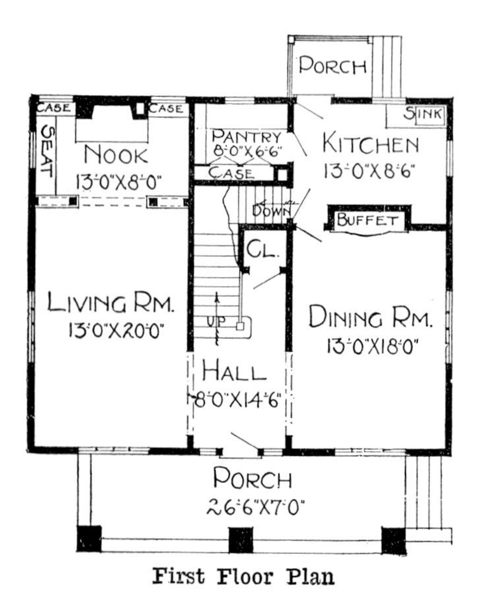

First Floor Plan

Blue prints consist of basement plan; first and second floor plans; front, rear, two side elevations; wall sections and all necessary interior details. Specifications consist of twenty-two pages of typewritten matter.

PRICE

of Blue Prints, together with a complete set of typewritten specifications

ONLY

$12.00

We mail Plans and Specifications the same day order is received.

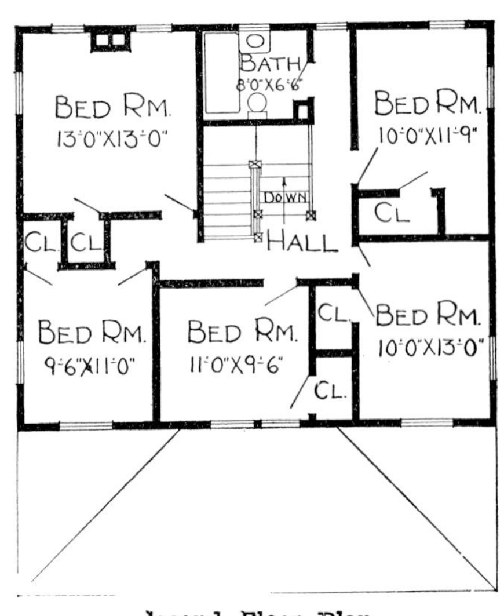

Second Floor Plan

Design No. 5049

Size: Width, 24 feet; Length, 28 feet 6 inches

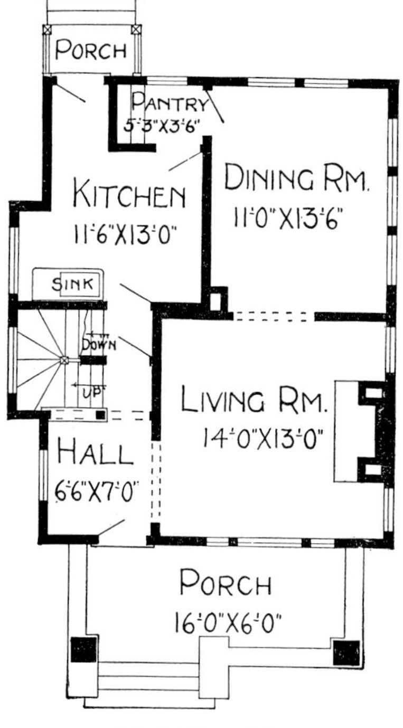

First Floor Plan

Blue prints consist of basement plan; roof plan; first and second floor plans; front, rear, two side elevations; wall sections and all necessary interior details. Specifications consist of twenty-two pages of typewritten matter.

PRICE

of Blue Prints, together with a complete set of typewritten specifications

ONLY

We mail Plans and Specifications the same day order is received.

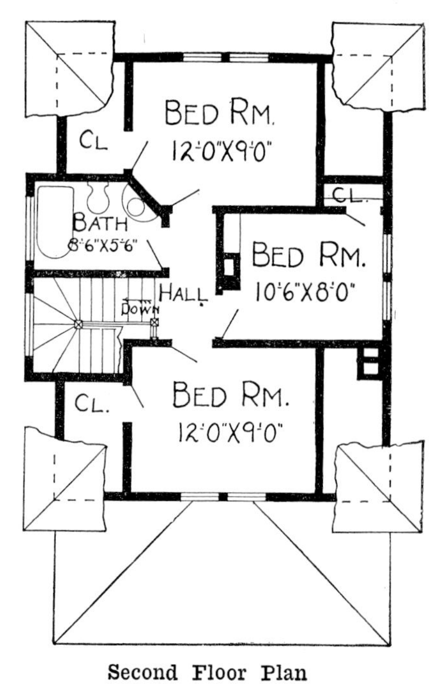

Second Floor Plan

Design No. 5040

Size: Width, 30 feet; Length, 39 feet

PRICE

of Blue Prints, together with a complete set of typewritten specifications

ONLY

$10.00

We mail Plans and Specifications the same day order is received.

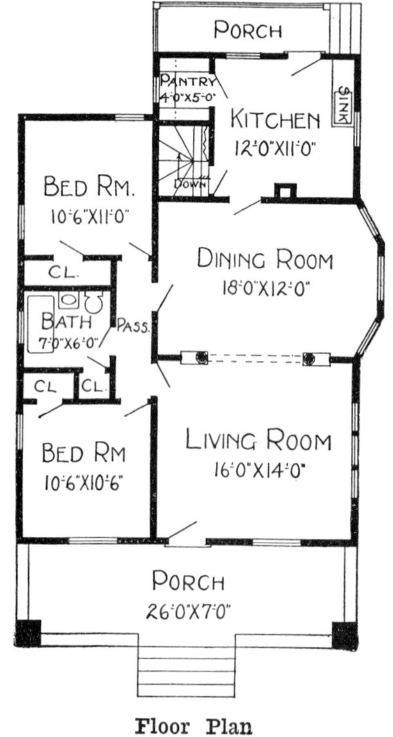

Floor Plan

Blue prints consist of basement plan; roof plan; floor plan; front, rear, two side elevations; wall sections and all necessary interior details. Specifications consist of twenty-two pages of typewritten matter.

Design No. 5108

Size: Width, 26 feet; Length, 53 feet

Blue prints consist of basement plan; roof plan; floor plan; front, rear, two side elevations; wall sections and all necessary interior details. Specifications consist of twenty-two pages of typewritten matter.

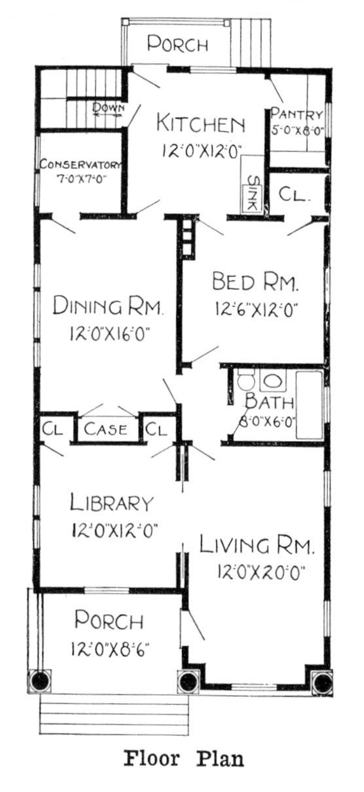

Floor Plan

PRICE

of Blue Prints, together with a complete set of typewritten specifications

ONLY

$10.00

We mail Plans and Specifications the same day order is received.

Design No. 9039=B

Size: Width, 37 feet; Length, 31 feet 6 inches

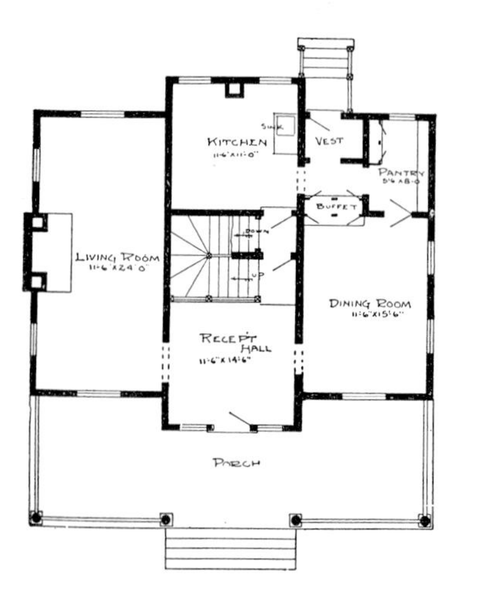

First Floor Plan

Blue prints consist of basement plan; roof plan; first and second floor plans; front, rear, two side elevations; wall sections and all necessary interior details. Specifications consist of twenty-two pages of typewritten matter.

PRICE

of Blue Prints, together with a complete set of typewritten specifications

ONLY

$12.00

We mail Plans and Specifications the same day order is received.

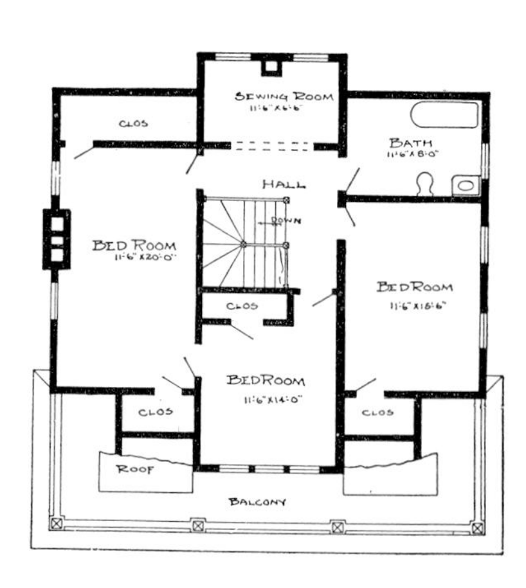

Second Floor Plan

Design No. 7047=B

Size: Width, 25 feet 6 inches; Length, 30 feet 6 inches

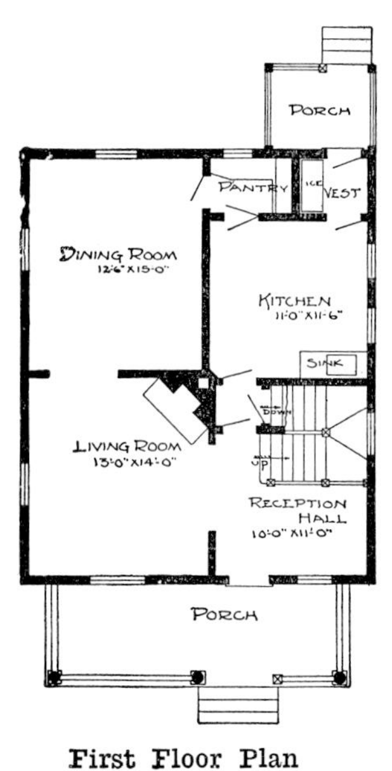

First Floor Plan

Blue prints consist of basement plan; first and second floor plans; front, rear, two side elevations; wall sections and all necessary interior details. Specifications consist of twenty-two pages of typewritten matter.

PRICE

of Blue Prints, together with a complete set of typewritten specifications

ONLY

$12.00

We mail Plans and Specifications the same day order is received.

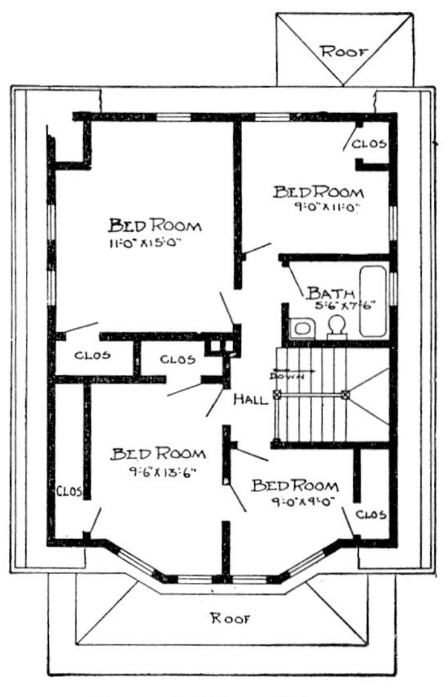

Second Floor Plan

Design No. 5066

Size: Width, 23 feet 6 inches; Length, 32 feet 6 inches

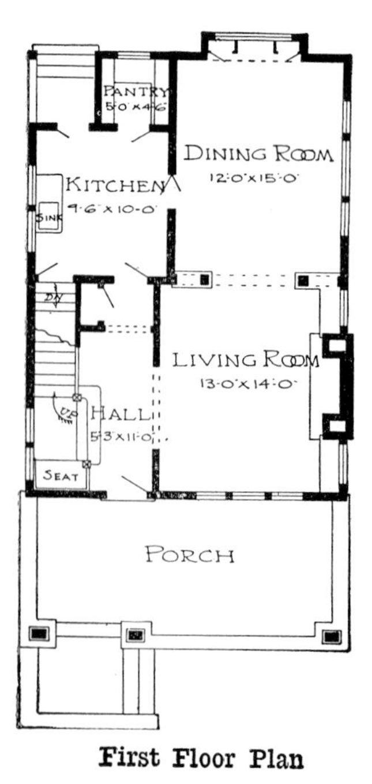

First Floor Plan

Blue prints consist of foundation plan; roof plan; first and second floor plan; front, rear, two side elevations; wall sections and all necessary interior details. Specifications consist of twenty-two pages of typewritten matter.

PRICE

of Blue Prints, together with a complete set of typewritten specifications

ONLY

$15.00

We mail Plans and Specifications the same day order is received.

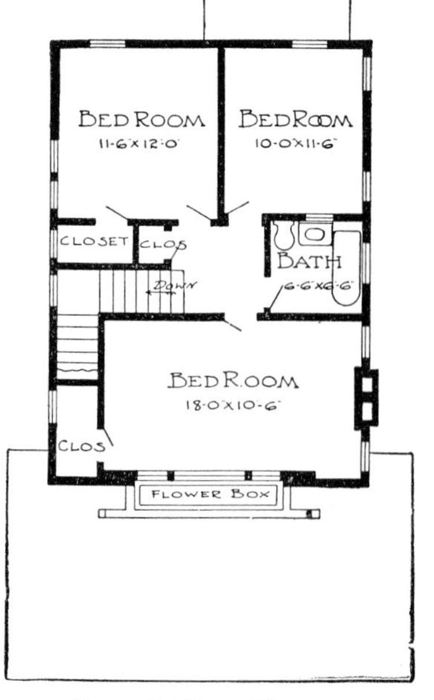

Second Floor Plan

Design No. 5071

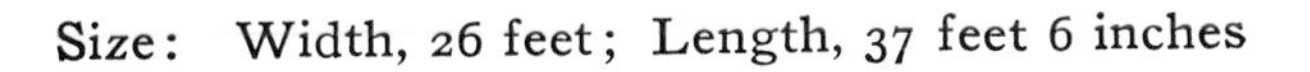

Size: Width, 26 feet; Length, 37 feet 6 inches

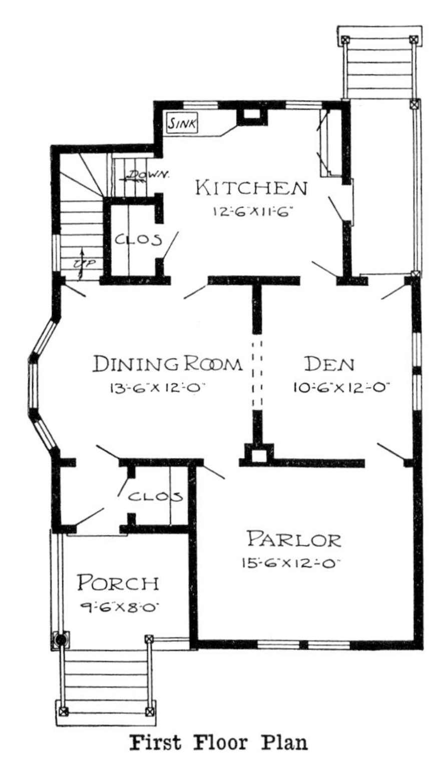

First Floor Plan

Blue prints consist of basement plan; first and second floor plans; front, rear, two side elevations; wall sections and all necessary interior details. Specifications consist of twenty-two pages of typewritten matter.

PRICE

of Blue Prints, together with a complete set of typewritten specifications

ONLY

$12.00

We mail Plans and Specifications the same day order is received.

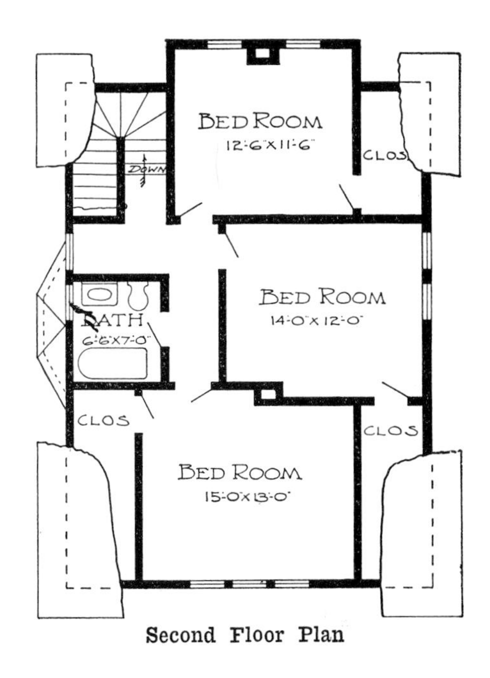

Second Floor Plan

Design No. 6078=B

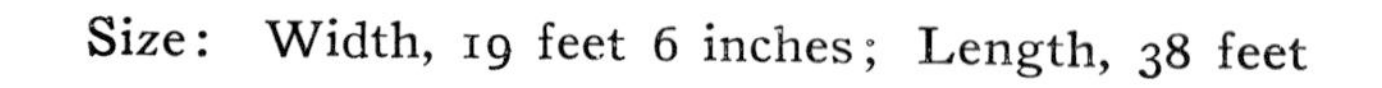

Size: Width, 19 feet 6 inches; Length, 38 feet

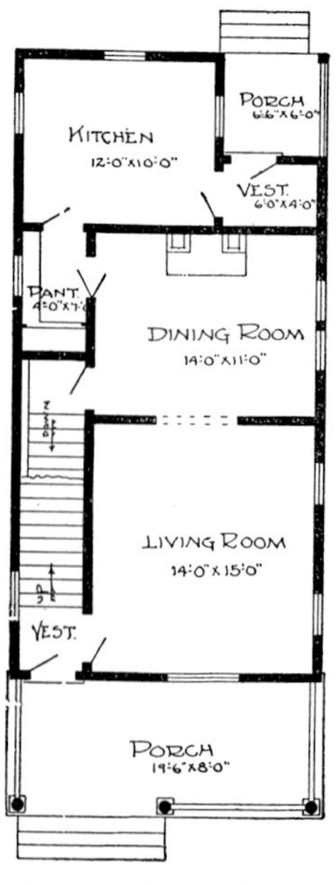

First Floor Plan

Blue prints consist of basement plan; first and second floor plans; front, rear, two side elevations; wall sections and all necessary interior details. Specifications consist of twenty-two pages of typewritten matter.

PRICE

of Blue Prints, together with a complete set of typewritten specifications

ONLY

$12.00

We mail Plans and Specifications the same day order is received.

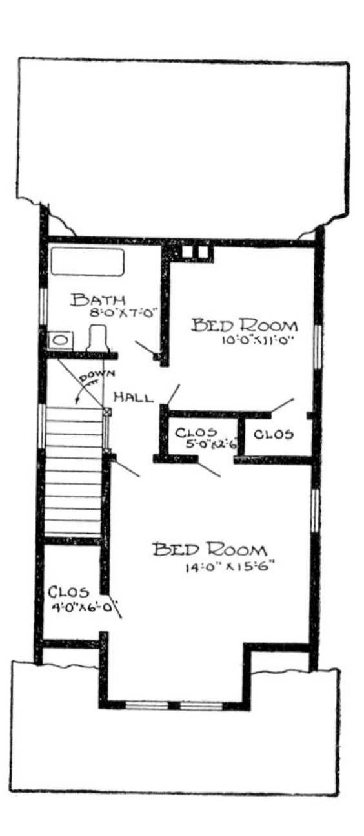

Second Floor Plan

Design No. 5136

Size: Width, 23 feet 6 inches; Length, 29 feet 6 inches

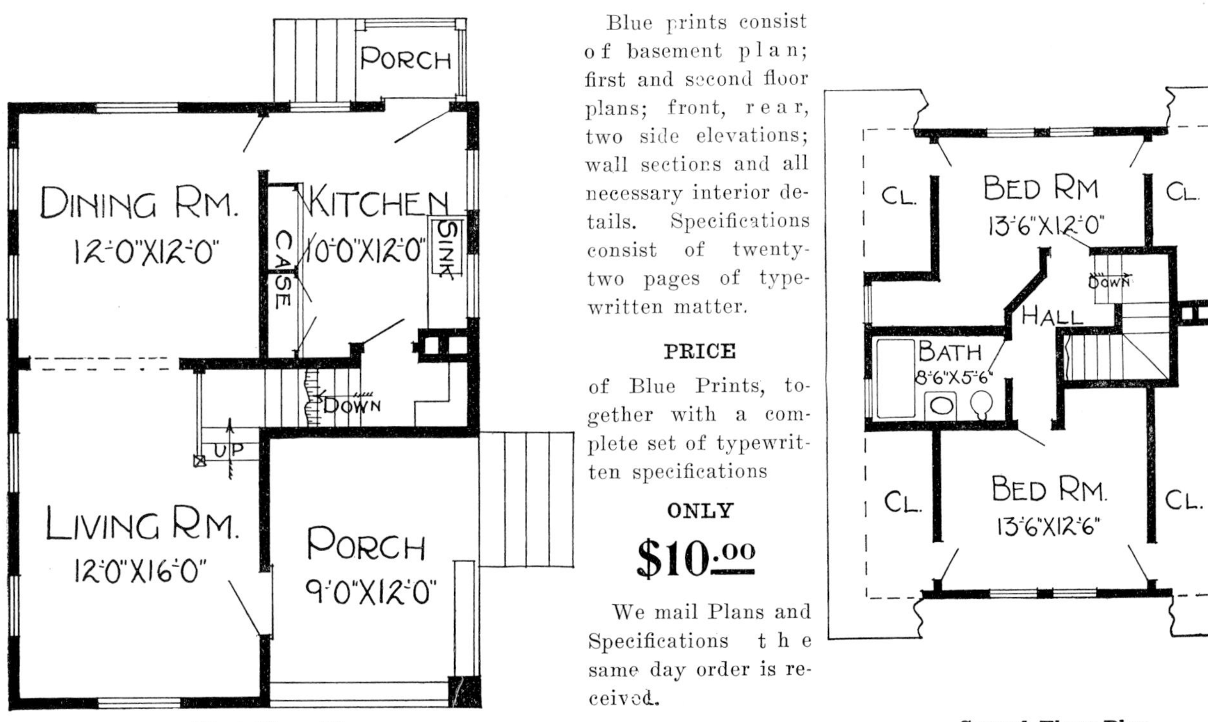

Blue prints consist of basement plan; first and second floor plans; front, rear, two side elevations; wall sections and all necessary interior details. Specifications consist of twenty-two pages of typewritten matter.

PRICE

of Blue Prints, together with a complete set of typewritten specifications

ONLY

$10.00

We mail Plans and Specifications the same day order is received.

First Floor Plan

Second Floor Plan

Design No. 7081-B

Size: Width, 23 feet 6 inches; Length, 35 feet

PRICE
of Blue Prints, together with a complete set of typewritten specifications

ONLY

$10.00

We mail Plans and Specifications the same day order is received.

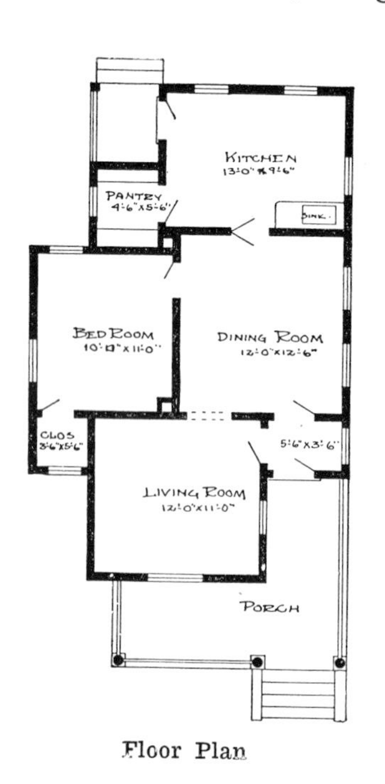

Floor Plan

Blue prints consist of foundation plan; roof plan; floor plan; front, rear, two side elevations; wall sections and all necessary interior details. Specifications consist of twenty-two pages of typewritten matter.

Design No. 5069

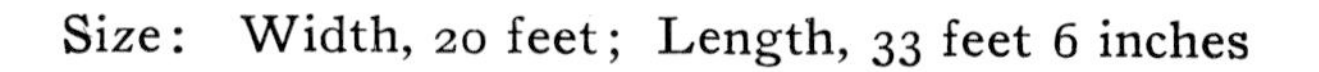

Size: Width, 20 feet; Length, 33 feet 6 inches

Blue prints consist of foundation plan; roof plan; floor plan; front, rear, two side elevations; wall sections and all necessary interior details. Specifications consist of twenty-two pages of typewritten matter.

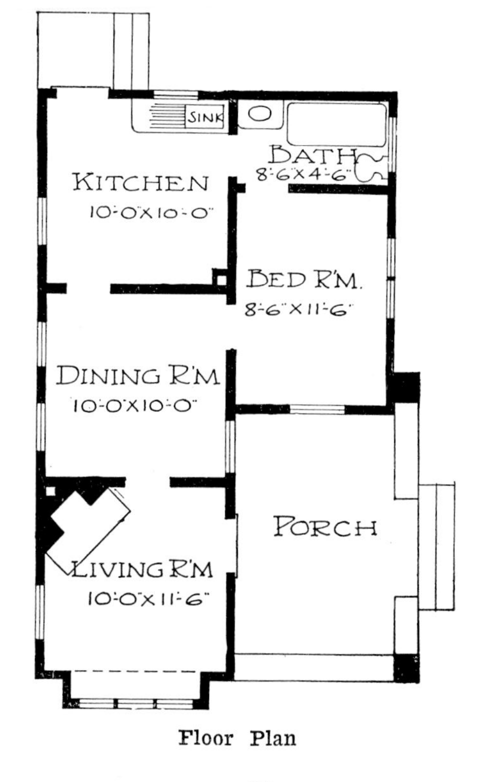

Floor Plan

PRICE

of Blue Prints, together with a complete set of typewritten specifications

ONLY

$10.00

We mail Plans and Specifications the same day order is received.

Design No. 7067-B

Size: Width, 28 feet 6 inches; Length, 28 feet

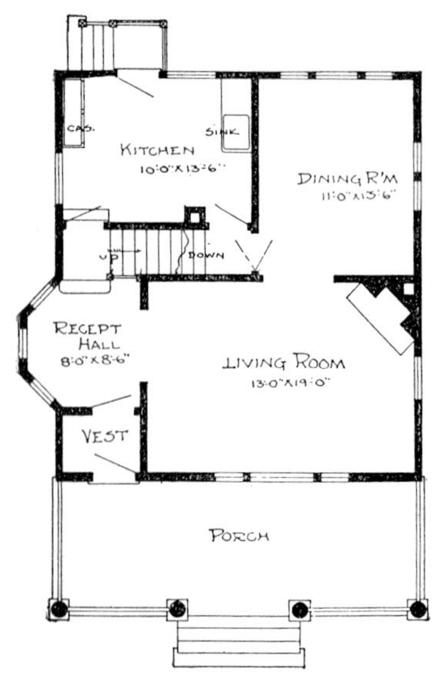

First Floor Plan

Blue prints consist of basement plan; roof plan; first and second floor plans; front, rear and two side elevations; wall sections and all necessary interior details. Specifications consist of twenty-two pages of typewritten matter.

PRICE

of Blue Prints, together with a complete set of typewritten specifications

ONLY

$12.00

We mail Plans and Specifications the same day order is received.

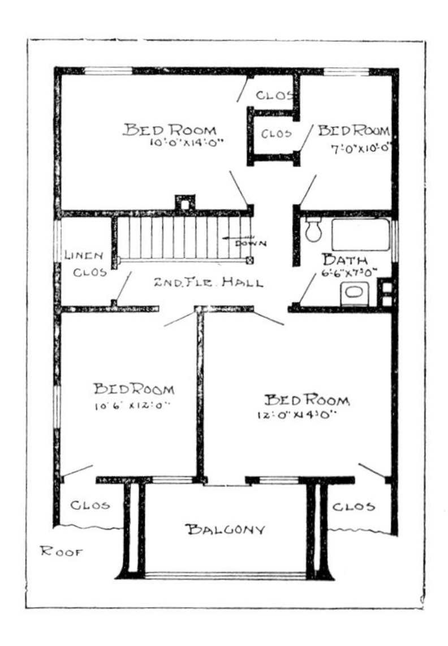

Second Floor Plan

Design No. 5089

Size: Width, 24 feet; Length, 30 feet

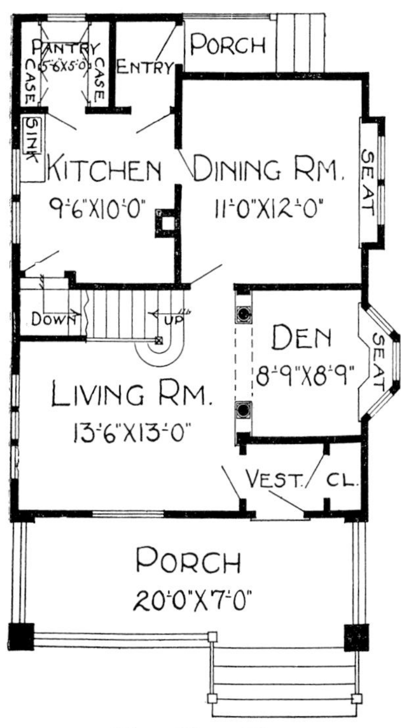

First Floor Plan

Blue prints consist of basement plan; roof plan; first and second floor plans; front, rear, two side elevations; wall sections and all necessary interior details. Specifications consist of twenty-two pages of typewritten matter.

PRICE

of Blue Prints, together with a complete set of typewritten specifications

ONLY

We mail Plans and Specifications the same day order is received.

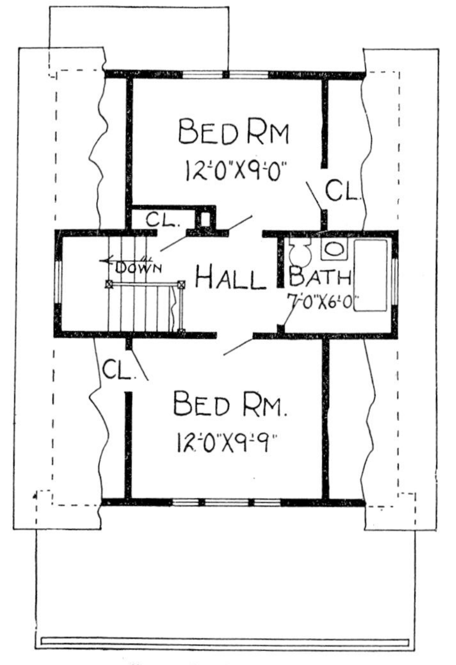

Second Floor Plan

Design No. 5060

Size: Width, 26 feet 6 inches; Length, 28 feet

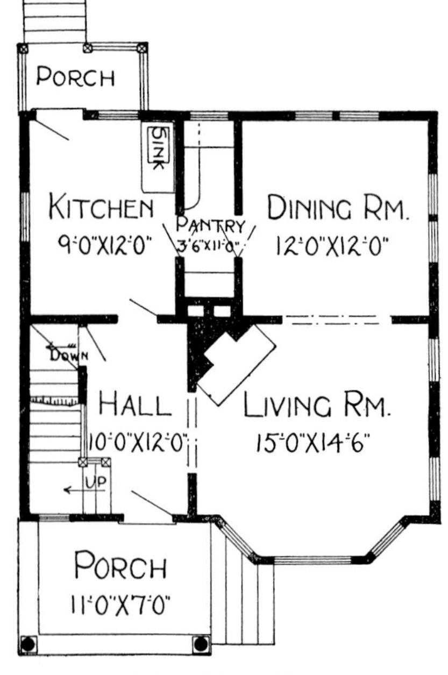

First Floor Plan

Blue prints consist of basement plan; roof plan; first and second floor plans; front, rear, two side elevations; wall sections and all necessary interior details. Specifications consist of twenty-two pages of typewritten matter.

PRICE

of Blue Prints, together with a complete set of typewritten specifications

ONLY

We mail Plans and Specifications the same day order is received.

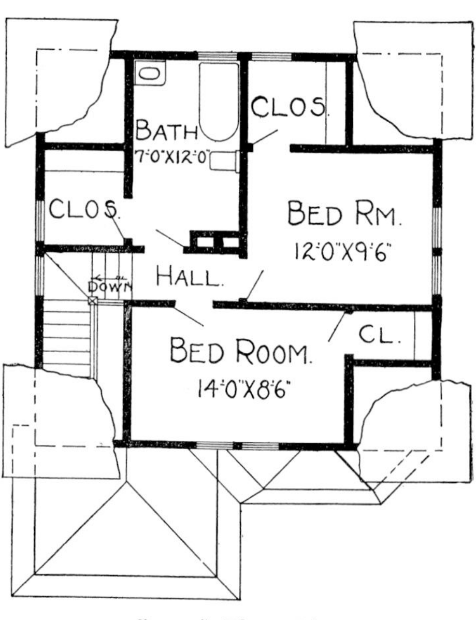

Second Floor Plan

Design No. 5117

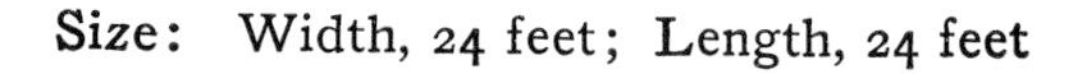

Size: Width, 24 feet; Length, 24 feet

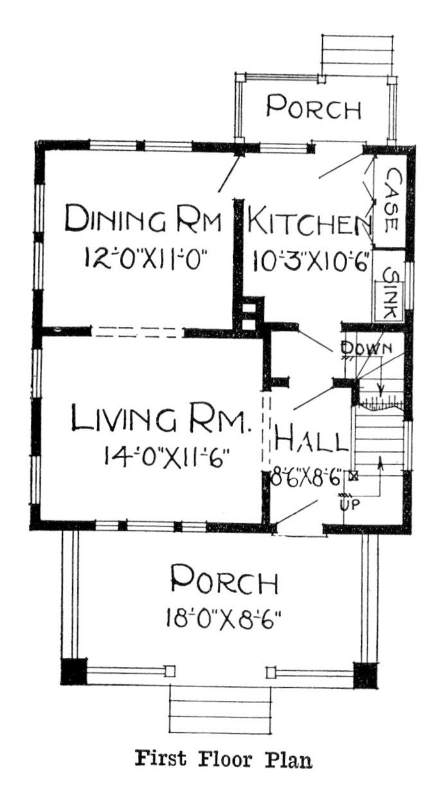

First Floor Plan

Blue prints consist of basement plan; first and second floor plans; front, rear, two side elevations; wall sections and all necessary interior details. Specifications consist of twenty-two pages of typewritten matter.

PRICE

of Blue Prints, together with a complete set of typewritten specifications

ONLY

$10.00

We mail Plans and Specifications the same day order is received.

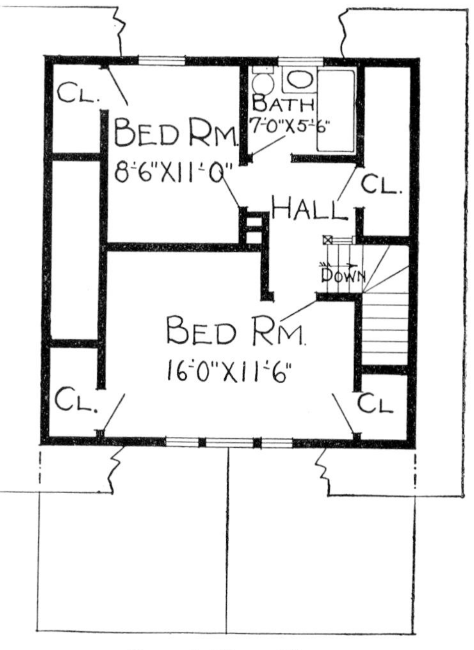

Second Floor Plan

Design No. 5077

Size: Width, 25 feet; Length, 34 feet

PRICE

of Blue Prints, together with a complete set of typewritten specifications

ONLY

We mail Plans and Specifications the same day order is received.

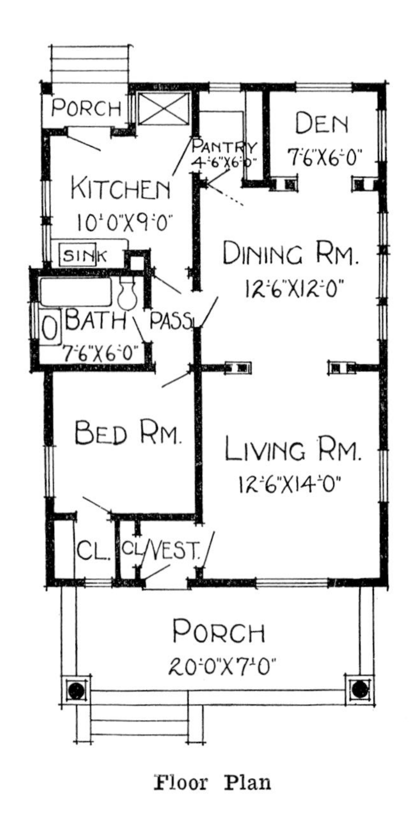

Floor Plan

Blue prints consist of foundation plan; roof plan; floor plan; front, rear, two side elevations wall sections and all necessary interior details. Specifications consist of twenty-two pages of typewritten matter.

Design No. 5123

Size: Width, 24 feet; Length, 34 feet

Blue prints consist of foundation plan; attic and roof plans; floor plan, front, rear, two side elevations; wall sections and all necessary interior details. Specifications consist of twenty-two pages of typewritten matter.

PORCH
SINK
KITCHEN 10'0"X10'0"
PANTRY 3'6"X6'6"
BATH 8'6"X6'6"
CL.
DINING RM. 14'0"X11'0"
BED RM. 8'6"X11'0"
TERRACE 8'0"X10'6"
LIVING RM. 14'0"X11'0"

Floor Plan

PRICE

of Blue Prints, together with a complete set of typewritten specifications

ONLY

We mail Plans and Specifications the same day order is received.

Design No. 8295-B

Size: Width, 37 feet 8 inches; Length, 33 feet 4 inches

PRICE

of Blue Prints, together with a complete set of typewritten specifications

ONLY

$10.00

We mail Plan and Specifications the same day order is received.

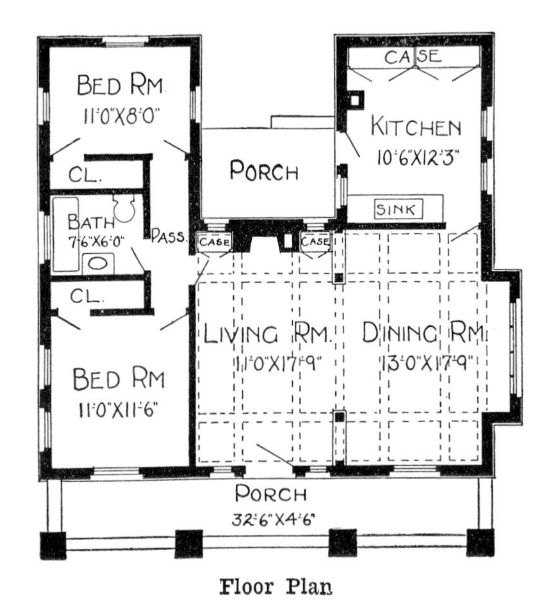

Floor Plan

Blue prints consist of foundation plan; floor plan; front, two side elevations; wall sections and all necessary interior details. Specifications consist of twenty-two pages of typewritten matter.

Design No. 8329=B

Size: Width, 30 feet 6 inches; Length, 31 feet 6 inches

Blue prints consist of basement plan; floor plan; front, rear, two side elevations; wall sections and all necessary interior details. Specifications consist of twenty-two pages of typewritten matter.

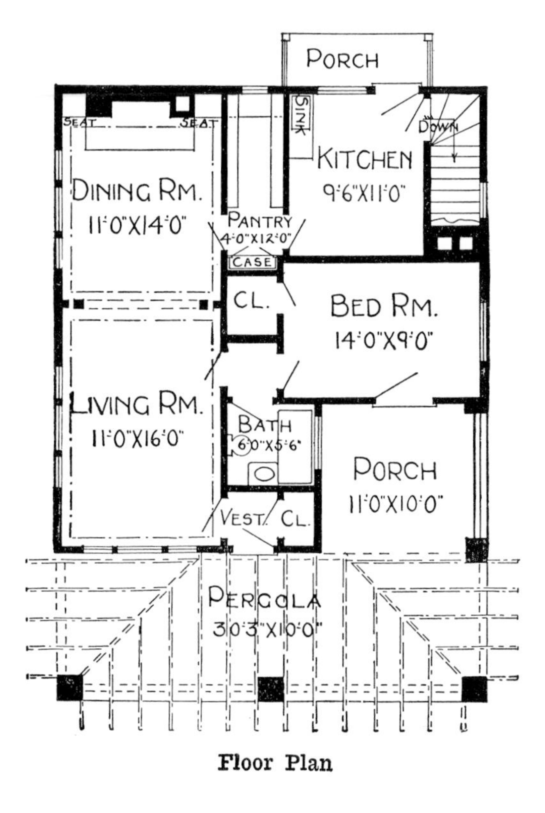

Floor Plan

PRICE

of Blue Prints, together with a complete set of typewritten specifications

ONLY

$10.00

We mail Plans and Specifications the same day order is received.

Design No. 5012

Size: Width, 24 feet; Length, 24 feet

PRICE

of Blue Prints, together with a complete set of typewritten specifications

ONLY

We mail Plans and Specifications the same day order is received.

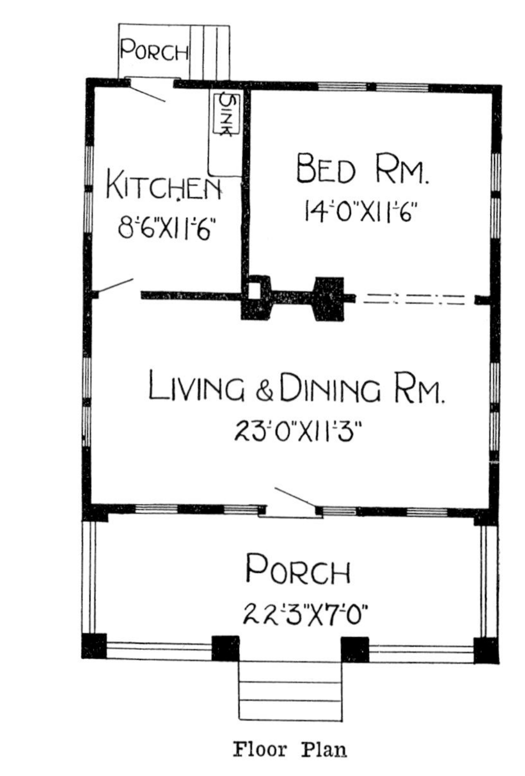

Floor Plan

Blue prints consist of foundation plan; floor plan; front, rear, two side elevations; wall sections and all necessary interior details. Specifications consist of twenty-two pages of typewritten matter.

Design No. 5009

Size: Width, 34 feet 6 inches; Width, 33 feet

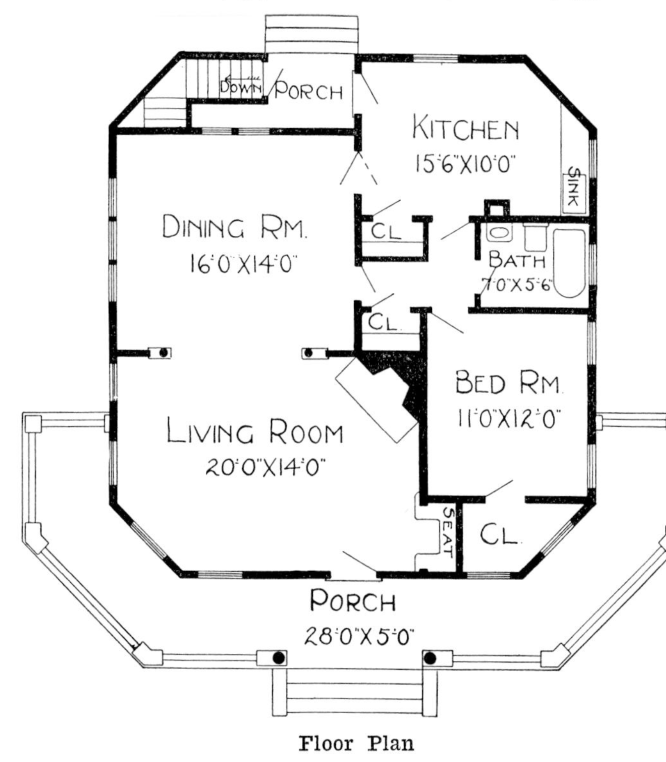

Floor Plan

Blue prints consist of basement plan: floor plan; front, rear, two side elevations; wall sections and all necessary interior details. Specifications consist of twenty-two pages of typewritten matter.

PRICE

of Blue Prints, together with a complete set of typewritten specifications

ONLY

We mail Plans and Specifications the same day order is received.

Design No. 5090

Size: Width, 27 feet; Length, 16 feet

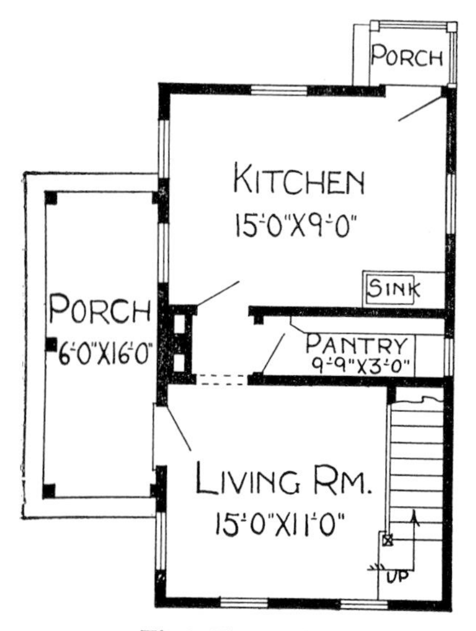

First Floor Plan

Blue prints consist of basement plan; roof plan; first and second floor plans; front, rear and two side elevations; wall sections and all necessary interior details. Specifications consist of twenty-two pages of typewritten matter.

PRICE

of Blue Prints, together with a complete set of typewritten specifications

ONLY

We mail Plans and Specifications the same day order is received.

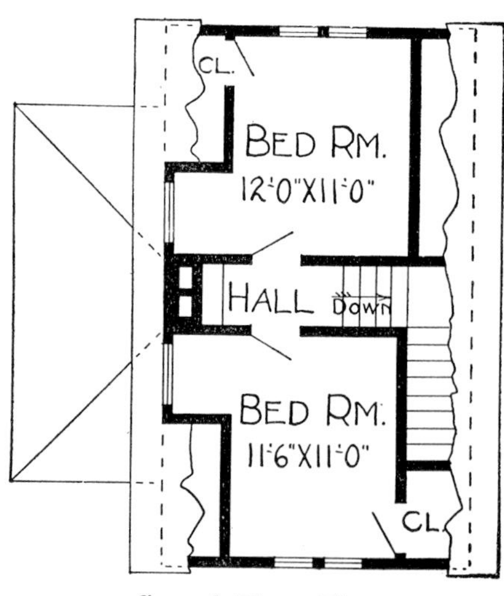

Second Floor Plan

Design No. 5080

Size: Width, 22 feet; Length, 29 feet

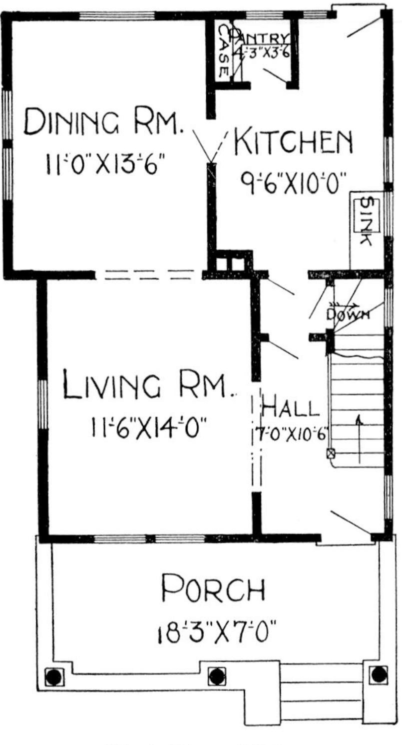

First Floor Plan

Blue prints consist of cellar and foundation plan; roof plan; first and second floor plans; front, rear, two side elevations; wall sections and all necessary interior details. Specifications consist of twenty-two pages of typewritten matter.

PRICE

of Blue Prints, together with a complete set of typewritten specifications

ONLY

We mail Plans and Specifications the same day order is received.

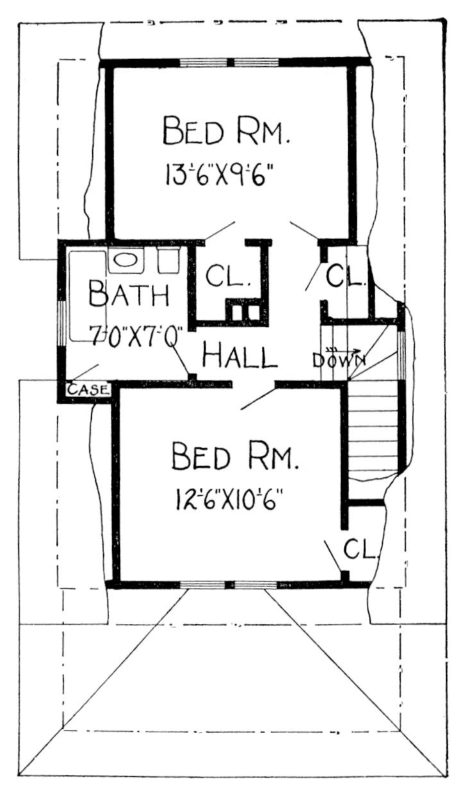

Second Floor Plan

Design No. 5125

Size: Width, 42 feet 6 inches; Width, 28 feet

PRICE

of Blue Prints, together with a complete set of typewritten specifications

ONLY

$8.00

We mail Plans and Specifications the same day order is received.

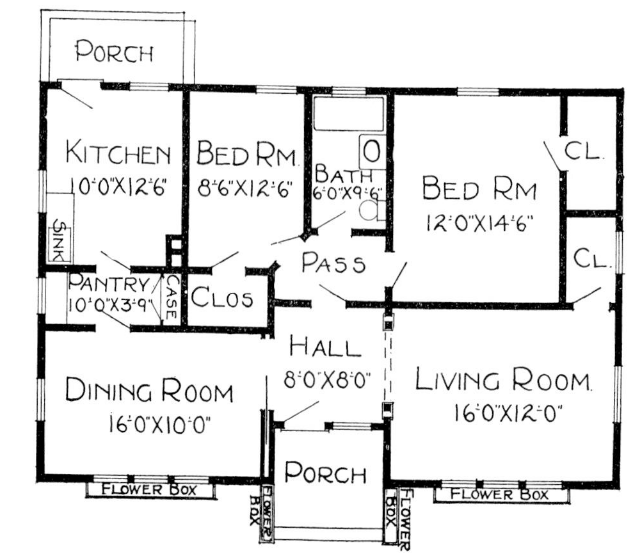

Floor Plan

Blue prints consist of foundation plan; floor plan; front, rear, two side elevations; wall sections and all necessary interior details. Specifications consist of twenty-two pages of typewritten matter.

Design No. 5004

Size: Width, 27 feet; Length, 37 feet 6 inches

Blue prints consist of basement plan; floor plan; front, rear, two side elevations; wall sections and all necessary interior details. Specifications consist of twenty-two pages of typewritten matter.

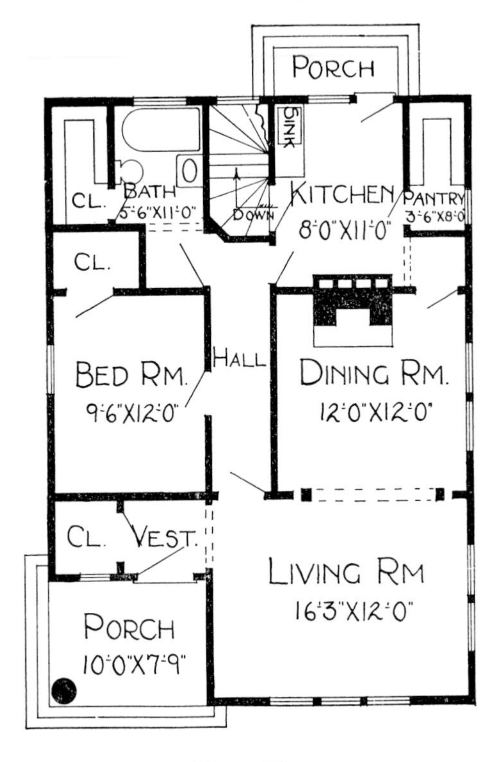

Floor Plan

PRICE

of Blue Prints, together with a complete set of typewritten specifications

ONLY

$8.00

We mail Plans and Specifications the same day order is received.

Design No. 5019

Size: Width, 53 feet 6 inches; Length, 31 feet 6 inches

ENTRY
KITCHEN
9'6"X12'0"
SERVANTS RM.
10'0"X10'6"
SINK
PANTRY
CASE
PANTRY
UP
VEST.
PORCH
6'0"X20'0"
DINING ROOM
20'0"X14'0"
LIVING RM.
16'0"X26'6"
PORCH
6'0"X20'0"
TERRACE

First Floor Plan

Blue prints consist of foundation plan; roof plan; first and second floor plans; front, rear, two side elevations; wall sections and all necessary interior details. Specifications consist of twenty-two pages of typewritten matter.

PRICE

of Blue Prints, together with a complete set of typewritten specifications

ONLY

$10.00

We mail Plans and Specifications the same day order is received.

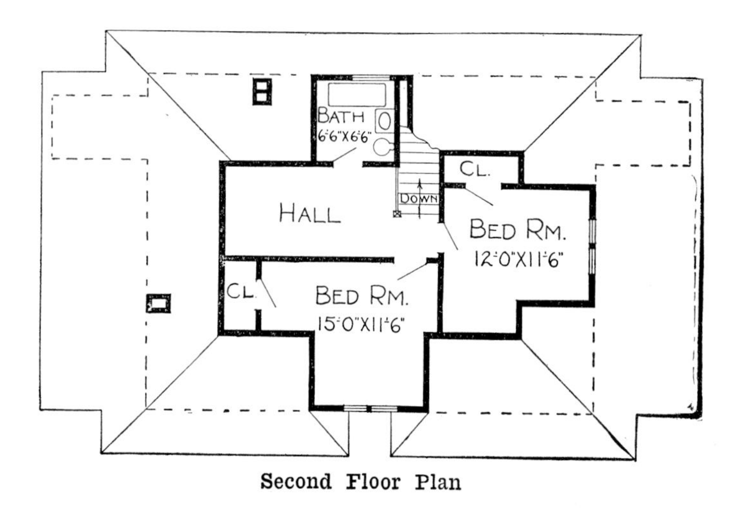

Second Floor Plan

Design No. 5075

Size: Width, 41 feet 6 inches;
Length, 31 feet

Blue prints consist of cellar and foundation plan; roof plan; first and second floor plans; front, rear, two side elvations; wall sections and all necessary interior details. Specifications consist of twenty-two pages of typewritten matter.

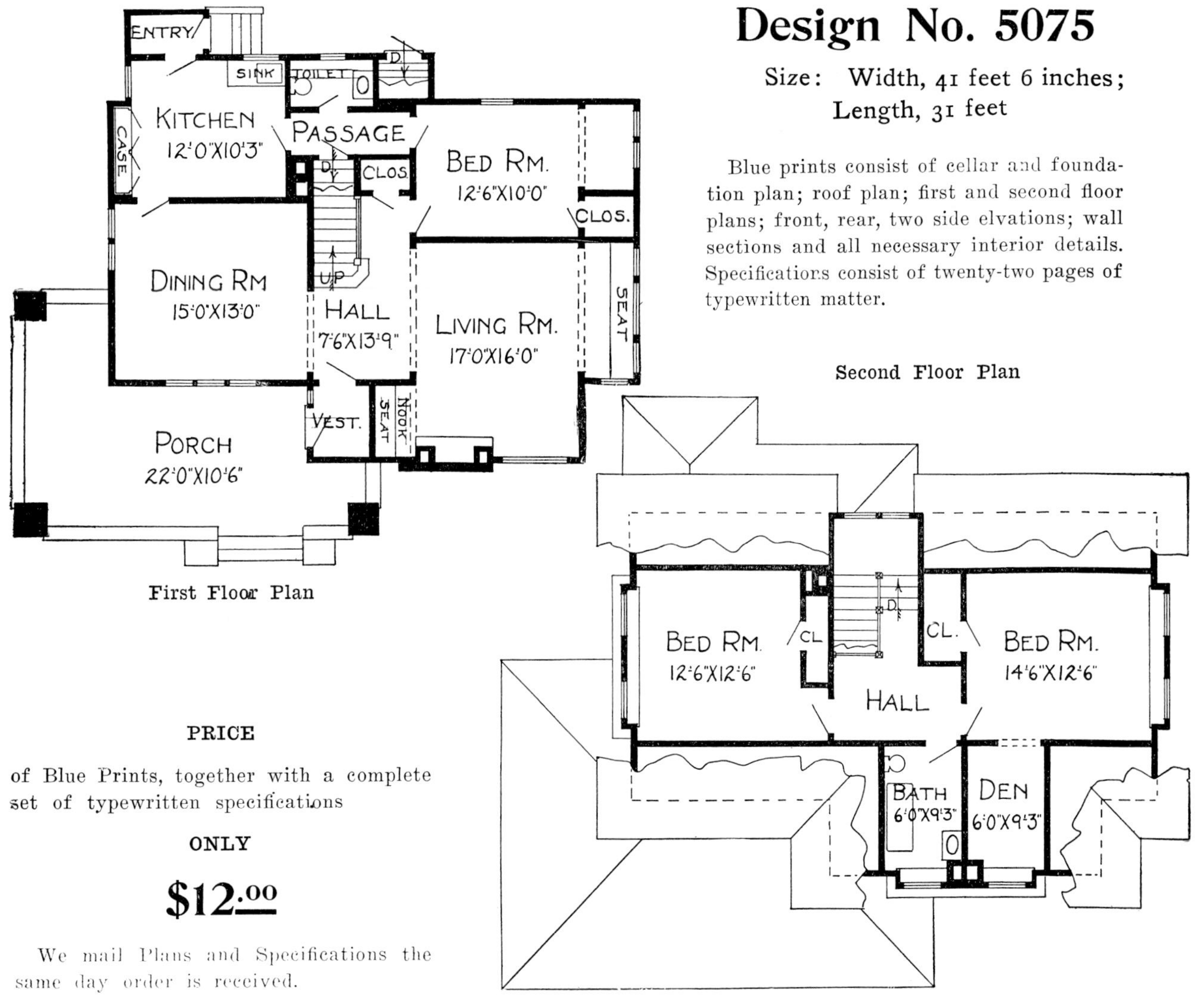

First Floor Plan

Second Floor Plan

PRICE

of Blue Prints, together with a complete set of typewritten specifications

ONLY

$12.00

We mail Plans and Specifications the same day order is received.

Design No. 5130

Size: Width, 22 feet; Length, 43 feet

PRICE

of Blue Prints, together with a complete set of typewritten specifications

ONLY

$8.00

We mail Plans and Specifications the same day order is received.

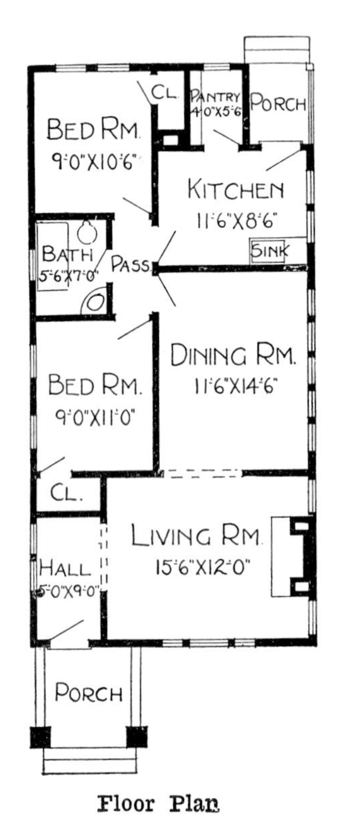

Floor Plan

Blue prints consist of foundation plan; floor plan; front, rear, two side elevations; wall sections and all necessary interior details. Specifications consist of twenty-two pages of typewritten matter.

Design No. 5127

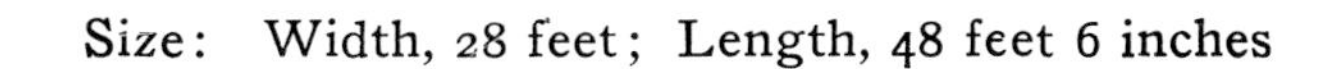

Size: Width, 28 feet; Length, 48 feet 6 inches

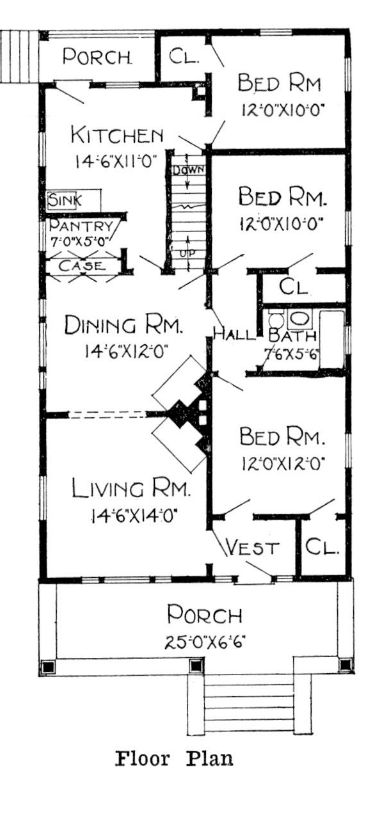

Floor Plan

Blue prints consist of basement plan; roof plan; floor plan; front, rear, two side elevations; wall sections and all necessary interior details. Specifications consist of twenty-two pages of typewritten matter.

PRICE

of Blue Prints, together with a complete set of typewritten specifications

ONLY

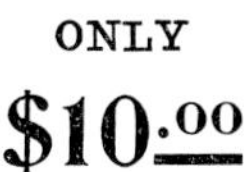

$10.00

We mail Plans and Specifications the same day order is received.

Design No. 5006

Size: Width, 24 feet; Length, 40 feet

PRICE

of Blue Prints, together with a complete set of typewritten specifications

ONLY

$8.00

We mail Plans and Specifications the same day order is received.

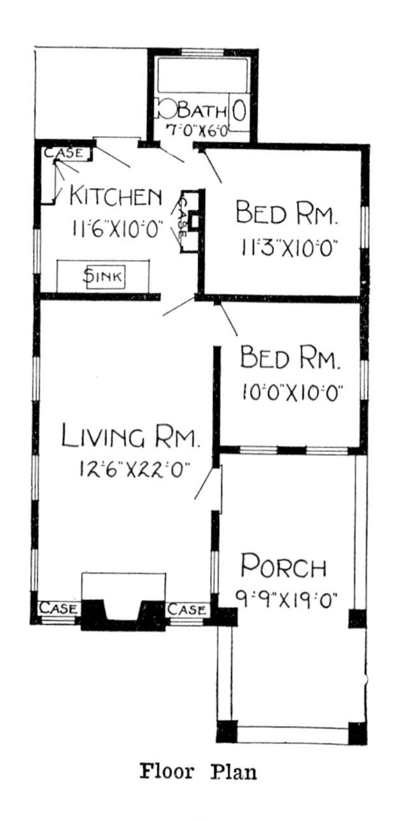

Floor Plan

Blue prints consist of foundation plan; floor plan; front, two side elevations; wall sections and all necessary interior details. Specifications consist of twenty-two pages of typewritten matter.

Design No. 5097

Size: Width, 23 feet; Length, 48 feet 6 inches

Blue prints consist of basement plan; floor plan; front, rear, two side elevations; wall sections and all necessary interior details. Specifications consist of twenty-two pages of typewritten matter.

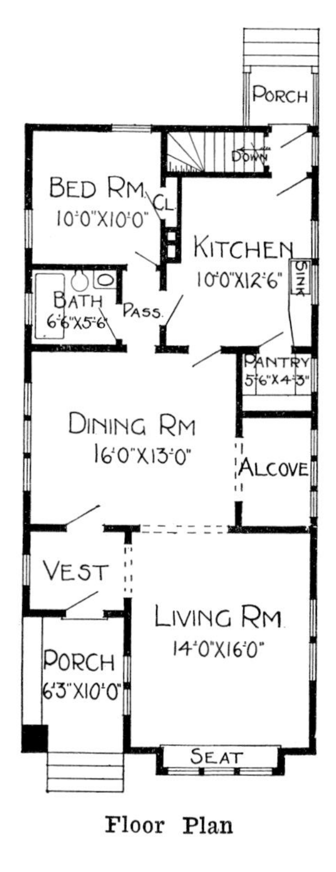

Floor Plan

PRICE

of Blue Prints, together with a complete set of typewritten specifications

ONLY

We mail Plans and Specifications the same day order is received.

Design No. 5065

Size: Width, 20 feet; Length, 28 feet

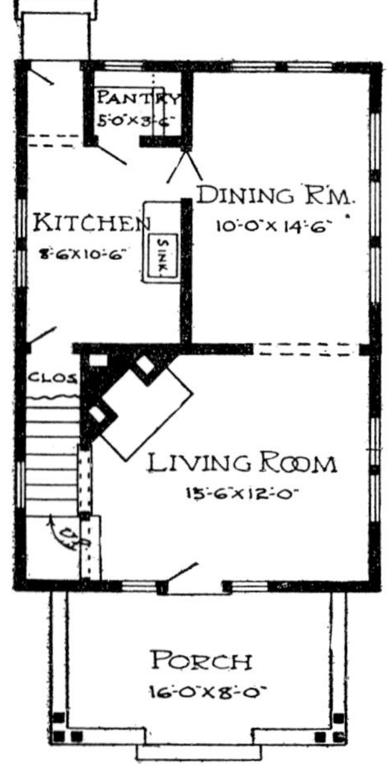

First Floor Plan

Blue prints consist of foundation plan; roof plan; first and second floor plans; front, rear, two side elevations; wall sections and all necessary interior details. Specifications consist of twenty-two pages of typewritten matter.

PRICE

of Blue Prints, together with a complete set of typewritten specifications

ONLY

We mail Plans and Specifications the same day order is received.

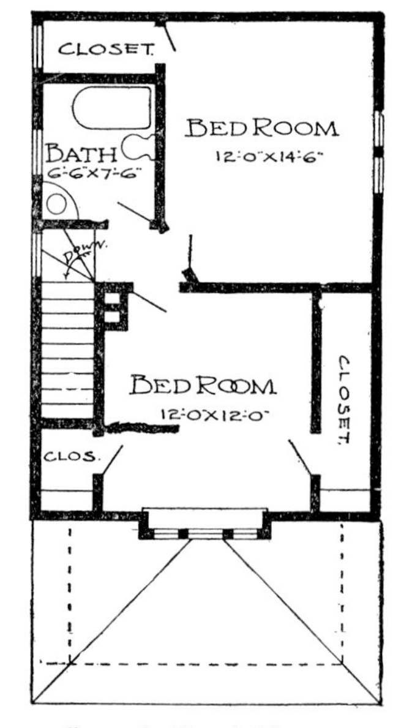

Second Floor Plan

Design No. 7040=B

Size: Width, 21 feet; Length, 28 feet

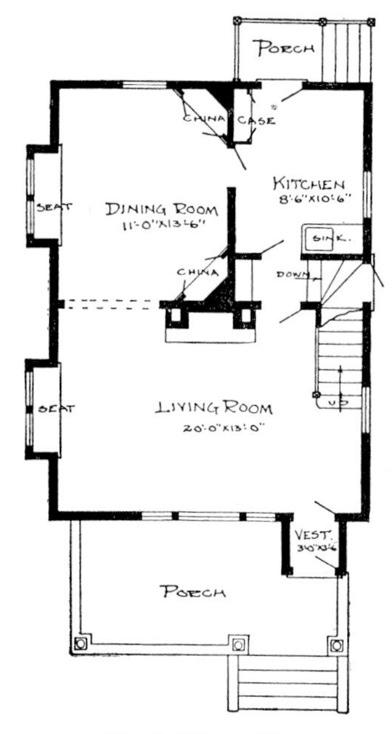

First Floor Plan

Blue prints consist of basement plan; first and second floor plans; front, rear, two side elevations; wall sections and all necessary interior details. Specifications consist of twenty-two pages of typewritten matter.

PRICE

of Blue Prints, together with a complete set of typewritten specifications

ONLY

$10.00

We mail Plans and Specifications the same day order is received.

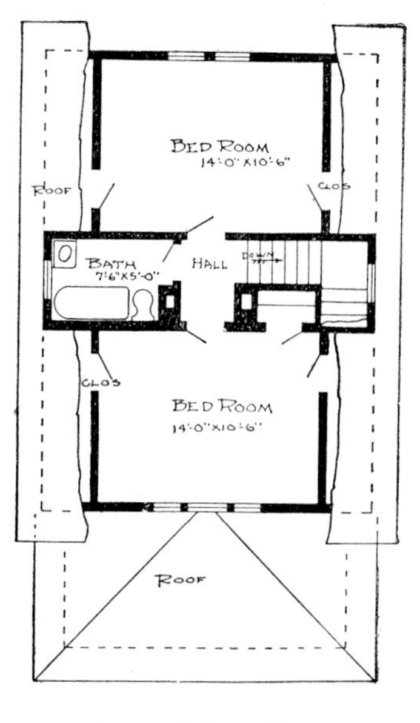

Second Floor Plan

Design No. 5072

Size: Width, 35 feet 6 inches; Length, 27 feet 6 inches

PRICE

of Blue Prints, together with a complete set of typewritten specifications

ONLY

$10.00

We mail Plans and Specifications the same day order is received.

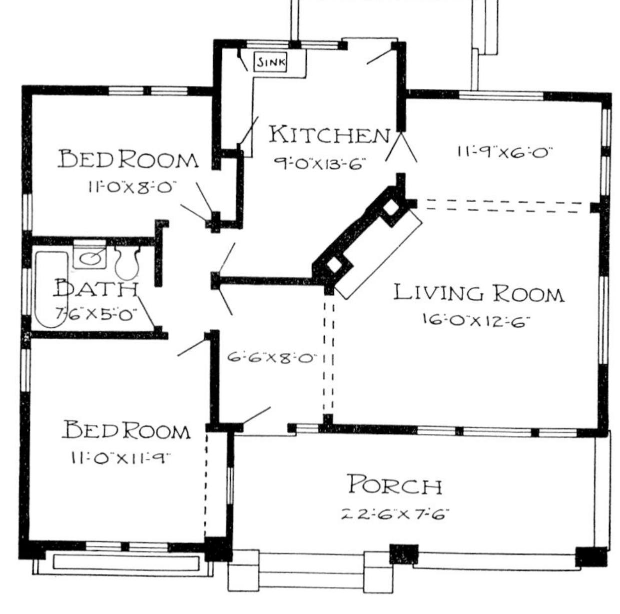

Floor Plan

Blue prints consist of foundation plan; floor plan; front, rear, two side elevations; wall sections and all necessary interior details. Specifications consist of twenty-two pages of typewritten matter.

Design No. 8209=B

Size: Width, 34 feet 4 inches; Length, 35 feet 6 inches

Blue prints consist of basement plan; roof plan; floor plan; front, rear, two side elevations; wall sections and all necessary interior details. Specifications consist of twenty-two pages of typewritten matter.

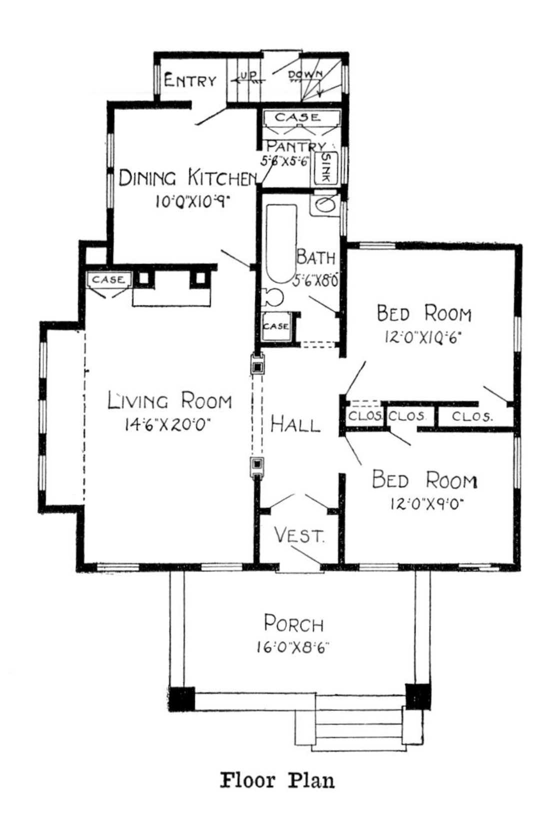

Floor Plan

PRICE

of Blue Prints, together with a complete set of typewritten specifications

ONLY

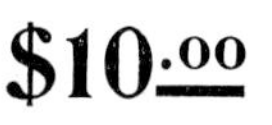

We mail Plans and Specifications the same day order is received.

Design No. 5015

Size: Width, 25 feet; Length, 29 feet

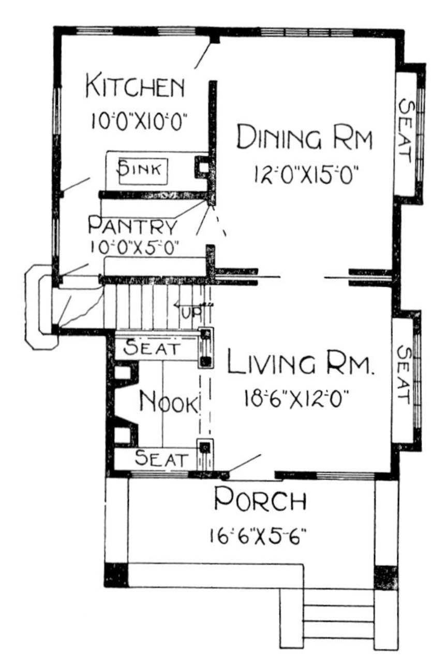

First Floor Plan

Blue prints consist of basement plan; roof plan; first and second floor plans; front, rear, and two side elevations; wall sections and all necessary interior details. Specifications consist of twenty-two pages of typewritten matter.

PRICE

of Blue Prints, together with a complete set of typewritten specifications

ONLY

$12.00

We mail Plans and Specifications the same day order is received.

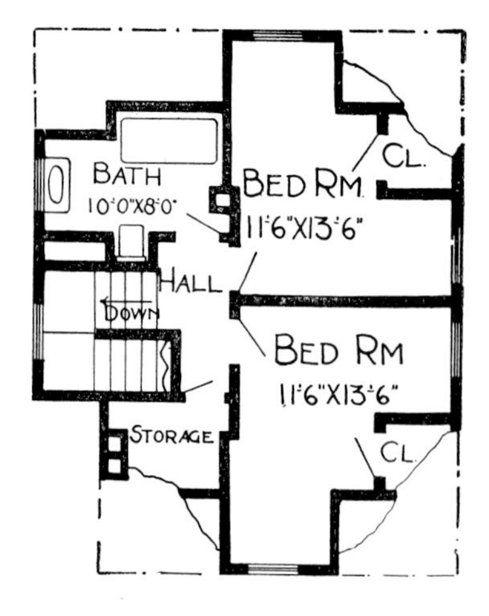

Second Floor Plan

Design No. 5084

Size: Width, 31 feet; Length, 42 feet 6 inches

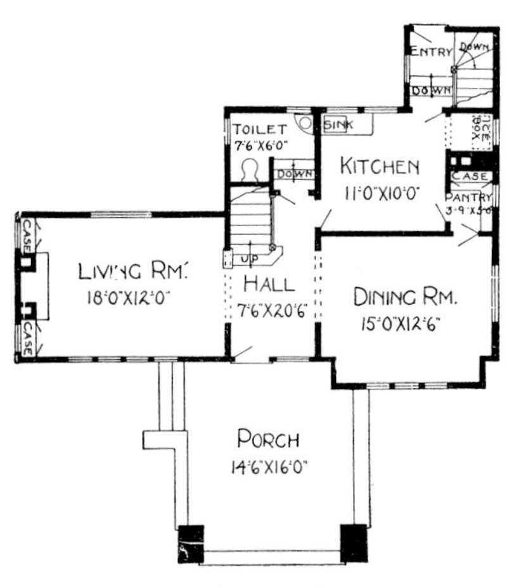

First Floor Plan

Blue prints consist of cellar and foundation plan; roof plan; first and second floor plans; front, rear, two side elevations; wall sections and all necessary interior details. Specifications consist of twenty-two pages of typewritten matter.

PRICE

of Blue Prints, together with a complete set of typewritten specifications

ONLY

$12.00

We mail Plans and Specifications the same day order is received.

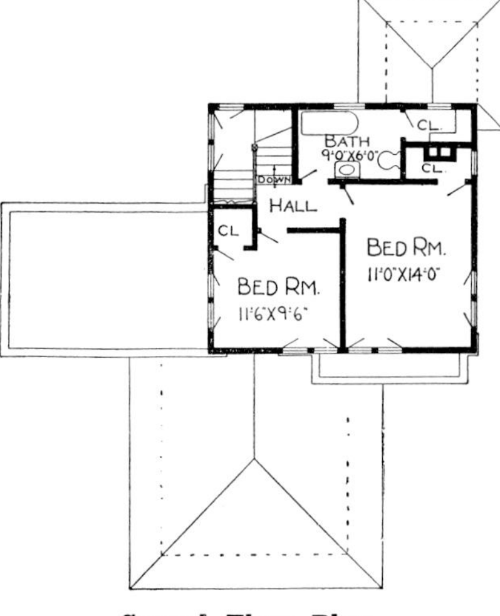

Second Floor Plan

Design No. 5036

Size: Width, 33 feet; Length, 30 feet 6 inches

PRICE

of Blue Prints, together with a complete set of typewritten specifications

ONLY

$10.00

We mail Plans and Specifications the same day order is received.

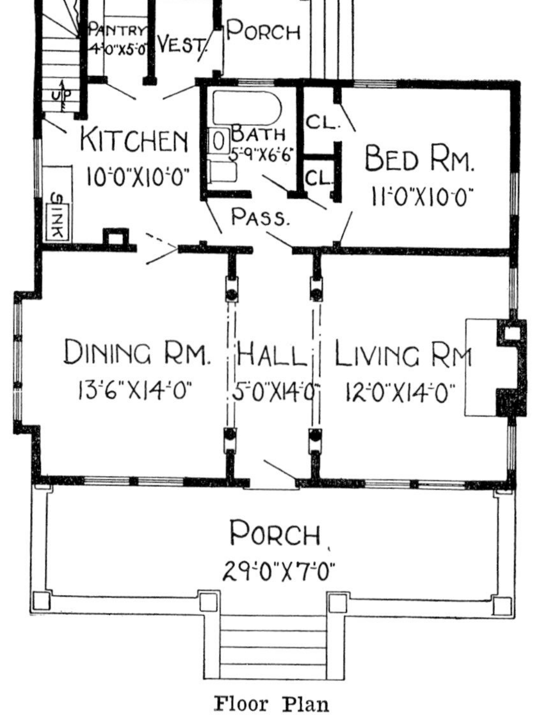

Floor Plan

Blue prints consist of foundation plan; attic and roof plans; floor plan; front, rear, two side elevations; wall sections and all necessary interior details. Specifications consist of twenty-two pages of typewritten matter.

Design No. 5081

Size: Width, 20 feet 8 inches; Length, 30 feet 8 inches

Blue prints consist of foundation plan; floor plan; front, rear, two side elevations; wall sections and all necessary interior details. Specifications consist of twenty-two pages of typewritten matter.

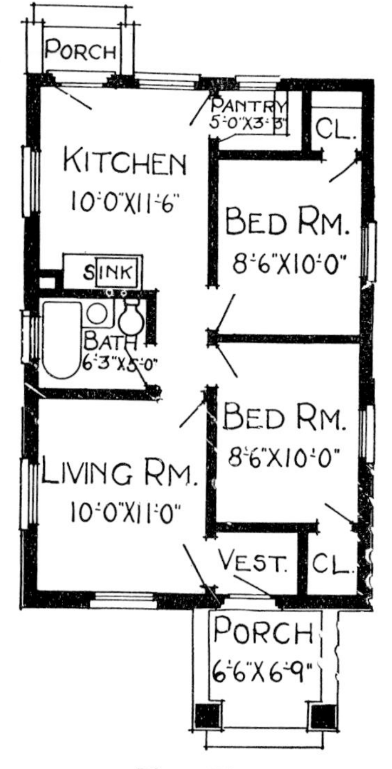

Floor Plan

PRICE

of Blue Prints, together with a complete set of typewritten specifications

ONLY

$8.00

We mail Plans and Specifications the same day order is received.

Design No. 5124

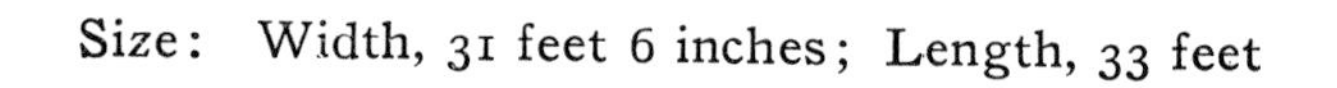

Size: Width, 31 feet 6 inches; Length, 33 feet

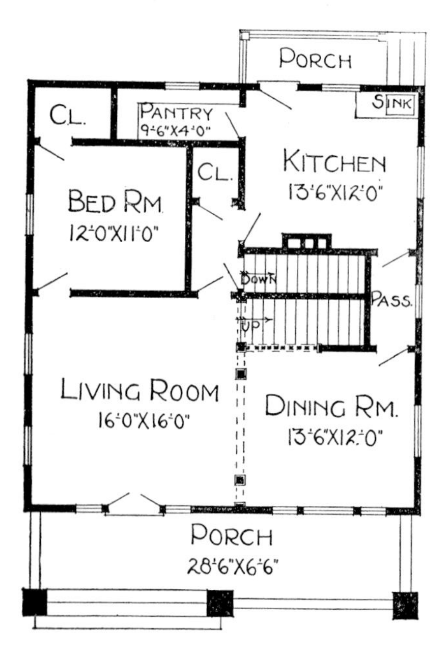

First Floor Plan

Blue prints consist of cellar and foundation plan; first and second floor plans; front, rear, two side elevations; wall sections and all necessary interior details. Specifications consist of twenty-two pages of typewritten matter.

PRICE

of Blue Prints, together with a complete set of typewritten specifications

ONLY

$12.00

We mail Plans and Specifications the same day order is received.

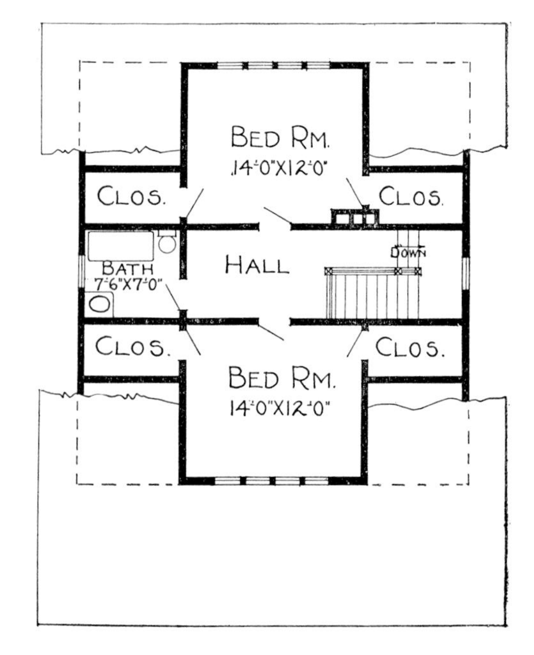

Second Floor Plan

Design No. 5104

Size: Width, 25 feet 6 inches; Length, 37 feet

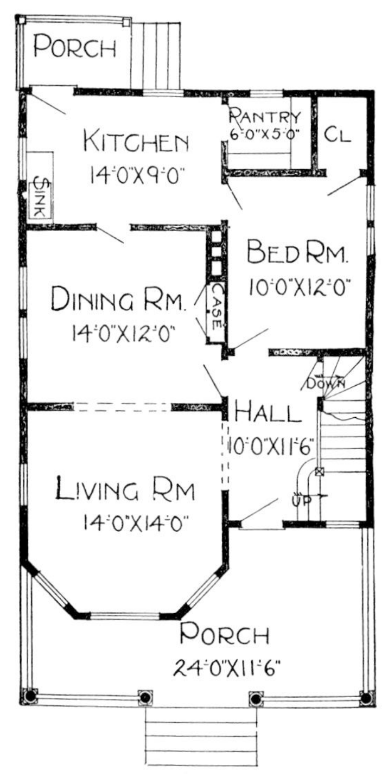

First Floor Plan

Blue prints consist of basement plan; roof plan; first and second floor plans; front, rear, two side elevations; wall sections and all necessary interior details. Specifications consist of twenty-two pages of typewritten matter.

PRICE

of Blue Prints, together with a complete set of typewritten specifications

ONLY

We mail Plans and Specifications the same day order is received.

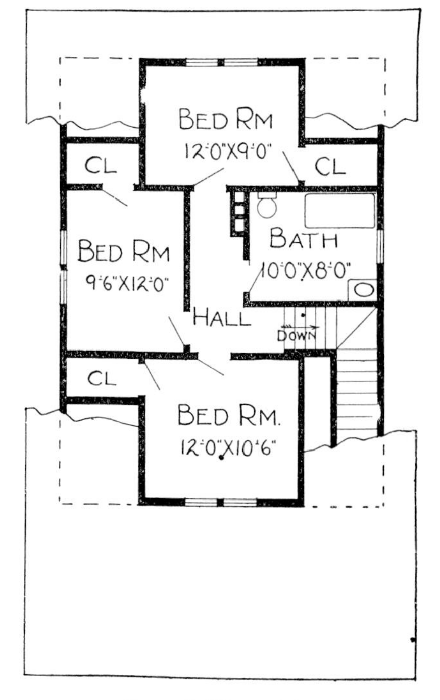

Second Floor Plan

Design No. 5022

Size: Width, 33 feet 6 inches; Length, 32 feet

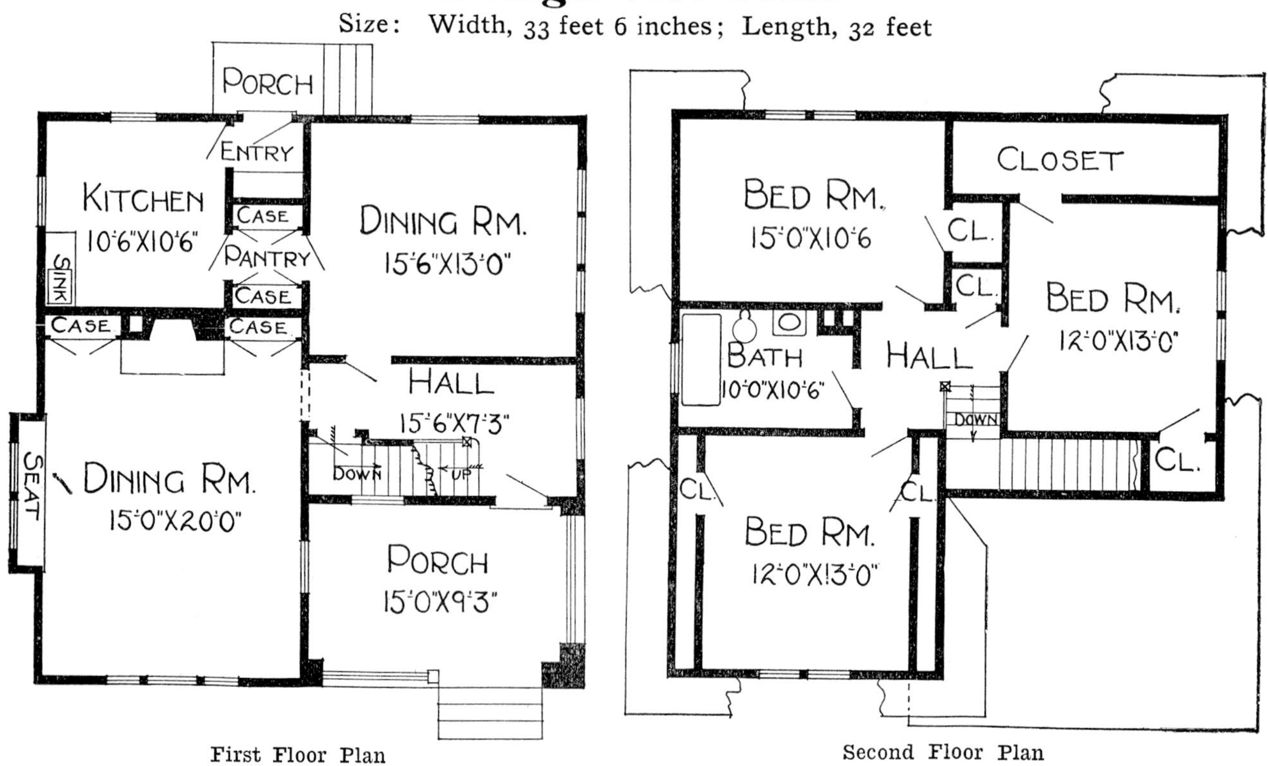

First Floor Plan

Second Floor Plan

PRICE

of Blue Prints, together with a complete set of typewritten specifications

ONLY

$12.00

We mail Plans and Specifications the same day order is received.

Blue prints consist of basement plan; roof plan; first and second floor plans; front, rear, two side elevations; wall sections and all necessary interior details. Specifications consist of twenty-two pages of typewritten matter.

Design No. 5121

Size: Width, 29 feet; Length, 38 feet 6 inches

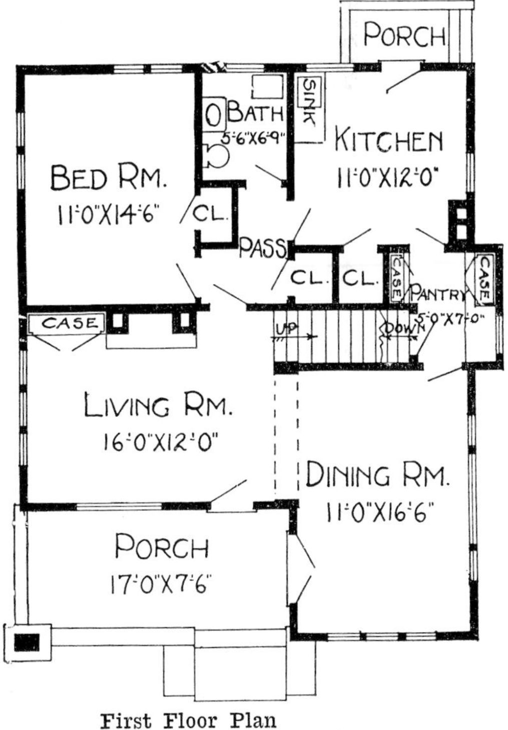

First Floor Plan

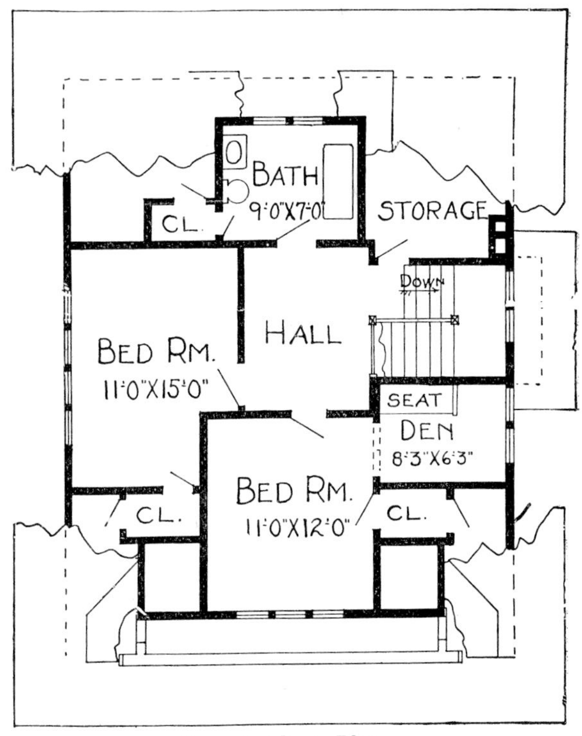

Second Floor Plan

Blue prints consist of basement plan; roof plan; first and second floor plans; front, rear, two side elevations; wall sections and all necessary interior details. Specifications consist of twenty-two pages of typewritten matter.

PRICE

of Blue Prints, together with a complete set of typewritten specifications

ONLY

$12.00

We mail Plans and Specifications the same day order is received.

Design No. 5114

Size: Width, 29 feet 6 inches; Length, 40 feet

PRICE

of Blue Prints, together with a complete set of typewritten specifications

ONLY

$10.00

We mail Plans and Specifications the same day order is received.

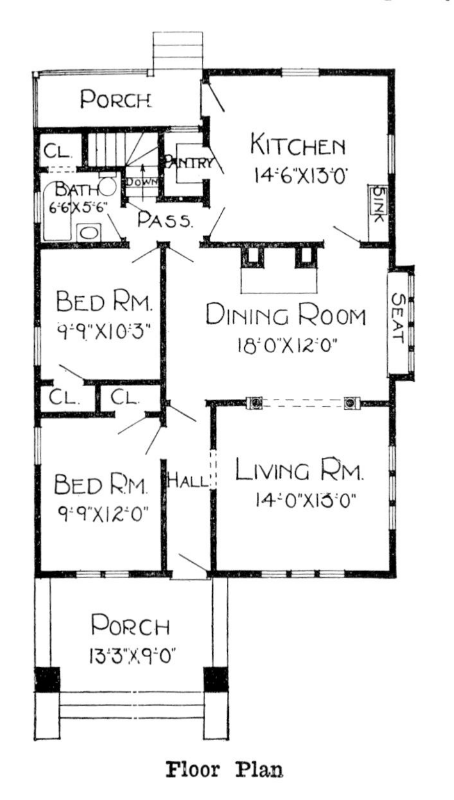

Floor Plan

Blue prints consist of cellar plan; floor plan; attic plan; front, rear, two side elevations; wall sections and all necessary interior details. Specifications consist of twenty-two pages of typewritten matter.

Design No. 7021=B

Size: Width, 31 feet; Length, 47 feet

Blue prints consist of basement plan; roof plan; floor plan; front, rear, two side elevations; wall sections and all necessary interior details. Specifications consist of twenty-two pages of typewritten matter.

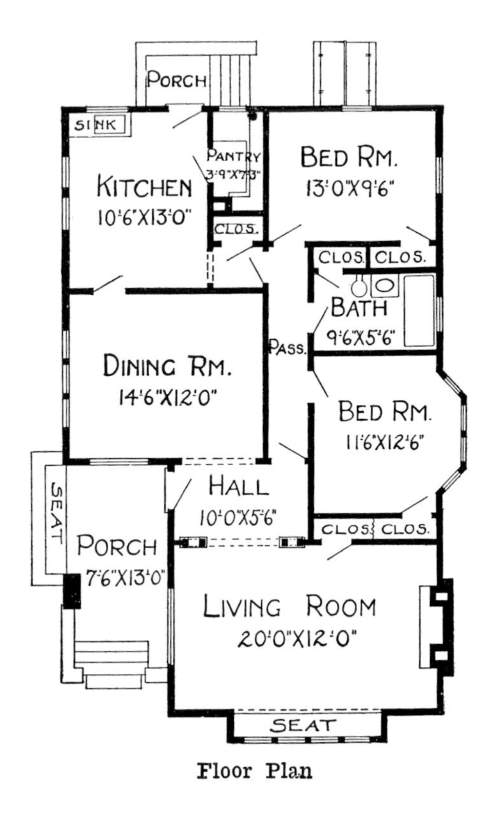

Floor Plan

PRICE

of Blue Prints together with a complete set of typewritten specifications

ONLY

$12.00

We mail Plans and Specifications the same day order is received.

Design No. 5074

Size: Width, 21 feet; Length, 36 feet

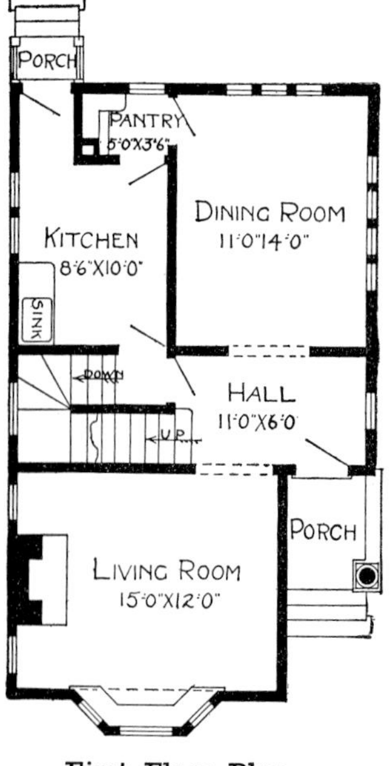

First Floor Plan

Blue prints consist of cellar and foundation plan; roof plan; first and second floor plans; front, two side elevations; wall sections and all necessary interior details. Specifications consist of twenty-two pages of typewritten matter.

PRICE

of Blue Prints, together with a complete set of typewritten specifications

ONLY

$12.00

We mail Plans and Specifications the same day order is received.

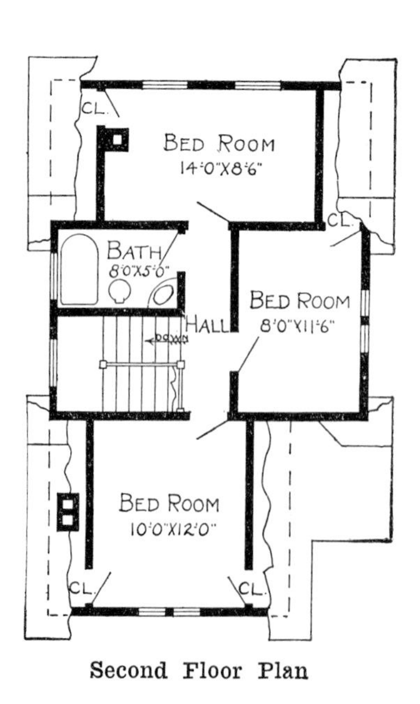

Second Floor Plan

Design No. 5076

Size: Width, 28 feet; Length, 49 feet

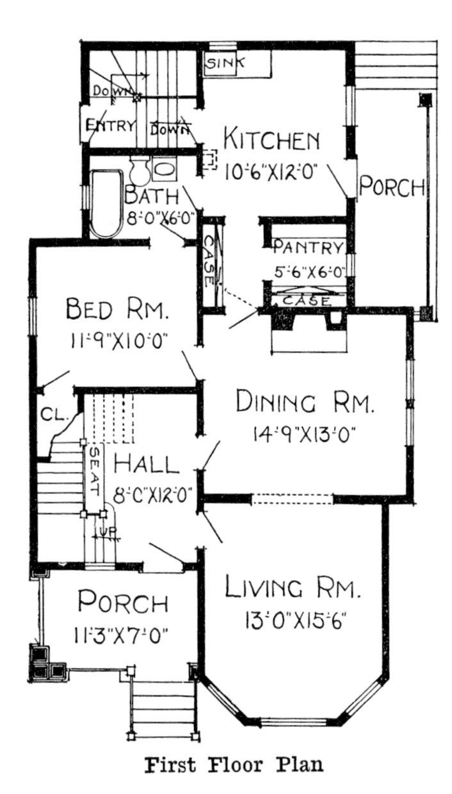

First Floor Plan

Blue prints consist of basement plan; roof plan; first and second floor plans; front, rear, two side elevations; wall sections and all necessary interior details. Specifications consist of twenty-two pages of typewritten matter.

PRICE

of Blue Prints, together with a complete set of typewritten specifications

ONLY

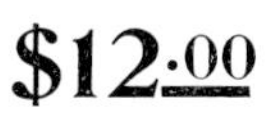

We mail Plans and Specifications the same day order is received.

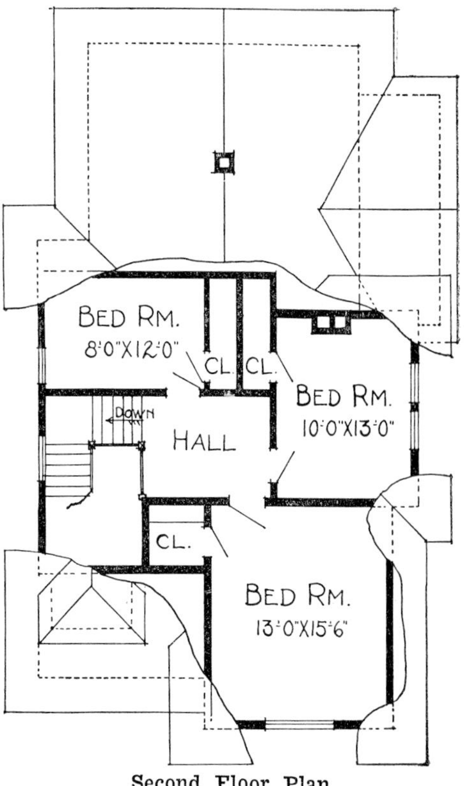

Second Floor Plan

Design No. 5050

Size: Width, 68 feet 6 inches; Length, 40 feet

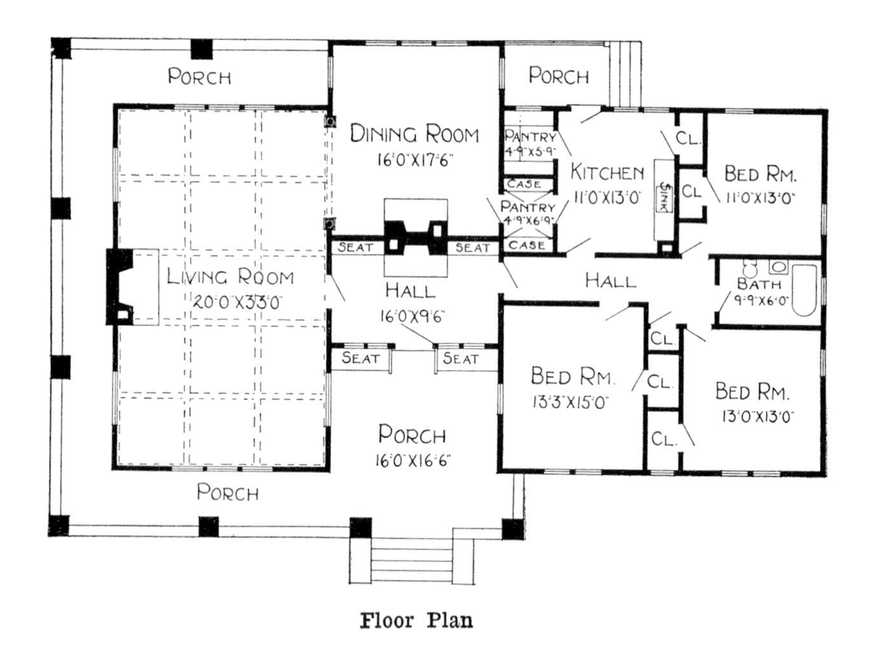

Floor Plan

Blue prints consist of foundation plan; floor plan; front, rear, two side elevations; wall sections and all necessary interior details. Specifications consist of twenty-two pages of typewritten matter.

PRICE

of Blue Prints, together with a complete set of typewritten specifications

ONLY

$10.00

We mail Plans and Specifications the same day order is received.

Design No. 5056

Size: Width, 42 feet 6 inches; Length, 26 feet

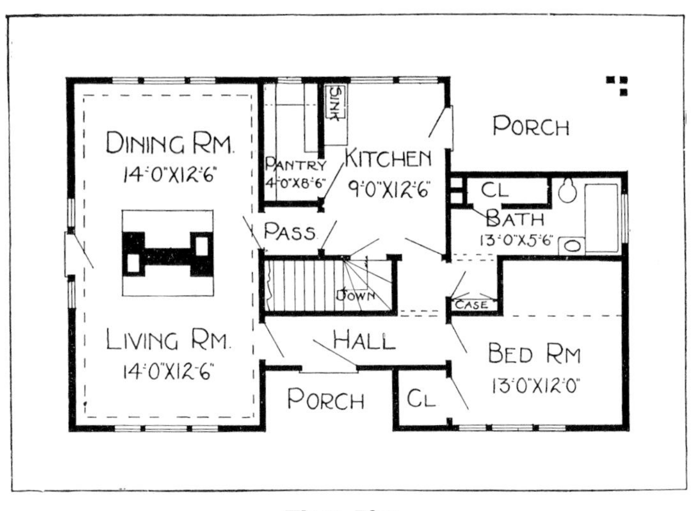

Floor Plan

Blue prints consist of basement plan; floor plan; front, rear, two side elevations; wall sections and all necessary interior details. Specifications consist of twenty-two pages of typewritten matter.

PRICE

of Blue Prints, together with a complete set of typewritten specifications

ONLY

$8.00

We mail Plans and Specifications the same day order is received.

Design No. 9074=B

Size: Width, 30 feet; Length, 40 feet

PRICE

of Blue Prints, together with a complete set of typewritten specifications

ONLY

$10.00

We mail Plans and Specifications the same day order is received.

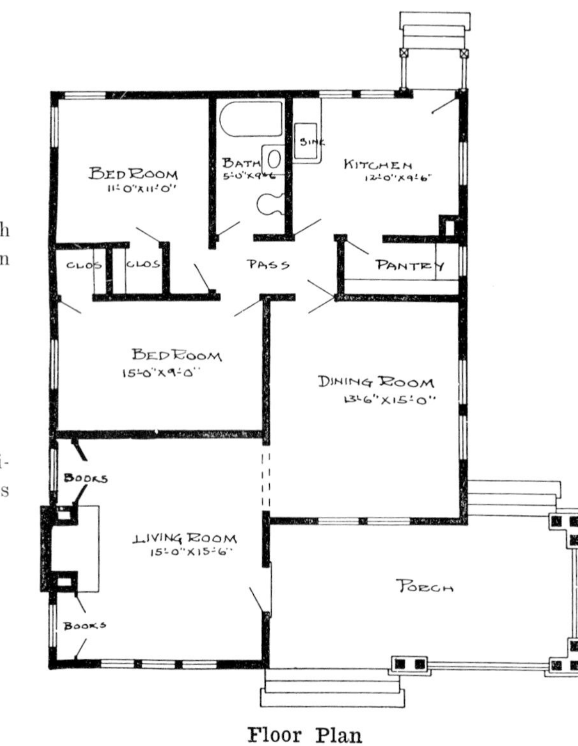

Floor Plan

Blue prints consist of foundation plan; roof plan; floor plan; front, rear, two side elevations; wall sections and all necessary interior details. Specifications consist of twenty-two pages of typewritten matter.

Design No. 5088

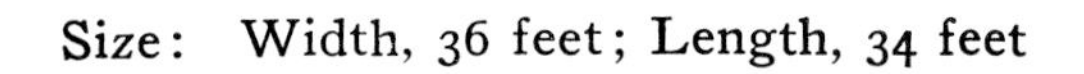

Size: Width, 36 feet; Length, 34 feet

Blue prints consist of basement plan; attic and roof plan; floor plan; front, rear, two side elevations; wall sections and all necessary interior details. Specifications consist of twenty-two pages of typewritten matter.

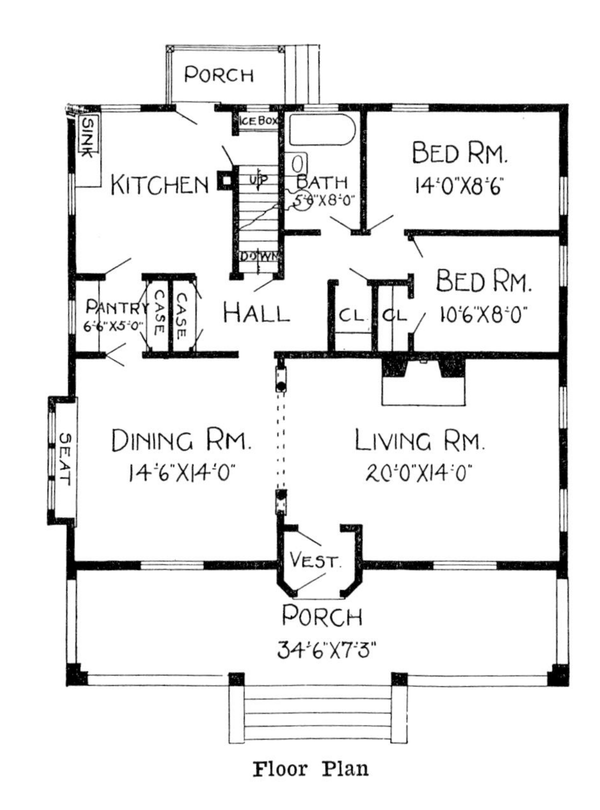

Floor Plan

PRICE

of Blue Prints together with a complete set of typewritten specifications

ONLY

$10.00

We mail Plans and Specifications the same day order is received.

Design No. 5140

Size: Width, 21 feet 6 inches; Length, 34 feet

PRICE

of Blue Prints, together with a complete set of typewritten specifications

ONLY

$8.00

We mail Plans and Specifications the same day order is received.

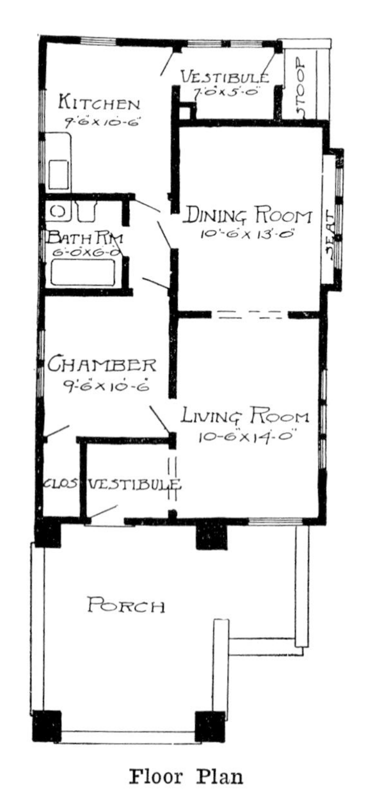

Floor Plan

Blue prints consist of foundation plan; floor plan; front, rear, two side elevations; wall sections and all necessary interior details. Specifications consist of twenty-two pages of typewritten matter.

Design No. 5135

Size: Width, 24 feet 6 inches; Length, 36 feet

Blue prints consist of foundation plan; floor plan; front, rear, two side elevations; wall sections and all necessary interior details. Specifications consist of twenty-two pages of typewritten matter.

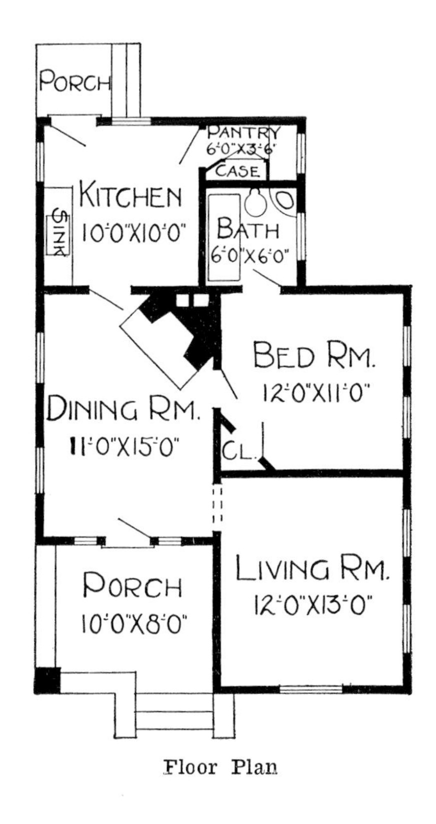

Floor Plan

PRICE

of Blue Prints, together with a complete set of typewritten specifications

ONLY

We mail Plans and Specifications the same day order is received.

Design No. 5103

Size: Width, 26 feet; Length, 42 feet

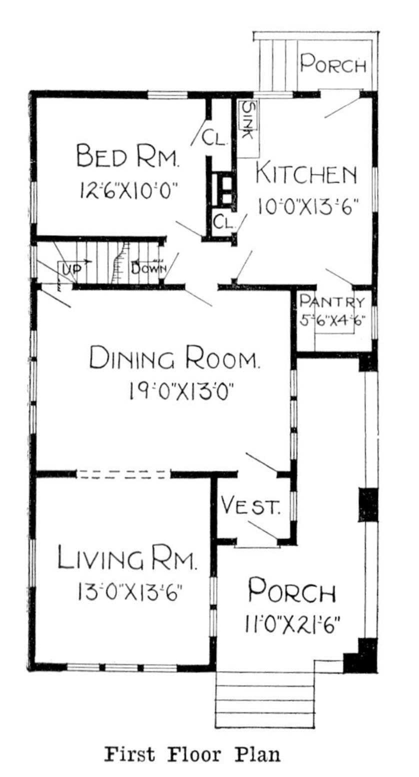

First Floor Plan

Blue prints consist of basement plan; roof plan; first and second floor plans; front, rear, two side elevations; wall sections and all necessary interior details. Specifications consist of twenty-two pages of typewritten matter.

PRICE

of Blue Prints, together with a complete set of typewritten specifications

ONLY

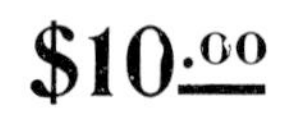

We mail Plans and Specifications the same day order is received.

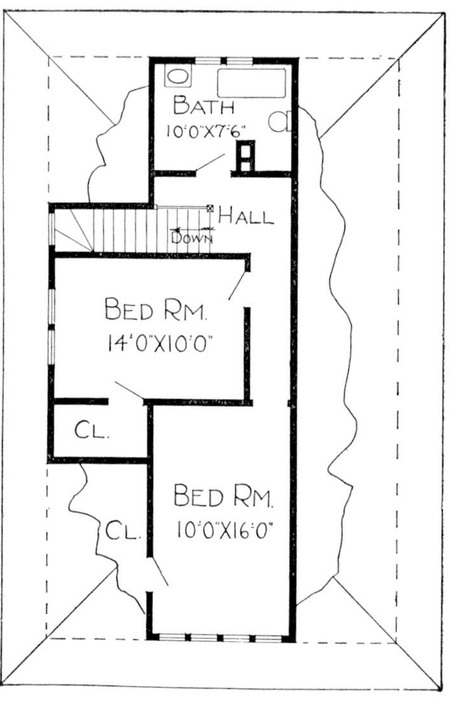

Second Floor Plan

Design No. 5133

Size: Width, 25 feet; Length, 30 feet 6 inches

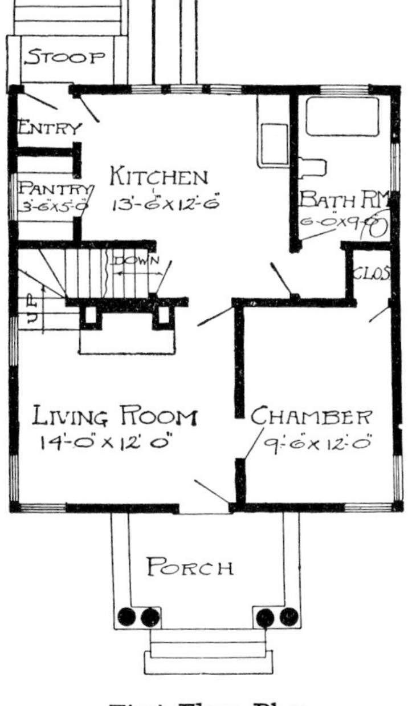

First Floor Plan

Blue prints consist of basement plan; roof plan; first and second floor plan; front, rear, two side elevations, wall sections and all necessary interior details. Specifications consist of twenty-two pages of typewritten matter.

PRICE

of Blue Prints, together with a complete set of typewritten specifications

ONLY

We mail Plans and Specifications the same day order is received.

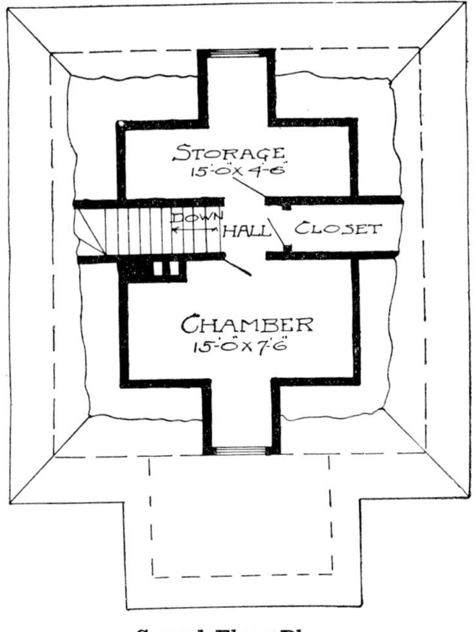

Second Floor Plan

Design No. 5139

Size: Width, 24 feet 8 inches; Length, 30 feet 4 inches

PRICE

of Blue Prints, together with a complete set of typewritten specifications

ONLY

$10.00

We mail Plans and Specifications the same day order is received.

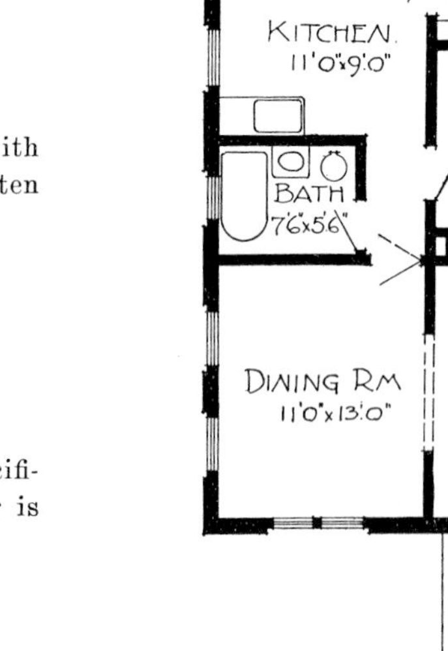

Floor Plan

Blue prints consist of foundation plan; floor plan; front, rear, two side elevations; wall sections and all necessary interior details. Specifications consist of twenty-two pages of typewritten matter.

Design No. 5134

Size: Width, 28 feet; Length, 41 feet

Blue prints consist of basement plan; first floor plan; roof plan; front, rear, right and left elevations; wall sections and all necessary interior details. Specifications consist of twenty-two pages of typewritten matter.

Floor Plan

PRICE

of Blue Prints, together with a complete set of typewritten specifications

ONLY

$10.00

We mail Plans and Specifications the same day order is received.

Design No. 5095

Size: Width, 24 feet; Length, 27 feet

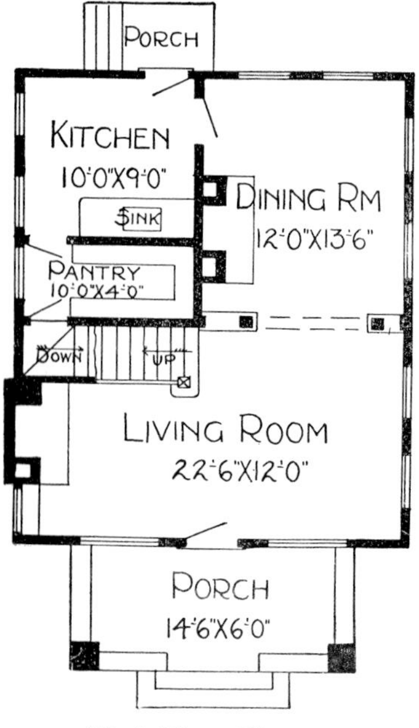

First Floor Plan

Blue prints consist of basement plan; roof plan; first and second floor plans; front, rear, two side elevations; wall sections and all necessary interior details. Specifications consist of twenty-two pages of typewritten matter.

PRICE

of Blue Prints, together with a complete set of typewritten specifications

ONLY

$10.00

We mail Plans and Specifications the same day order is received.

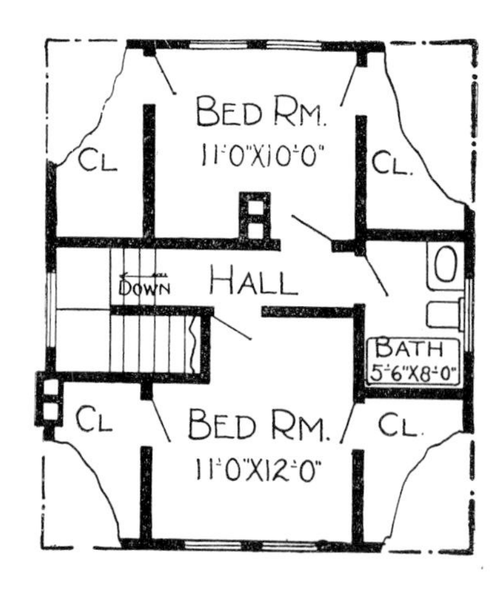

Second Floor Plan

Design No. 5010

Size: Width, 23 feet 6 inches; Length, 23 feet 6 inches

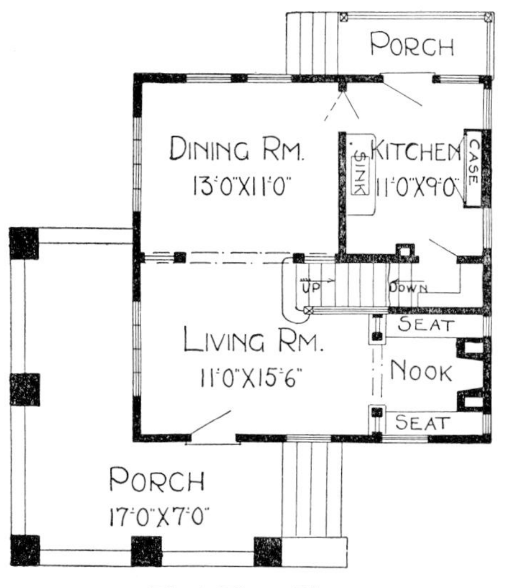

First Floor Plan

Blue prints consist of basement plan; first and second floor plans; front, two side elevations; wall sections and all necessary interior details. Specifications consist of twenty-two pages of typewritten matter.

PRICE

of Blue Prints, together with a complete set of typewritten specifications

ONLY

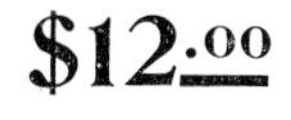

$12.00

We mail Plans and Specifications the same day order is received.

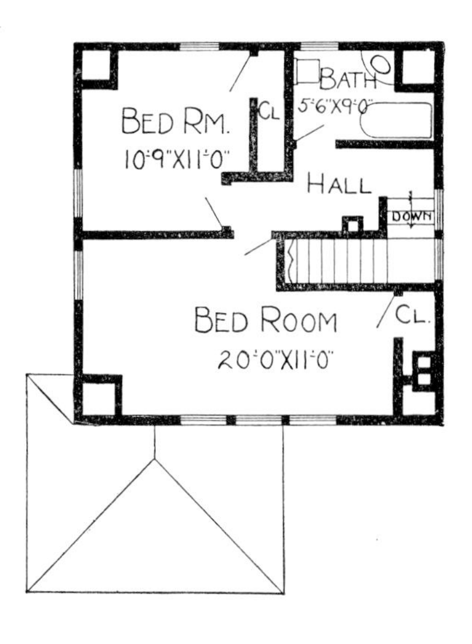

Second Floor Plan

Design No. 5062

Size: Width, 27 feet 6 inches; Length, 47 feet

PRICE

of Blue Prints, together with a complete set of typewritten specifications

ONLY

$10.00

We mail Plans and Specifications the same day order is received.

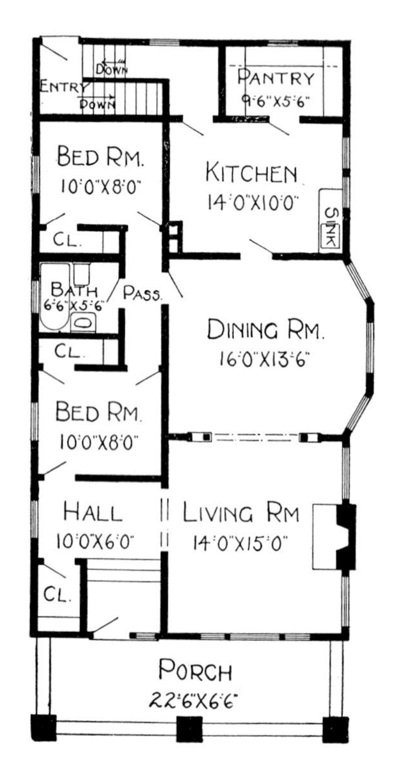

Floor Plan

Blue prints consist of basement plan; floor plan; front, rear, two side elevations; wall sections and all necessary interior details. Specifications consist of twenty-two pages of typewritten matter.

Design No. 5007

Size: Width, 30 feet; Length, 36 feet

Blue prints consist of foundation plan; floor plan; front, rear, two side elevations; wall sections and all necessary interior details. Specifications consist of twenty-two pages of typewritten matter.

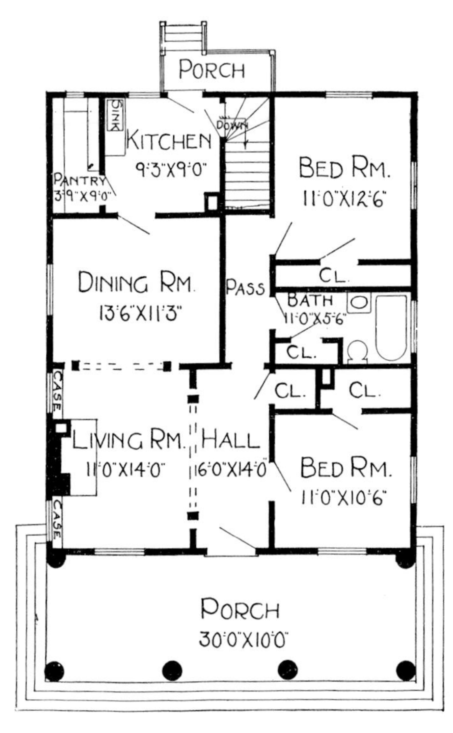

Floor Plan

PRICE

of Blue Prints, together with a complete set of typewritten specifications

ONLY

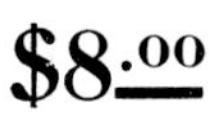

We mail Plans and Specifications the same day order is received.

Design No. 5119

Size: Width, 22 feet 6 inches; Length, 39 feet 6 inches

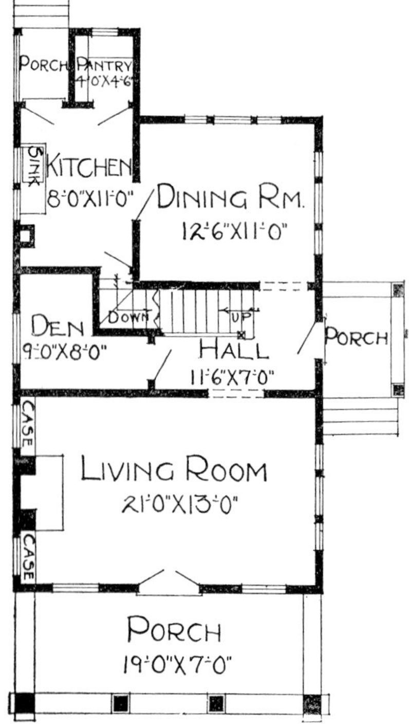

First Floor Plan

Blue prints consist of basement plan; first and second floor plans; front, two side elevations; wall sections and all necessary interior details. Specifications consist of twenty-two pages of typewritten matter.

PRICE

of Blue Prints, together with a complete set of typewritten specifications

ONLY

$12.00

We mail Plans and Specifications the same day order is received.

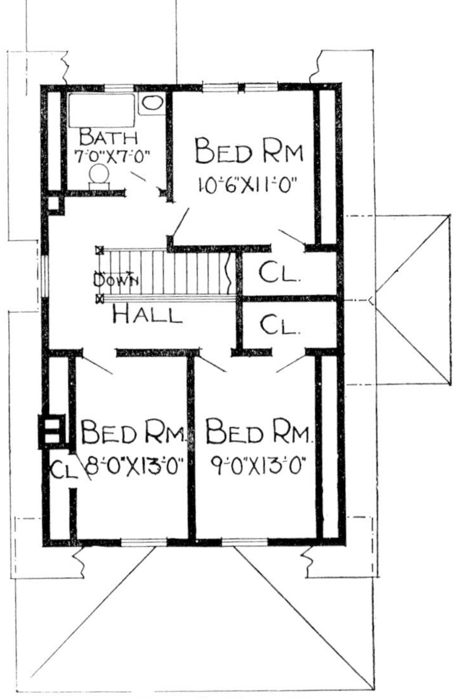

Second Floor Plan

Design No. 5032

Size: Width, 25 feet 6 inches; Length, 34 feet

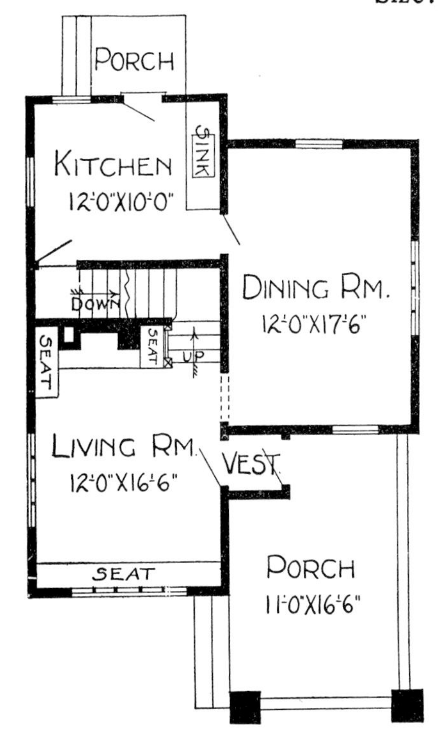

First Floor Plan

Blue Prints consist of basement plan; roof plan; first and second floor plans; front, rear, two side elevations; wall sections and all necessary interior details. Specifications consist of twenty-two pages of typewritten matter.

PRICE

of Blue Prints, together with a complete set of typewritten specifications

ONLY

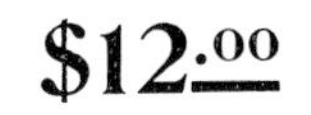

We mail Plans and Specifications the same day order is received.

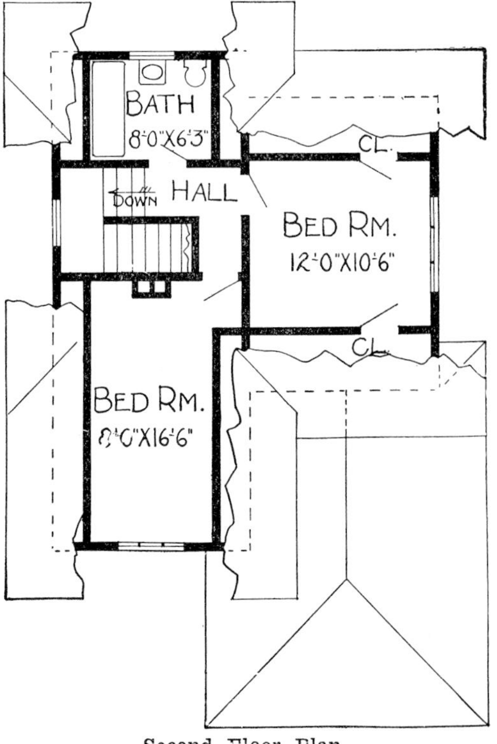

Second Floor Plan

Design No. 5145

Size: Width, 24 feet; Length, 38 feet

PRICE

of Blue Prints, together with a complete set of typewritten specifications

ONLY

We mail Plans and Specifications the same day order is received.

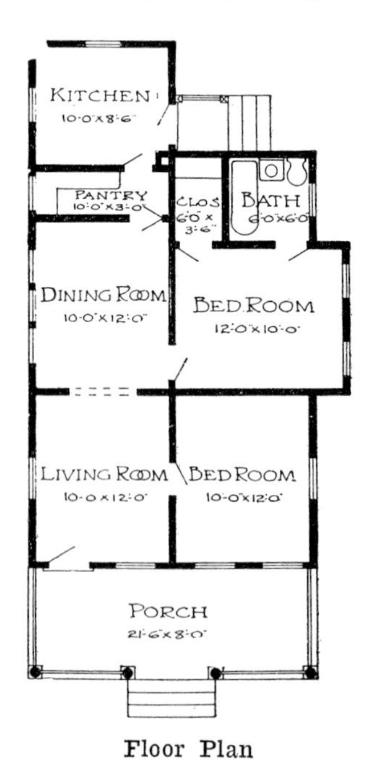

Floor Plan

Blue prints consist of foundation plan; roof plan; floor plan; front, rear, two side elevations; wall sections and all necessary interior details. Specifications consist of twenty-two pages of typewritten matter.

Design No. 5149

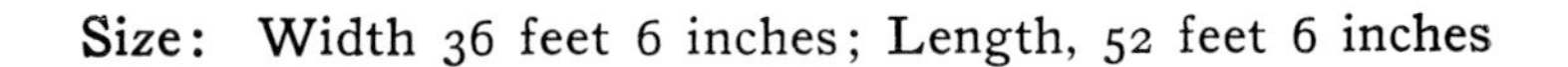

Size: Width 36 feet 6 inches; Length, 52 feet 6 inches

Blue prints consist of basement plan; roof plan; floor plan; front, rear, two side elevations; wall sections and all necessary interior details. Specifications consist of twenty-two pages of typewritten matter.

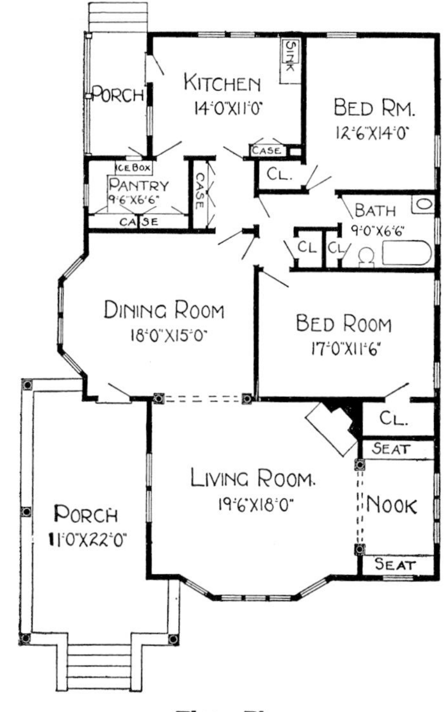

Floor Plan

PRICE

of Blue Prints, together with a complete set of typewritten specifications

ONLY

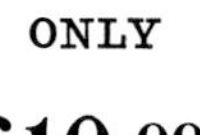

$10.00

We mail Plans and Specifications the same day order is received.

Design No. 7030-B

Size: Width, 35 feet; Length, 23 feet 6 inches

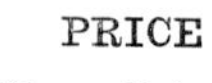

PRICE

of Blue Prints, together with a complete set of typewritten specifications

ONLY

$12.00

We mail Plans and Specifications the same day order is received.

Blue prints consist of basement plan; roof plan; first and second floor plans; front, rear, two side elevations; wall sections and all necessary interior details. Specifications consist of twenty-two pages of typewritten matter.

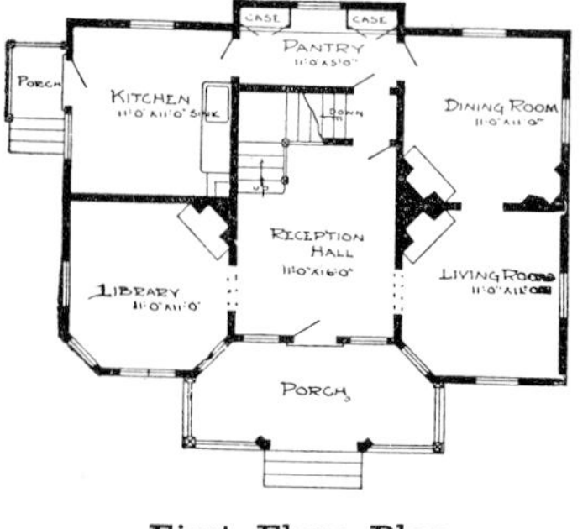

First Floor Plan

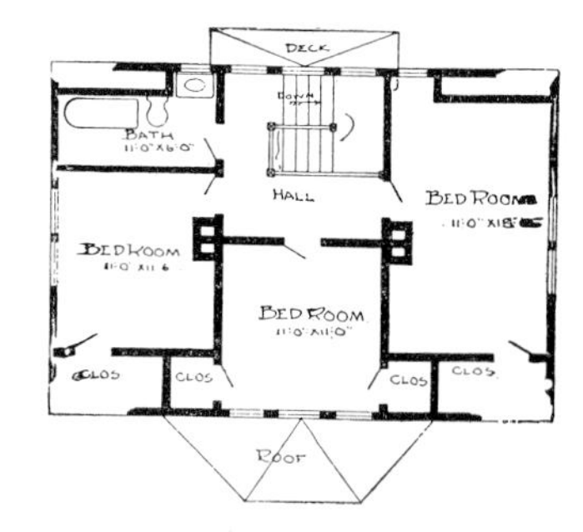

Second Floor Plan

Design No. 7044=B

Size: Width, 39 feet; Length, 25 feet 6 inches

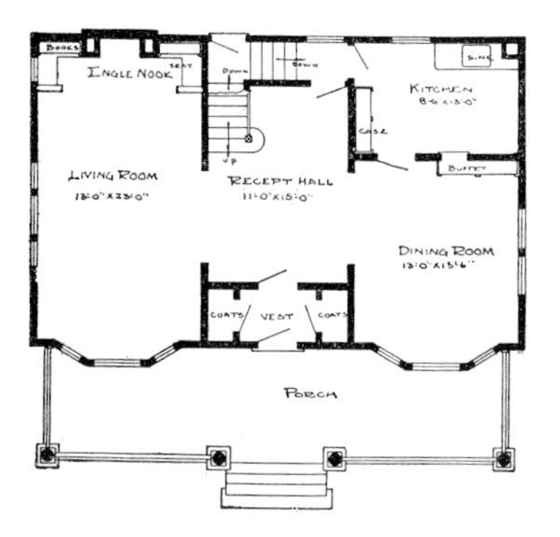

First Floor Plan

Blue prints consist of basement plan; roof plan; first and second floor plans; front, rear, two side elevations; wall sections and all necessary interior details. Specifications consist of twenty-two pages of typewritten matter.

PRICE

of Blue Prints, together with a complete set of typewritten specifications

ONLY

$12.00

We mail Plans and Specifications the same day order is received.

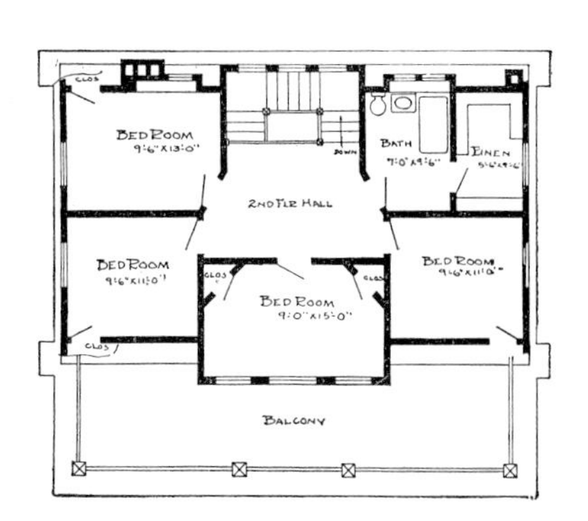

Second Floor Plan

Design No. 9519

Size: Width, 28 feet; Length, 48 feet

Blue prints consist of basement plan; roof plan; floor plan; front, rear, two side elevations; wall sections and all necessary interior details. Specifications consist of twenty-two pages of typewritten matter.

PRICE

of Blue Prints, together with a complete set of typewritten specifications

ONLY

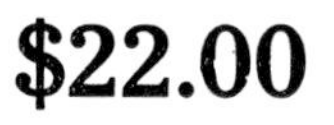

We mail Plans and Specifications the same day order is received.

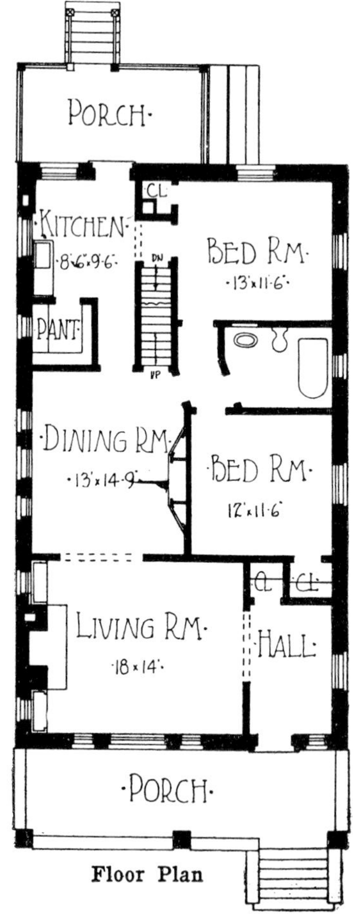

Floor Plan

Design No. 9515

Size: Width, 47 feet 6 inches; Length, 46 feet

Blue prints consist of basement plan; floor plan; front, rear, two side elevations; wall sections and all necessary interior details. Specifications consist of twenty-two pages of typewritten matter.

PRICE

of Blue Prints, together with a complete set of typewritten specifications

ONLY

$26.00

We mail Plans and Specifications the same day order is received.

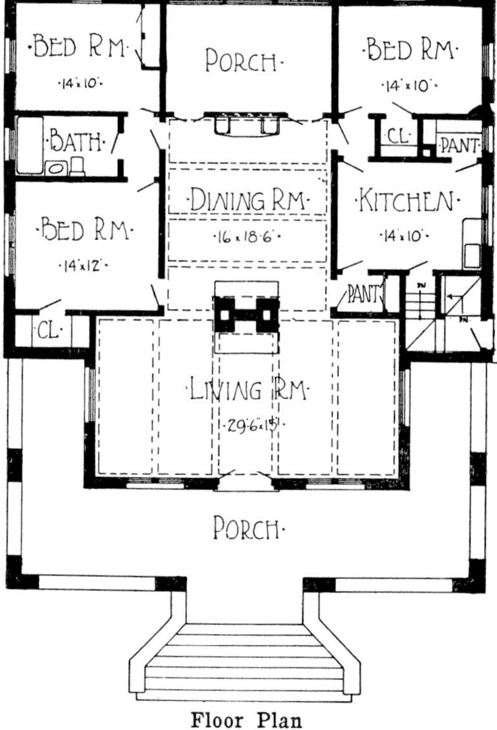

Floor Plan

ALTERATIONS. We can change any plans to suit your requirements, at a reasonable extra charge depending on amount of work involved.

Design No. 8206-B

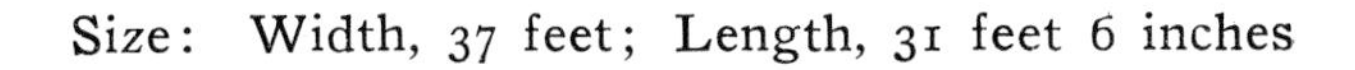

Size: Width, 37 feet; Length, 31 feet 6 inches

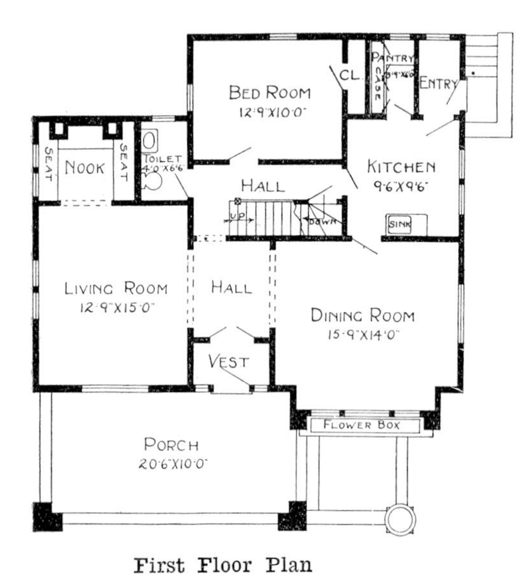

First Floor Plan

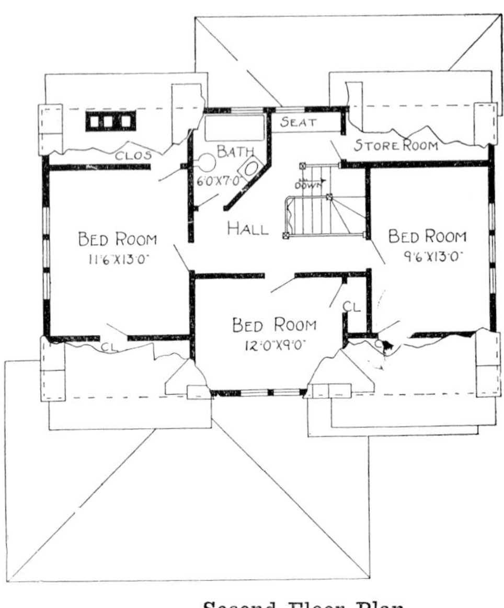

Second Floor Plan

PRICE

of Blue Prints, together with a complete set of typewritten specifications

ONLY

$15.00

We mail Plans and Specifications the same day order is received.

Blue prints consist of basement plan; roof plan; first and second floor plans; front, rear, two side elevations; wall sections and all necessary interior details. Specifications consist of twenty-two pages of typewritten matter.

Design No. 5021

Size: Width, 32 feet; Length, 32 feet

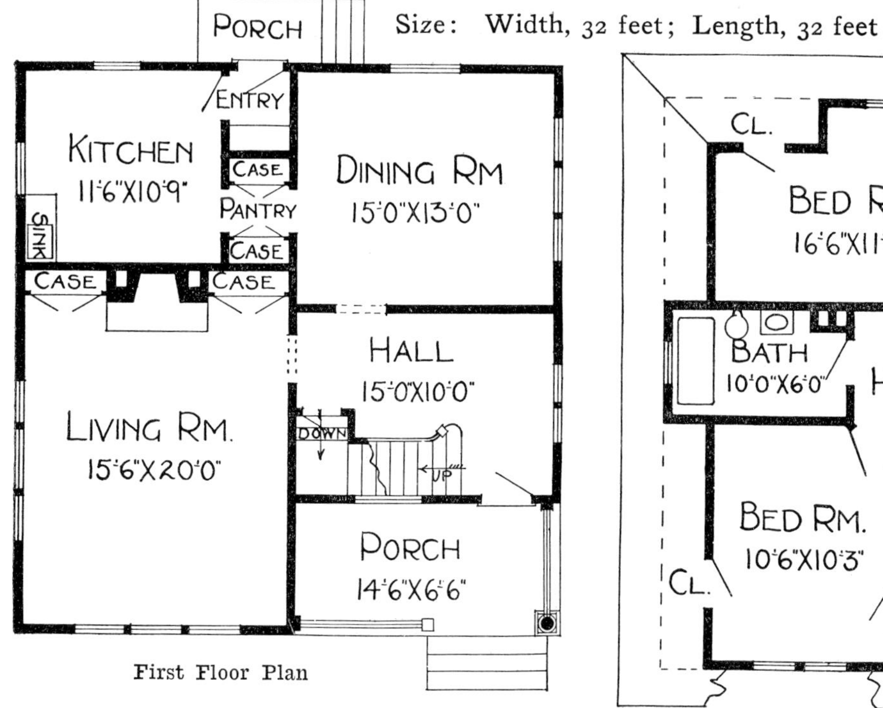

First Floor Plan

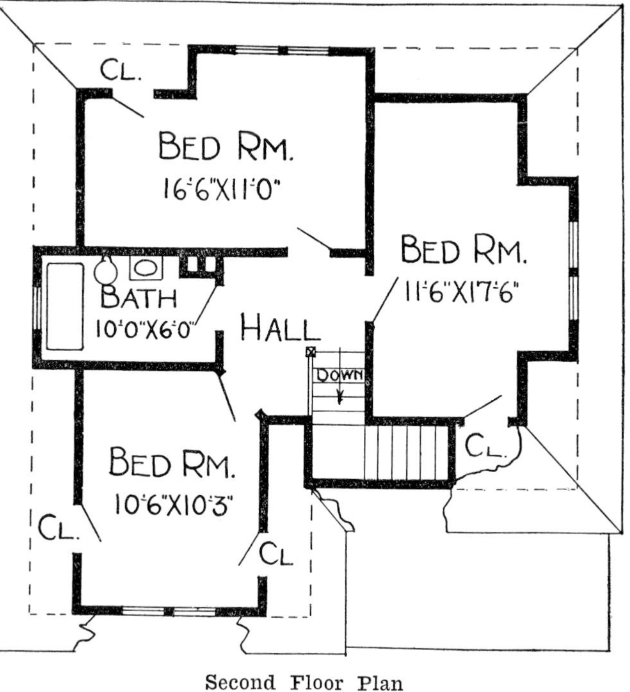

Second Floor Plan

PRICE

of Blue Prints, together with a complete set of typewritten specifications

ONLY

$10.00

We mail Plans and Specifications the same day order is received.

Blue prints consist of basement plan; roof plan; first and second floor plans; front, rear, two side elevations; wall sections and all necessary interior details. Specifications consist of twenty-two pages of typewritten matter.

Design No. 5020

Size: Width, 38 feet; Length, 21 feet

PRICE

of Blue Prints, together with a complete set of typewritten specifications

ONLY

$8.00

We mail Plans and Specifications the same day order is received.

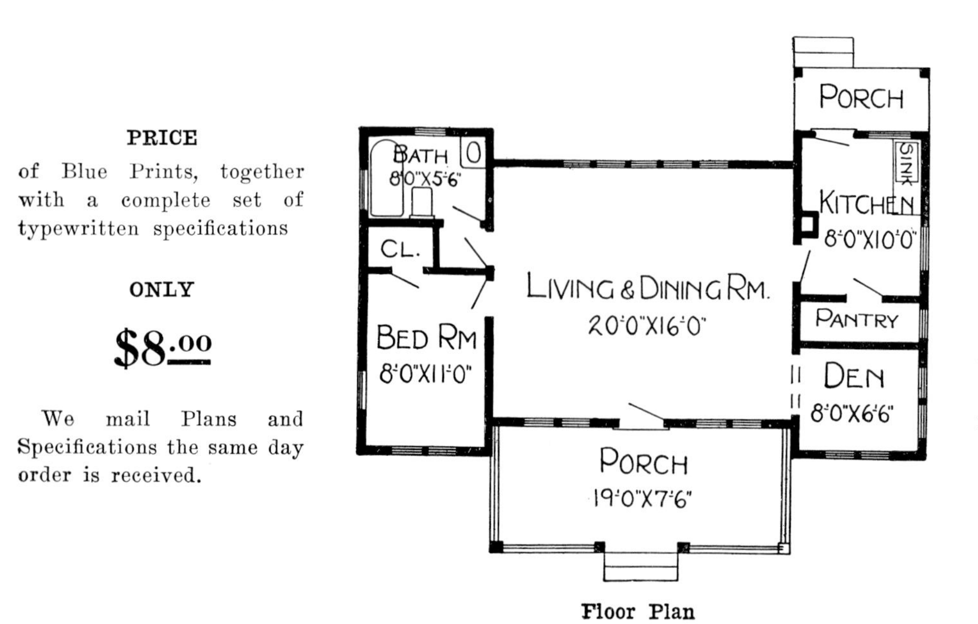

Floor Plan

Blue prints consist of foundation plan; roof plan; floor plan; front, rear, two side elevations; wall sections and all necessary interior details. Specifications consist of twenty-two pages of typewritten matter.

Design No. 5046

Size: Width, 43 feet; Length, 35 feet

Blue prints consist of basement plan; roof and attic plan; floor plan; front, rear, two side elevations; wall sections and all necessary interior details. Specifications consist of twenty-two pages of typewritten matter.

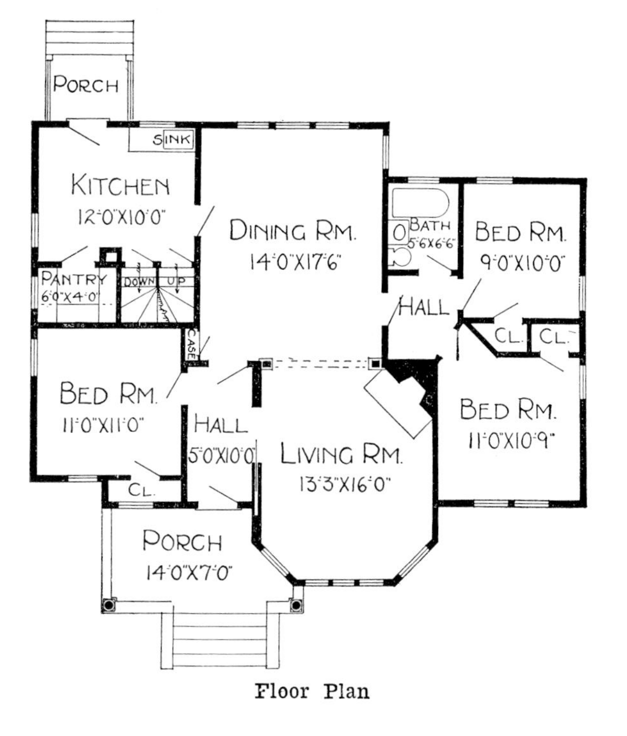

Floor Plan

PRICE

of Blue Prints, together with a complete set of typewritten specifications

ONLY

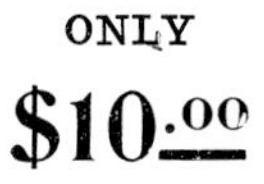

We mail Plans and Specifications the same day order is received.

Design No. 2138-B

Size: Width, 25 feet 6 inches; Length, 51 feet 6 inches

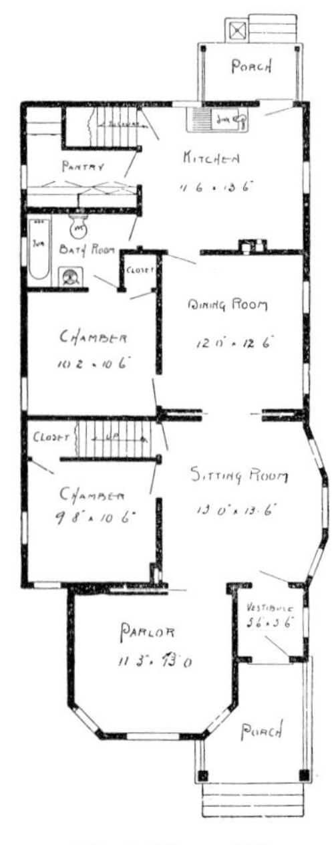

First Floor Plan

Blue prints consist of cellar and foundation plan; roof plan; first and second floor plans; front, rear, two side elevations; wall sections and all necessary interior details. Specifications consist of twenty-two pages of typewritten matter.

PRICE

of Blue Prints, together with a complete set of typewritten specifications

ONLY

$10.00

We mail Plans and Specifications the same day order is received.

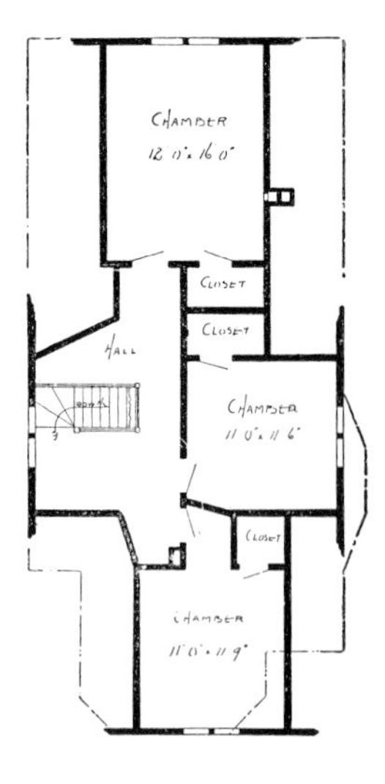

Second Floor Plan

Design No. 5052

Size: Width, 29 feet 6 inches; Length, 48 feet

PRICE

of Blue Prints, together with a complete set of typewritten specifications

ONLY

$10.00

We mail Plans and Specifications the same day order is received.

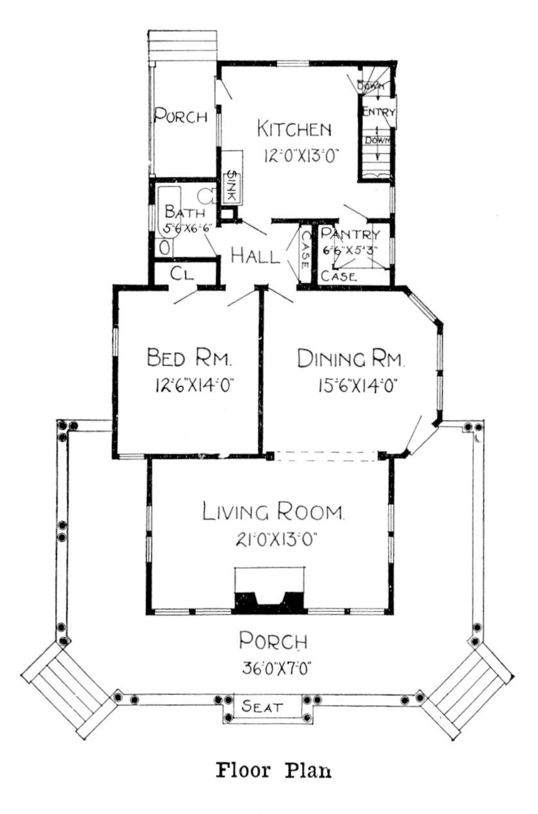

Floor Plan

Blue prints consist of basement plan; **roof plan;** floor plan; front, rear, two side elevations; wall sections and all necessary interior details. Specifications consist of twenty-two pages of typewritten matter.

Design No. 5137

Size: Width, 22 feet; Length, 30 feet

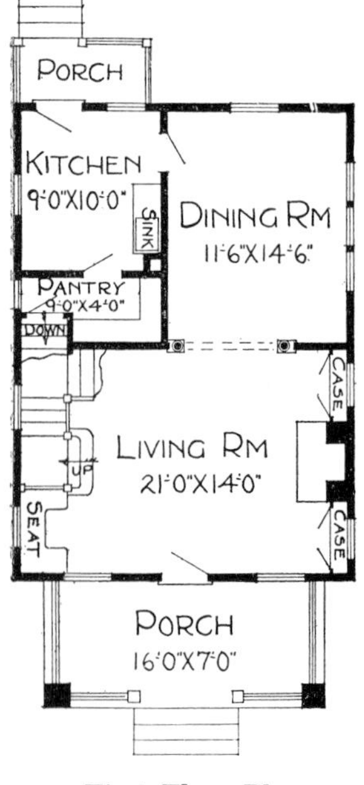

First Floor Plan

Blue prints consist of basement plan; first and second floor plans; front, rear, two side elevations; wall sections and all necessary interior details. Specifications consist of twenty-two pages of typewritten matter.

PRICE

of Blue Prints, together with a complete set of typewritten specifications

ONLY

We mail plans and specifications the same day order is received.

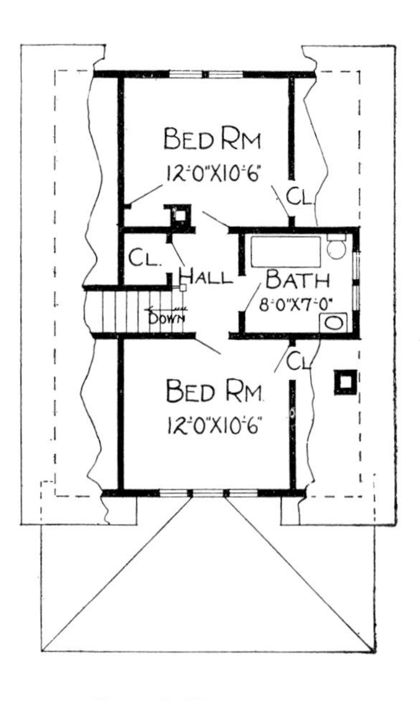

Second Floor Plan

Design No. 5041

Size: Width, 40 feet; Length, 38 feet

Blue prints consist of basement plan; roof plan; floor plan; front, rear, two side elevations; wall sections and all necessary interior details. Specifications consist of twenty-two pages of typewritten matter.

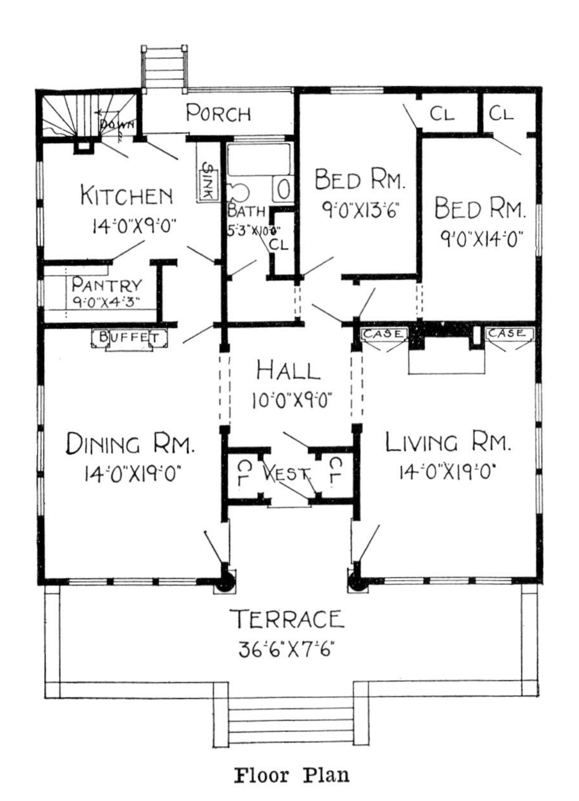

Floor Plan

PRICE

of Blue Prints, together with a complete set of typewritten specifications

ONLY

$10.00

We mail Plans and Specifications the same day order is received.

Design No. 5106

Size: Width, 27 feet 6 inches; Length, 43 feet

PRICE

of Blue Prints, together with a complete set of typewritten specifications

ONLY

We mail Plans and Specifications the same day order is received.

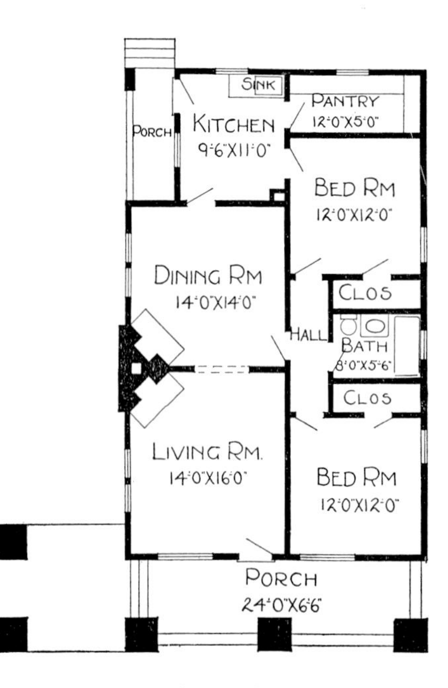

Floor Plan

Blue prints consist of foundation plan; floor plan; front, rear, two side elevations; wall sections and all necessary interior details. Specifications consist of twenty-two pages of typewritten matter.

Design No. 5051

Size: Width, 31 feet; Length, 31 feet

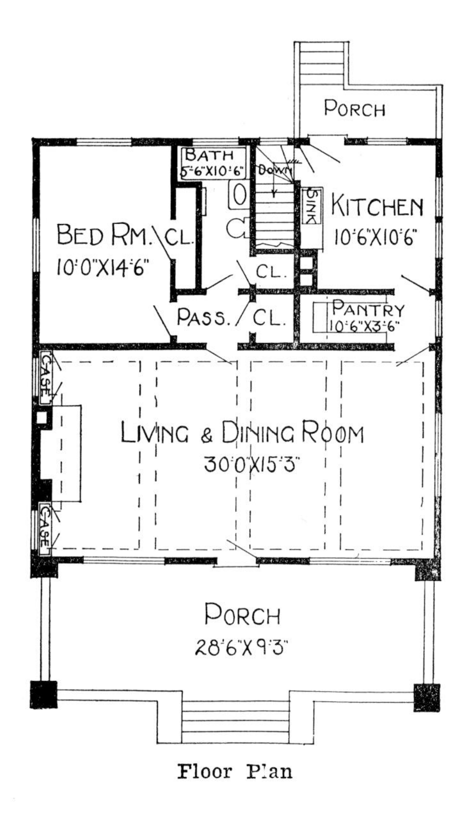

Floor Plan

Blue prints consist of basement plan; floor plan; front, two side elevations; wall sections and all necessary interior details. Specifications consist of twenty-two pages of typewritten matter.

PRICE

of Blue Prints, together with a complete set of typewritten specifications

ONLY

We mail Plans and Specifications the same day order is received.

Design No. 5042

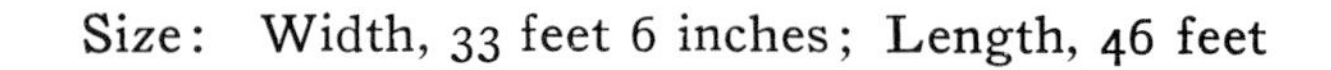

Size: Width, 33 feet 6 inches; Length, 46 feet

PRICE

of Blue Prints, together with a complete set of typewritten specifications

ONLY

$12.00

We mail Plans and Specifications the same day order is received.

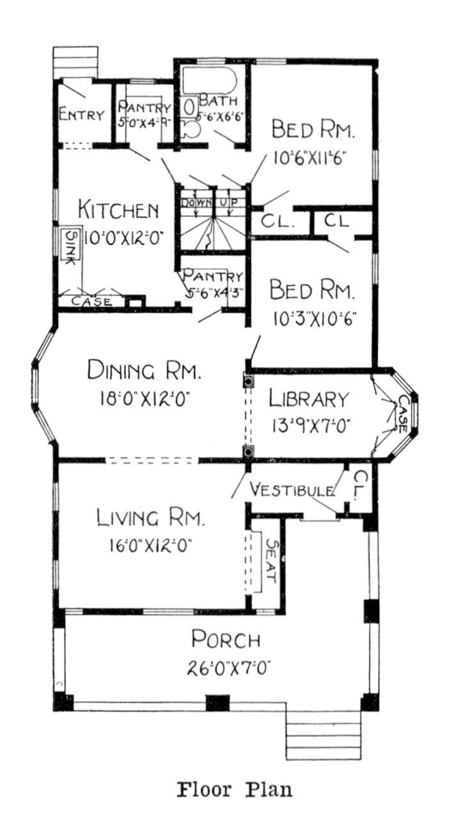

Floor Plan

Blue prints consist of foundation plan; attic and roof plan; floor plan; front, rear, two side elevations; wall sections and all necessary interior details. Specifications consist of twenty-two pages of typewritten matter.

Design No. 5039

Size: Width, 24 feet; Length, 58 feet 6 inches

Blue prints consist of basement plan; floor plan; front, rear, two side elevations; wall sections and all necessary interior details. Specifications consist of twenty-two pages of typewritten matter.

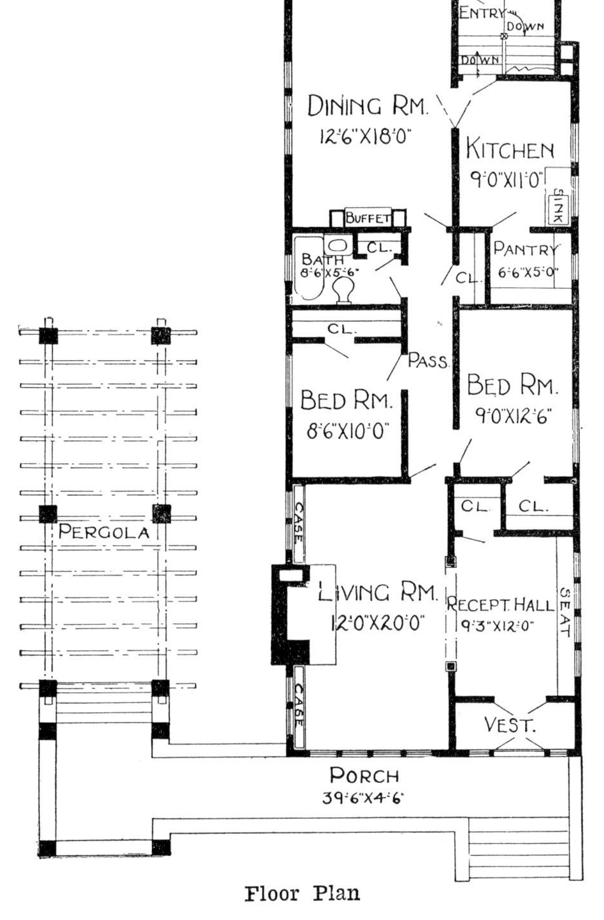

Floor Plan

PRICE

of Blue Prints, together with a complete set of typewritten specifications

ONLY

$10.00

We mail Plans and Specifications the same day order is received.

Design No. 2545-B

Size: Width, 46 feet 3 inches; Length, 24 feet 6 inches

Blue prints consist of cellar and foundation plan; roof plan; first and second floor plans; front, rear, two side elevations; wall sections and all necessary interior details. Specifications consist of twenty-two pages of typewritten matter.

PRICE

of Blue Prints, together with a complete set of typewritten specifications

ONLY

$15.00

We mail Plans and Specifications the same day order is received.

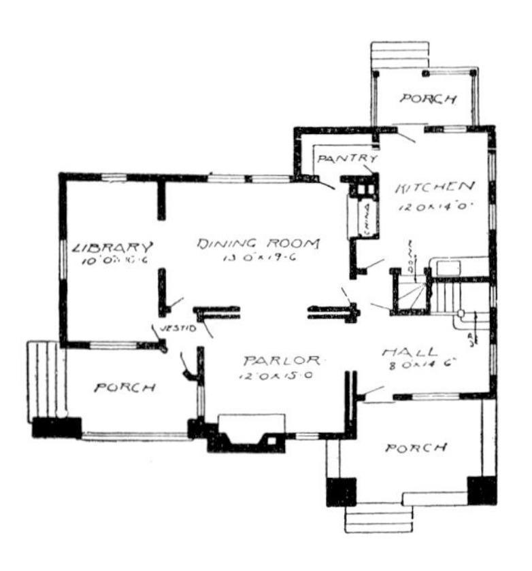

First Floor Plan

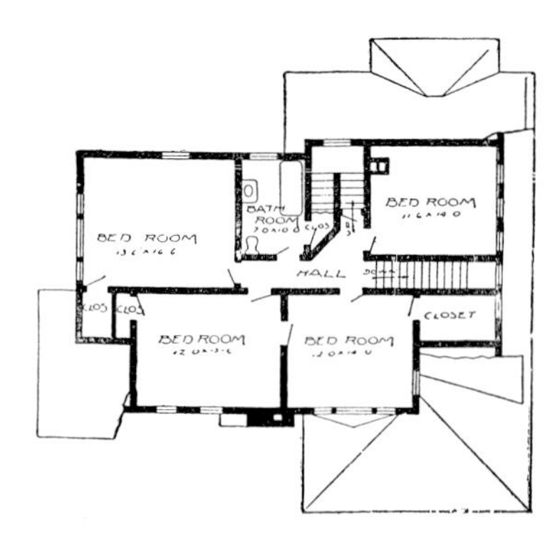

Second Floor Plan

Design No. 2544-B

Size: Width, 34 feet 6 inches; Length, 35 feet 6 inches

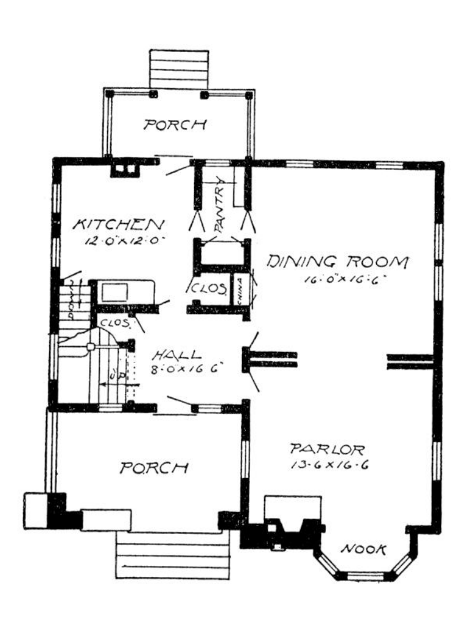

First Floor Plan

Blue prints consist of cellar and foundation plan; roof plan; first and second floor plans; front, rear, two side elevations; wall sections and all necessary interior details. Specifications consist of twenty-two pages of typewritten matter.

PRICE

of Blue Prints, together with a complete set of typewritten specifications

ONLY

$15.00

We mail Plans and Specifications the same day order is received.

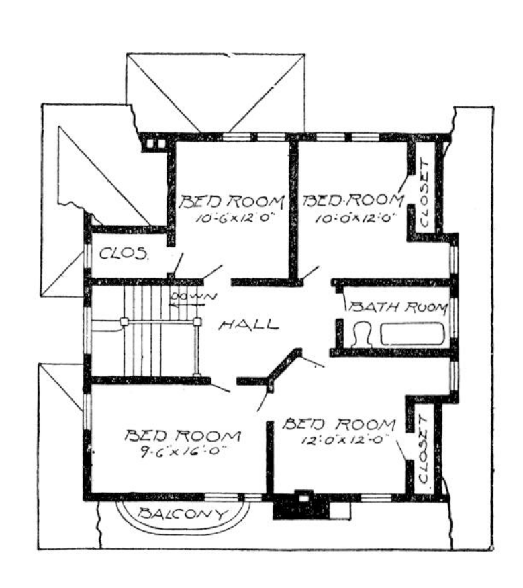

Second Floor Plan

Design No. 6086-B

Size: Width, 40 feet; Length, 49 feet

PRICE

of Blue Prints, together with a complete set of typewritten specifications

ONLY

$12.00

We mail Plans and Specifications the same day order is received.

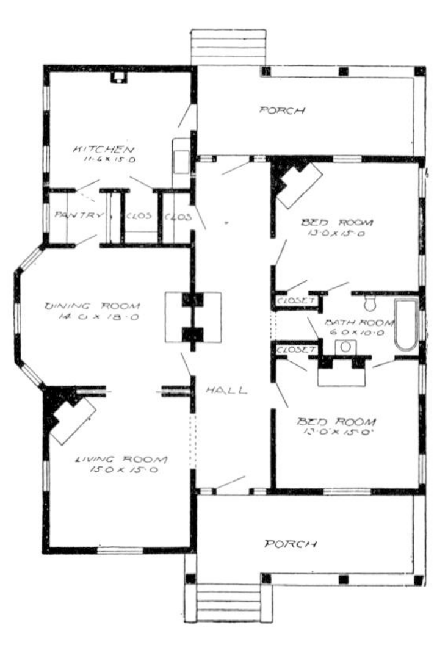

Floor Plan

Blue prints consist of foundation plan; roof plan; floor plan; front, rear, two side elevations; wall sections and all necessary interior details. Specifications consist of twenty-two pages of typewritten matter.

Design No. 5129

Size: Width, 30 feet; Length, 40 feet

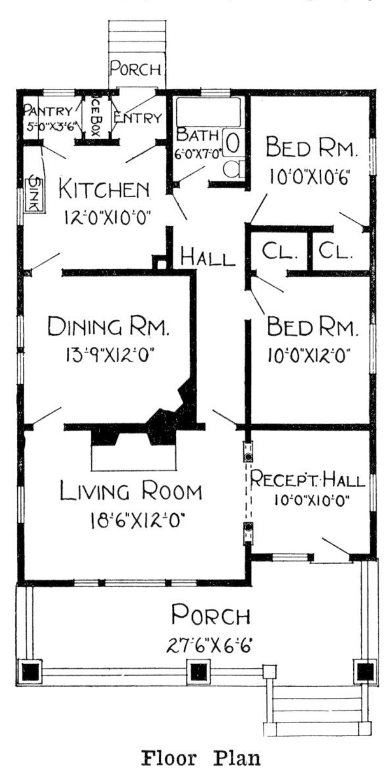

Floor Plan

Blue prints consist of foundation plan; floor plan; front, rear, two side elevations; wall sections and all necessary interior details. Specifications consist of twenty-two pages of typewritten matter

PRICE

of Blue Prints, together with a complete set of typewritten specifications

ONLY

$10.00

We mail Plans and Specifications the same day order is received.

Design No. 5047

Size: Width, 27 feet; Length, 35 feet

PRICE

of Blue Prints, together with a complete set of typewritten specifications

ONLY

$8.00

We mail Plans and Specifications the same day order is received.

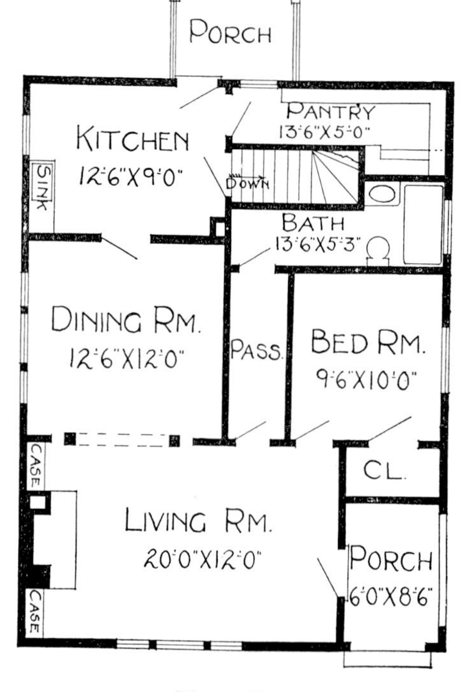

Floor Plan

Blue prints consist of foundation plan; roof plan; floor plan; front, rear, two side elevations; wall sections and all necessary interior details. Specifications consist of twenty-two pages of typewritten matter.

Design No. 5057

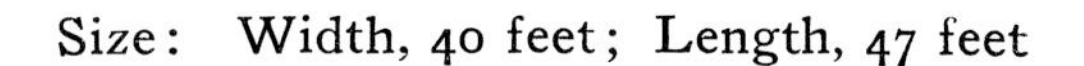

Size: Width, 40 feet; Length, 47 feet

Blue prints consist of basement plan; attic and roof plan; floor plan; front, rear, two side elevations; wall sections and all necessary interior details. Specifications consist of twenty-two pages of typewritten matter.

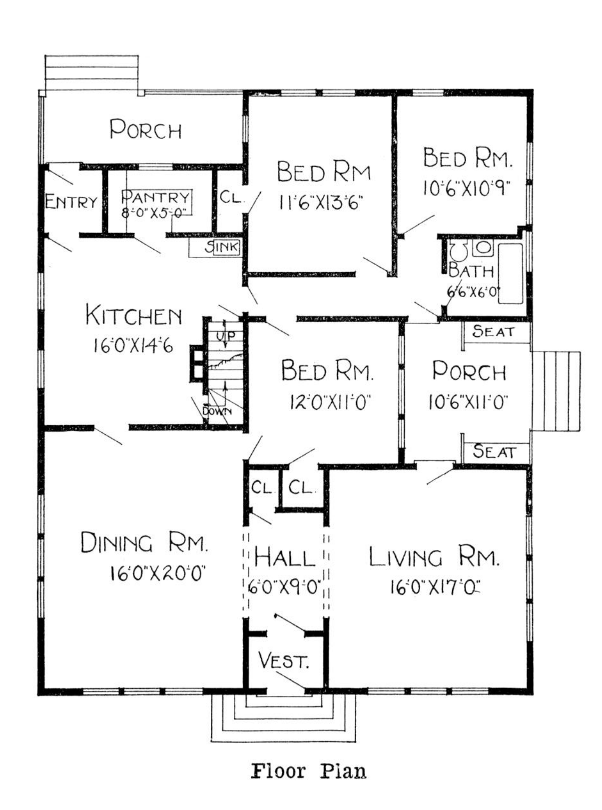

Floor Plan

PRICE

of Blue Prints, together with a complete set of typewritten specifications

ONLY

$10.00

We mail Plans and Specifications the same day order is received.

Design No. 5059

Size: Width, 27 feet 6 inches; Length, 36 feet 6 inches

PRICE

of Blue Prints, together with a complete set of typewritten specifications

ONLY

$8.00

We mail Plans and Specifications the same day order is received.

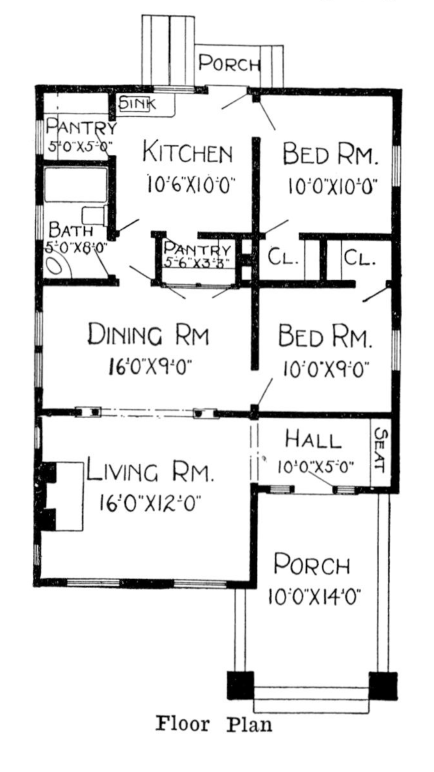

Floor Plan

Blue prints consist of foundation plan; floor plan; front, rear, two side elevations; wall sections and all necessary interior details. Specifications consist of twenty-two pages of typewritten matter.

Design No. 5048

Size: Width, 20 feet; Length, 26 feet 6 inches

Blue prints consist of foundation plan; floor plan; front, two side elevations; wall sections and all necessary interior details. Specifications consist of twenty-two pages of typewritten matter.

Porch
Kitchen 9'6"X9'6"
Sink
Toilet
Cl.
Bed Rm. 9'0"X11'0"
Pantry 5'0"X4'0"
Living Rm. 19'0"X11'0"
Porch 18'6"X5'3"

Floor Plan

PRICE

of Blue Prints, together with a complete set of typewritten specifications

ONLY

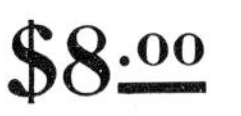

$8.00

We mail Plans and Specifications the same day order is received.

Design No. 2509-B

Size: Width, 30 feet; Length, 45 feet

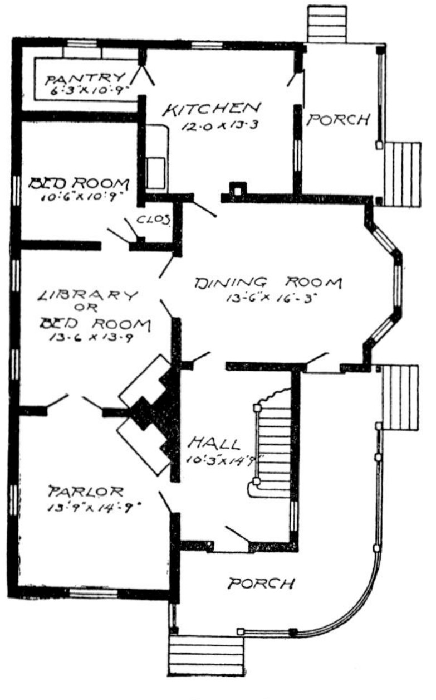

First Floor Plan

Blue prints consist of cellar and foundation plan; roof plan; first and second floor plans; front, two side elevations; wall sections and all necessary interior details. Specifications consist of twenty-two pages of typewritten matter.

PRICE

of Blue Prints, together with a complete set of typewritten specifications

ONLY

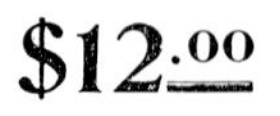

We mail Plans and Specifications the same day order is received.

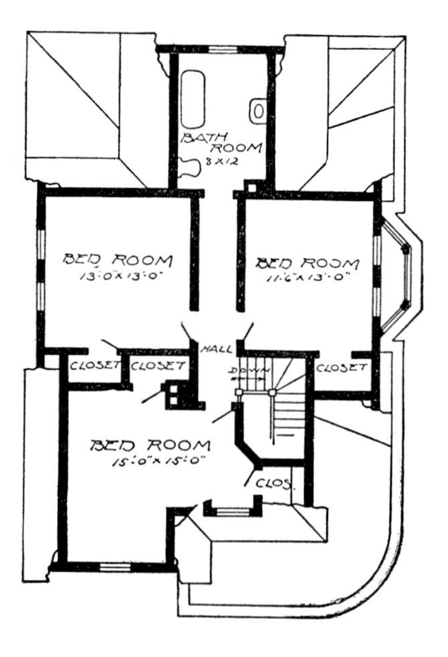

Second Floor Plan

Design No. 2121-B

Size: Width, 23 feet 6 inches; Length, 34 feet

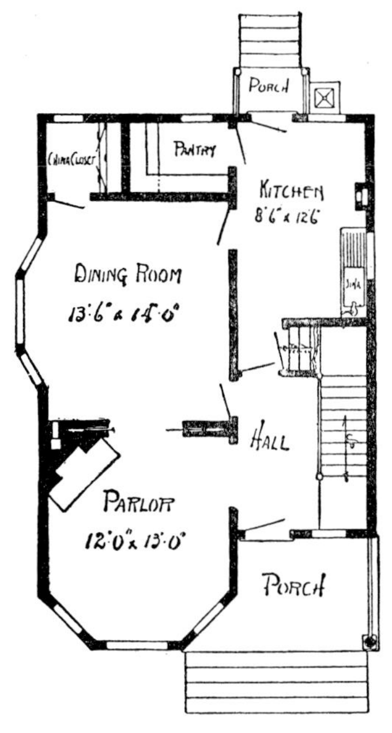

First Floor Plan

Blue prints consist of cellar and foundation plan; first and second floor plans; front, two side elevations; wall sections and all necessary interior details. Specifications consist of twenty-two pages of typewritten matter.

PRICE

of Blue Prints, together with a complete set of typewritten specifications

ONLY

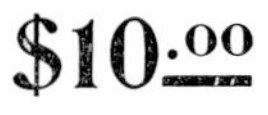

We mail Plans and Specifications the same day order is received.

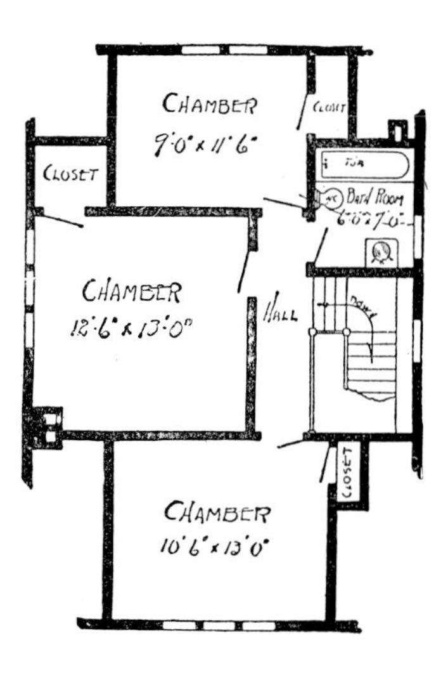

Second Floor Plan

Design No. 5101

Size: Width, 27 feet 6 inches; Length, 33 feet 6 inches

PRICE

of Blue Prints, together with a complete set of typewritten specifications

ONLY

We mail Plans and Specifications the same day order is received.

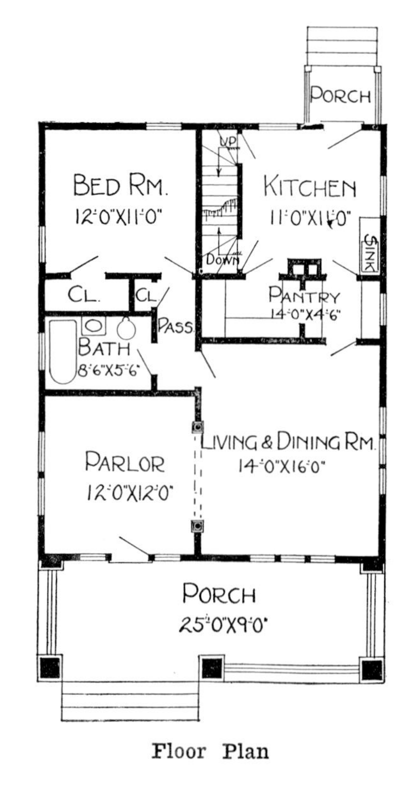

Floor Plan

Blue prints consist of basement plan; roof plan; floor plan; front, rear, two side elevations; wall sections and all necessary interior details. Specifications consist of twenty-two pages of typewritten matter.

Design No. 5128

Size: Width, 27 feet 6 inches; Length, 32 feet

Blue prints consist of foundation plan; roof plan; floor plan; front, rear, two side elevations; wall sections and all necessary interior details. Specifications consist of twenty-two pages of typewritten matter.

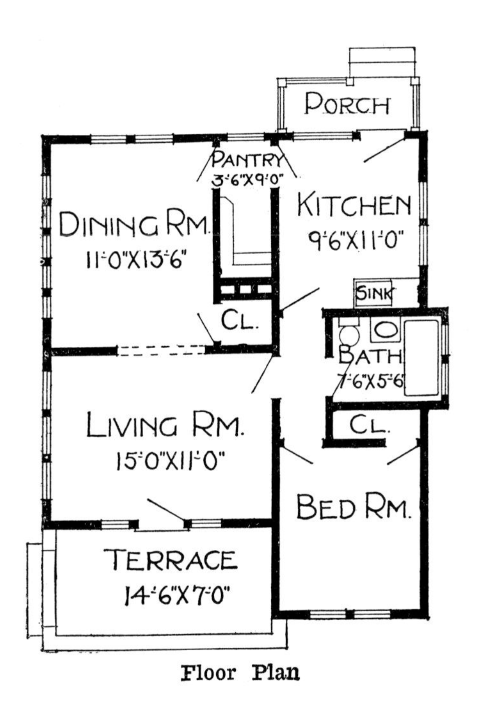

Floor Plan

PRICE

of Blue Prints, together with a complete set of typewritten specifications

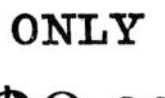

ONLY

$8.00

We mail Plans and Specifications the same day order is received.

Design No. 5027

Size: Width, 27 feet 6 inches; Length, 44 feet

PRICE

of Blue Prints, together with a complete set of typewritten specifications

ONLY

$10.00

We mail Plans and Specifications the same day order is received.

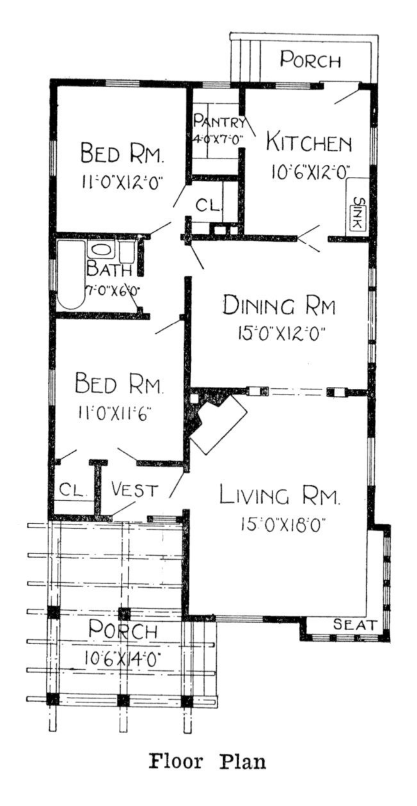

Floor Plan

Blue prints consist of foundation plan; floor plan; front, rear, two side elevations; wall sections and all necessary interior details. Specifications consist of twenty-two pages of typewritten matter.

Design No. 9065=B

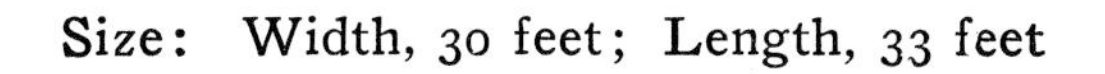

Size: Width, 30 feet; Length, 33 feet

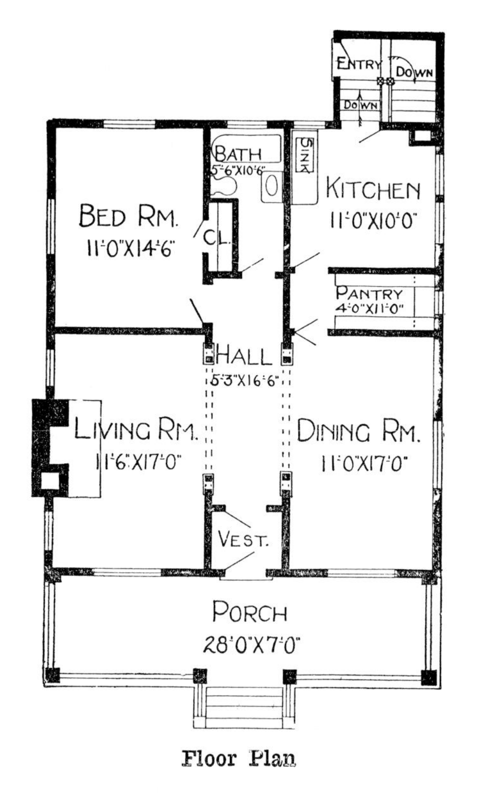

Floor Plan

Blue prints consist of basement plan; floor plan; front, rear, two side elevations; wall sections and all necessary interior details. Specifications consist of twenty-two pages of typewritten matter.

PRICE

of Blue Prints, together with a complete set of typewritten specifications

ONLY

$10.00

We mail Plans and Specifications the same day order is received.

Design No. 7045=B

Size: Width, 30 feet; Length, 25 feet

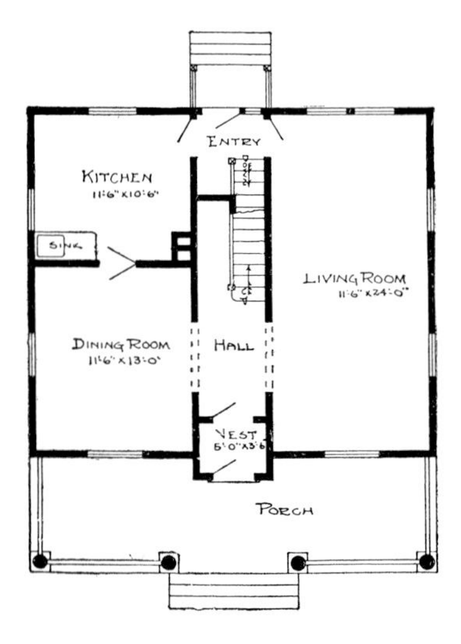

First Floor Plan

Blue prints consist of basement plan; roof plan; first and second floor plans; front, rear, two side elevations; wall sections and all necessary interior details. Specifications consist of twenty-two pages of typewritten matter.

PRICE

of Blue Prints, together with a complete set of typewritten specifications

ONLY

$12.00

We mail Plans and Specifications the same day order is received.

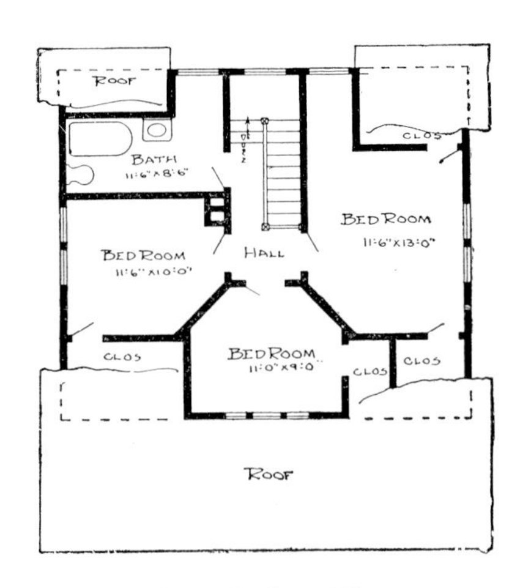

Second Floor Plan

Design No. 2525-B

Size: Width, 36 feet; Length, 36 feet

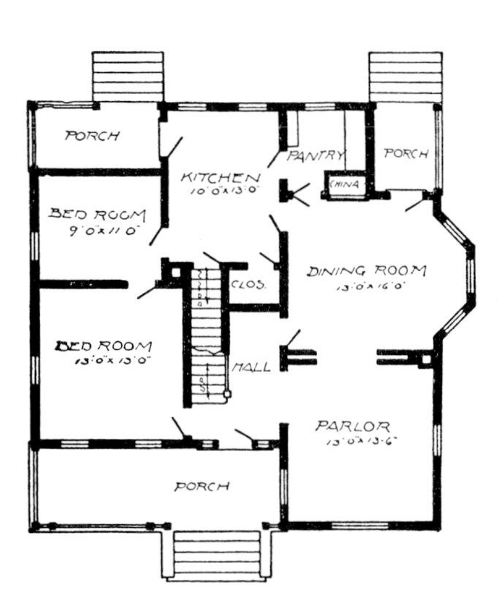

First Floor Plan

Blue prints consist of cellar and foundation plan; first and second floor plans; front, rear, two side elevations; wall sections and all necessary interior details. Specifications consist of twenty-two pages of typewritten matter.

PRICE

of Blue Prints, together with a complete set of typewritten specifications

ONLY

We mail Plans and Specifications the same day order is received.

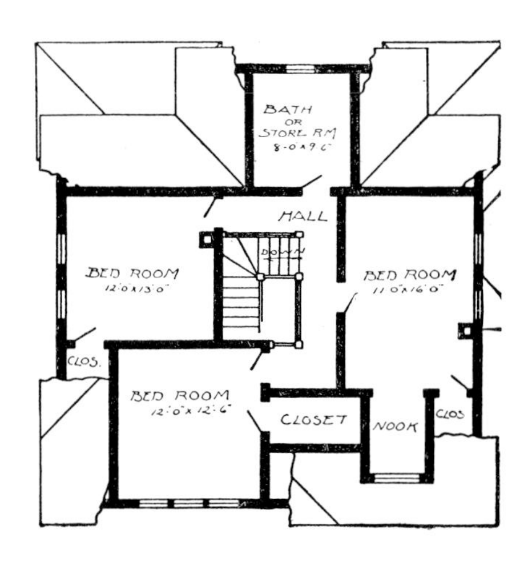

Second Floor Plan

Design No. 5023

Size: Width, 47 feet; Length, 21 feet

PRICE

of Blue Prints, together with a complete set of typewritten specifications

ONLY

$8.00

We mail Plans and Specifications the same day order is received.

Floor Plan

Blue prints consist of basement plan; floor plan; front, rear, two side elevations; wall sections and all necessary interior details. Specifications consist of twenty-two pages of typewritten matter.

Design No. 8245=B

Size: Width, 25 feet 6 inches; Length, 38 feet 4 inches

Blue prints consist of foundation plan; roof plan; floor plan; front, rear, two side elevations; wall sections and all necessary interior details. Specifications consist of twenty-two pages of typewritten matter.

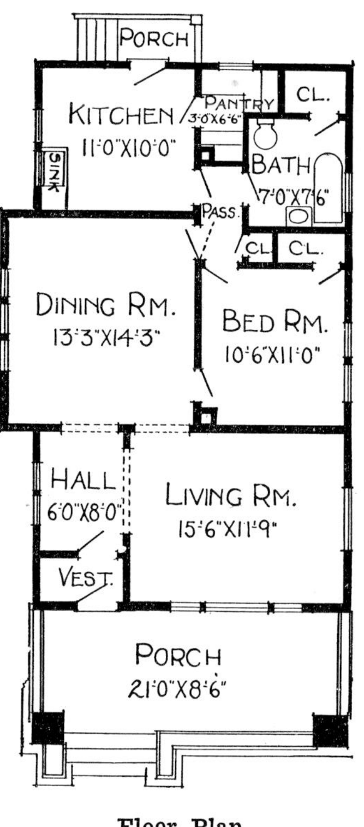

Floor Plan

PRICE

of Blue Prints, together with a complete set of typewritten specifications

ONLY

$12.00

We mail Plans and Specifications the same day order is received.

Design No. 5098

Size: Width, 30 feet; Length, 37 feet 6 inches

PRICE

of Blue Prints, together with a complete set of typewritten specifications

ONLY

$7.00

We mail Plans and Specifications the same day order is received.

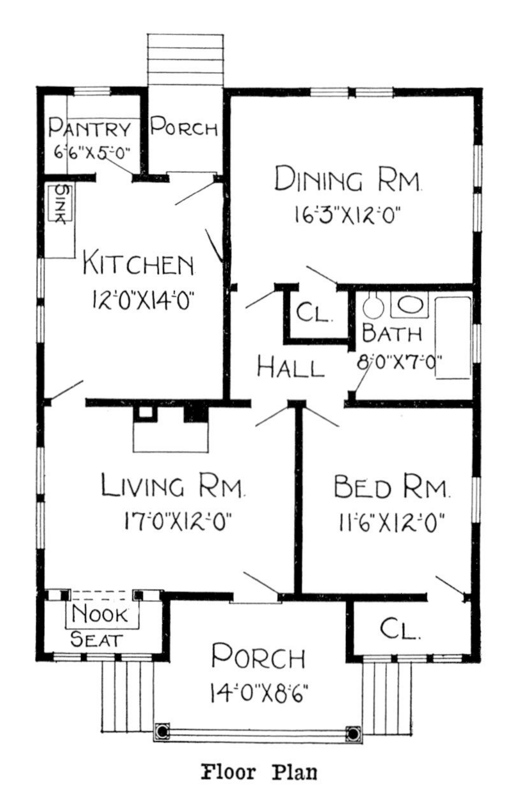

Floor Plan

Blue prints consist of basement plan; floor plan; front, rear, two side elevations; wall sections and all necessary interior details. Specifications consist of twenty-two pages of typewritten matter.

Design No. 8254=B

Size: Width, 27 feet 4 inches; Length, 36 feet 4 inches

Blue prints consist of basement plan; roof plan; floor plan; front, rear, two side elevations; wall sections and all necessary interior details. Specifications consist of twenty-two pages of typewritten matter.

DOWN
UP
SINK
BED RM.
10'6"X9'0"
KITCHEN
10'6"X13'6"
PANTRY
BATH
5'9"X5'6"
HALL
NOOK
SEAT
BED RM.
9'0"X9'0"
LIVING RM.
12'0"X14'6"
CL.
VEST.
PORCH
13'0"X11'0"

Floor Plan

PRICE

of Blue Prints, together with a complete set of typewritten specifications

ONLY

$10.00

We mail Plans and Specifications the same day order is received.

Design No. 2008=B

Size: Width, 28 feet; Length, 38 feet

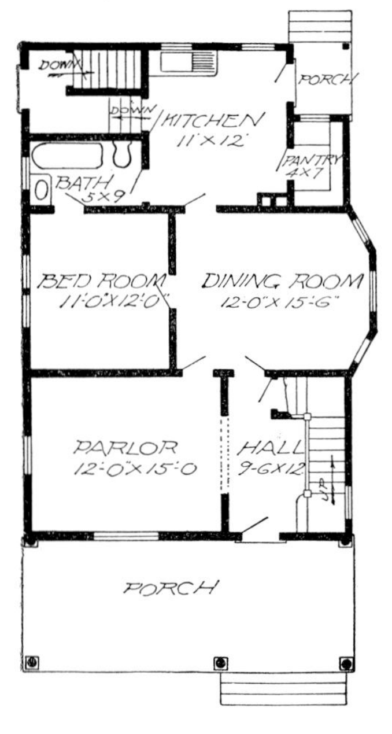

First Floor Plan

Blue prints consist of foundation plan; first and second floor plans; front, two side elevations; wall sections and all necessary interior details. Specifications consist of twenty-two pages of typewritten matter.

PRICE

of Blue Prints, together with a complete set of typewritten specifications

ONLY

We mail Plans and Specifications the same day order is received.

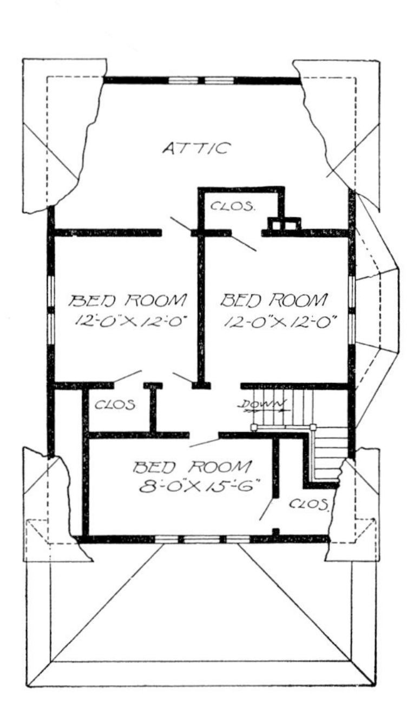

Second Floor Plan

Design No. 9009=B

Size: Width, 26 feet; Length, 48 feet

Blue prints consist of basement plan; floor plan; front, rear, two side elevations; wall sections and all necessary interior details. Specifications consist of twenty-two pages of typewritten matter.

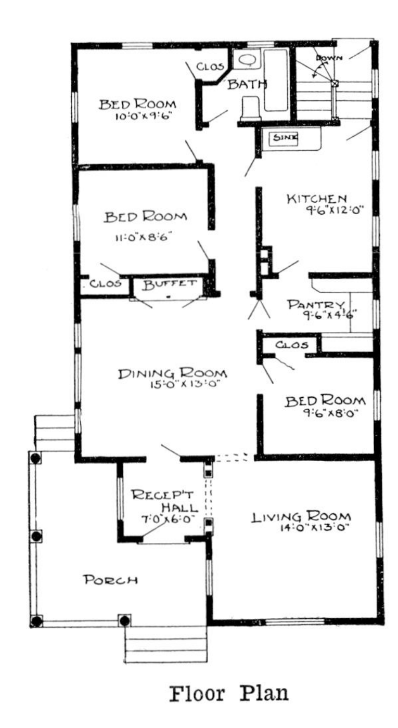

Floor Plan

PRICE

of Blue Prints, together with a complete set of typewritten specifications

ONLY

$10.00

We mail Plans and Specifications the same day order is received.

Design No. 5093

Size: Width, 32 feet; Length, 34 feet

PRICE

of Blue Prints, together with a complete set of typewritten specifications

ONLY

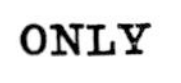

We mail Plans and Specifications the same day order is received.

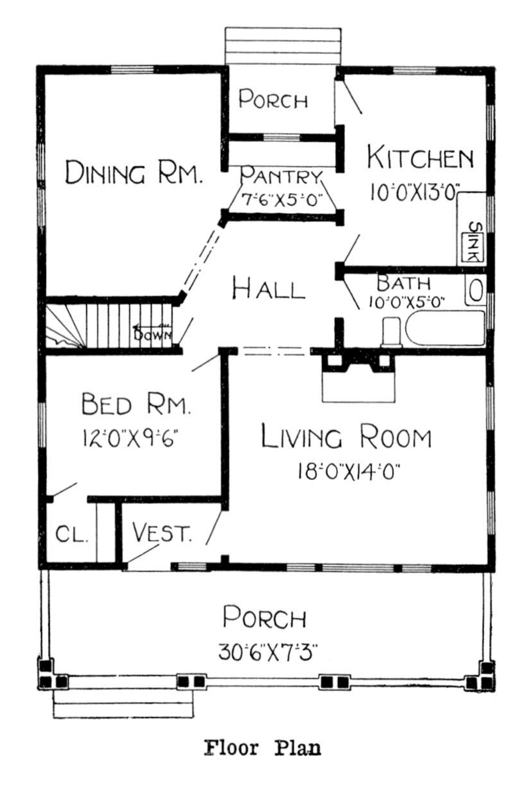

Floor Plan

Blue prints consist of basement plan; floor plan; front, rear, two side elevations; wall sections and all necessary interior details. Specifications consist of twenty-two pages of typewritten matter.

Design No. 5035

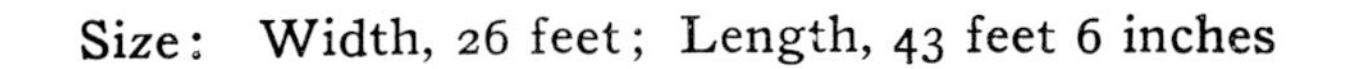

Size: Width, 26 feet; Length, 43 feet 6 inches

Blue prints consist of basement plan; roof plan; floor plan; front, rear, two side elevations; wall sections and all necessary interior details. Specifications consist of twenty-two pages of typewritten matter.

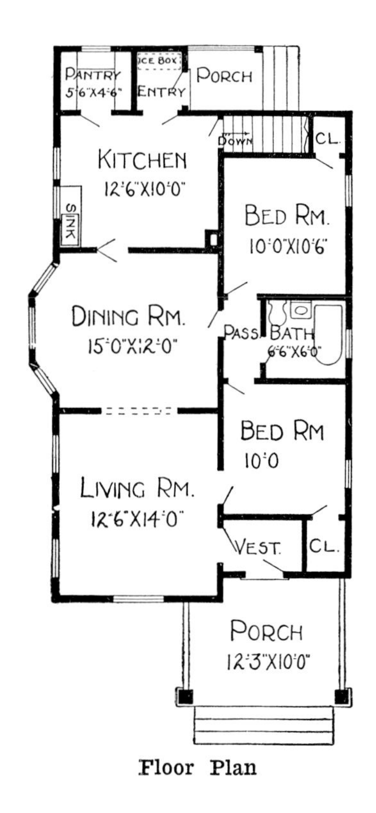

Floor Plan

PRICE

of Blue Prints, together with a complete set of typewritten specifications

ONLY

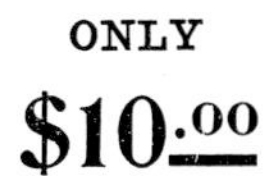

$10.00

We mail Plans and Specifications the same day order is received.

Design No. 5126

Size: Width, 24 feet 6 inches; Length, 33 feet

PRICE
of Blue Prints, together with a complete set of typewritten specifications

ONLY

$8.00

We mail Plans and Specifications the same day order is received.

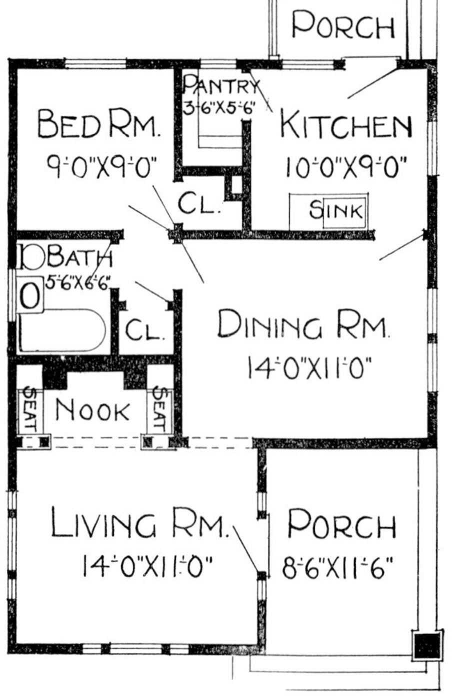

Floor Plan

Blue prints consist of foundation plan; floor plan; front, two side elevations; wall sections and all necessary interior details. Specifications consist of twenty-two pages of typewritten matter.

Design No. 6041=B

Size: Width, 35 feet 6 inches; Length, 40 feet

Blue prints consist of basement plan; roof plan; floor plan; front, rear, two side elevations; wall sections and all necessary interior details. Specifications consist of twenty-two pages of typewritten matter.

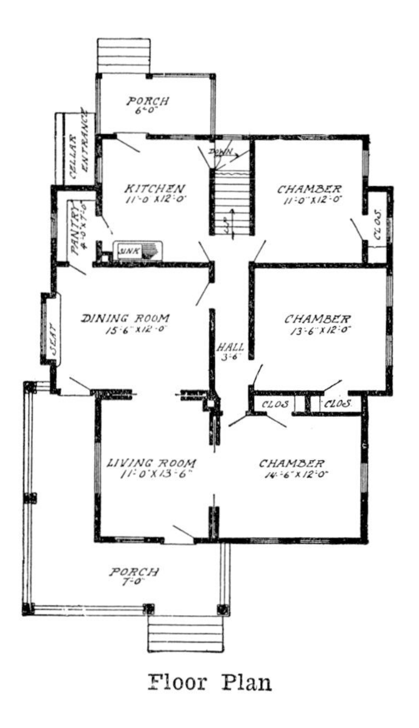

Floor Plan

PRICE

of Blue Prints, together with a complete set of typewritten specifications

ONLY

We mail Plans and Specifications the same day order is received.

Design No. 5092

Size: Width, 21 feet; Length, 35 feet

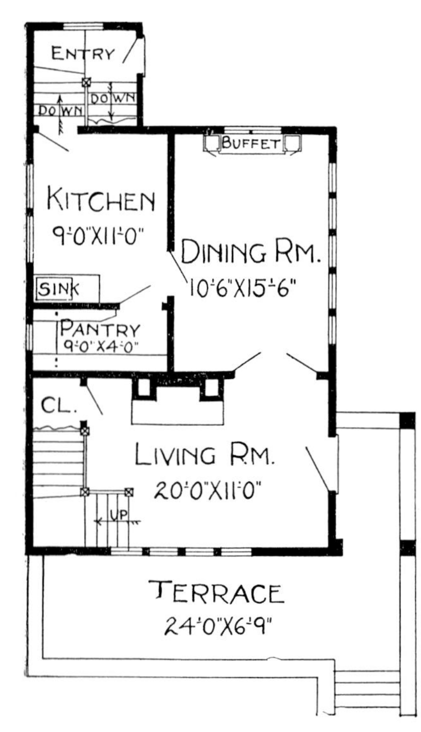

First Floor Plan

Blue prints consist of basement plan; first and second floor plans; front, rear, two side elevations; wall sections and all necessary interior details. Specifications consist of twenty-two pages of typewritten matter.

PRICE

of Blue Prints, together with a complete set of typewritten specifications

ONLY

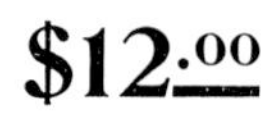

We mail Plans and Specifications the same day order is received.

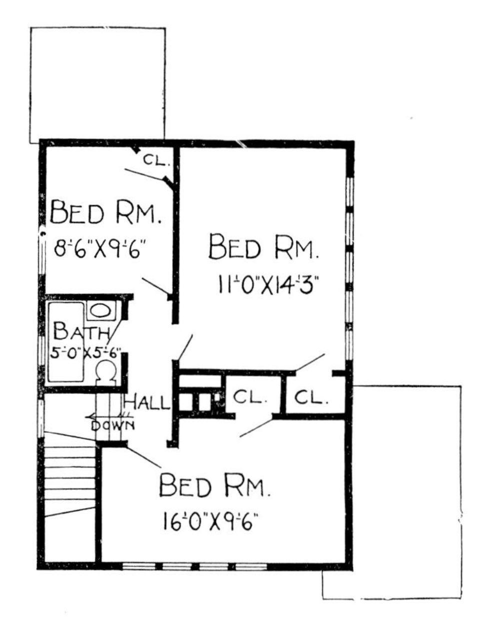

Second Floor Plan

Design No. 5091

Size: Width, 36 feet; Length, 33 feet

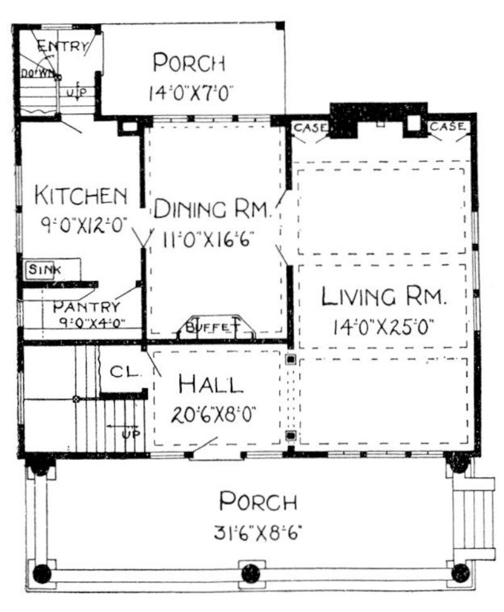

First Floor Plan

Blue prints consist of basement plan; first and second floor plans; front, rear, two side elevations; wall sections and all necessary interior details. Specifications consist of twenty-two pages of typewritten matter.

PRICE

of Blue Prints, together with a complete set of typewritten specifications

ONLY

$12.00

We mail Plans and Specifications the same day order is received.

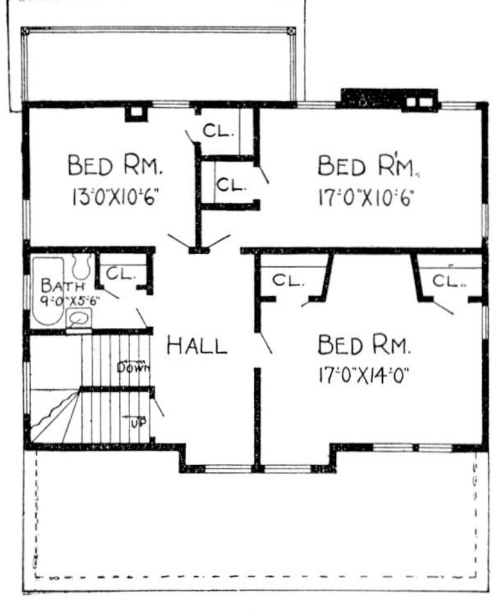

Second Floor Plan

Design No. 5003

Size: Width, 29 feet 6 inches; Length, 39 feet

PRICE

of Blue Prints, together with a complete set of typewritten specifications

ONLY

$7.00

We mail Plans and Specifications the same day order is received.

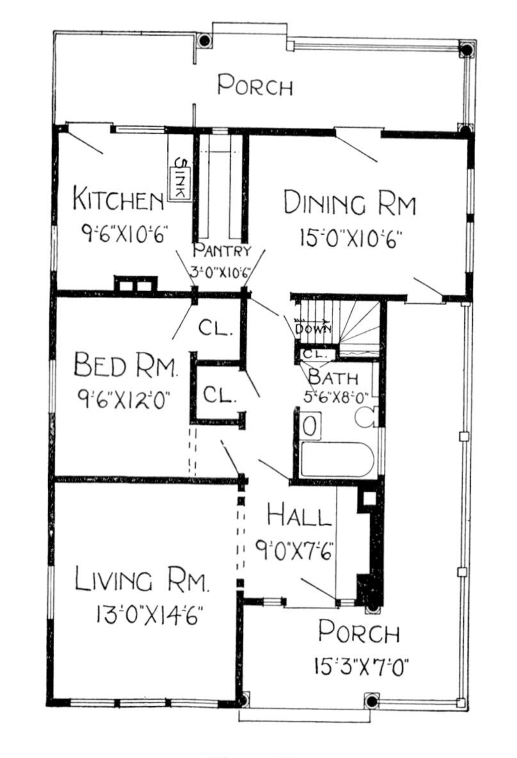

Floor Plan

Blue prints consist of basement plan; floor plan; front, rear, two side elevations; wall sections and all necessary interior details. Specifications consist of twenty-two pages of typewritten matter.

Design No. 5102

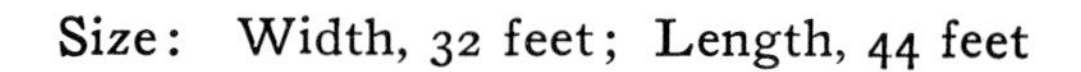

Size: Width, 32 feet; Length, 44 feet

Blue prints consist of basement plan; floor plan; front, two side elevations; wall sections and all necessary interior details. Specifications consist of twenty-two pages of typewritten matter.

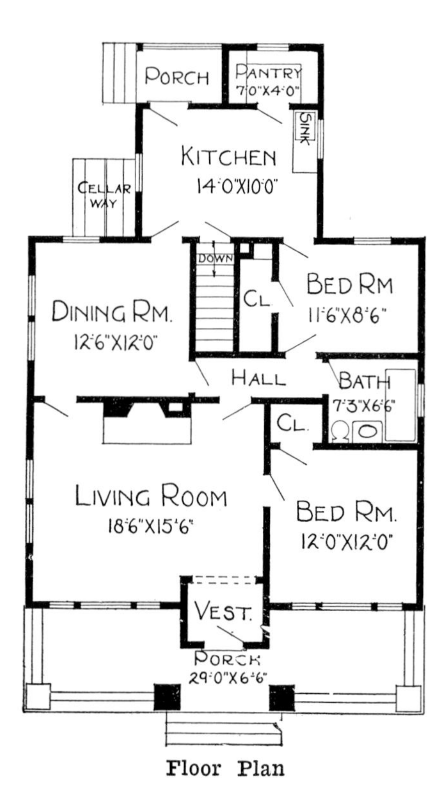

Floor Plan

PRICE

of Blue Prints, together with a complete set of typewritten specifications

ONLY

$8.00

We mail Plans and Specifications the same day order is received.

Design No. 5110

Size: Width, 34 feet; Length, 34 feet

PRICE

of Blue Prints, together with a complete set of typewritten specifications

ONLY

$8.00

We mail Plans and Specifications the same day order is received.

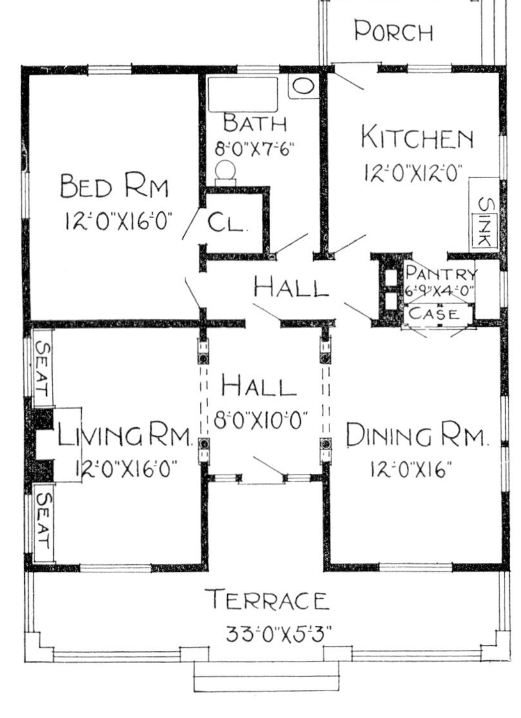

Floor Plan

Blue prints consist of foundation plan; floor plan; front, two side elevations; wall sections and all necessary interior details. Specifications consist of twenty-two pages of typewritten matter.

Design No. 5016

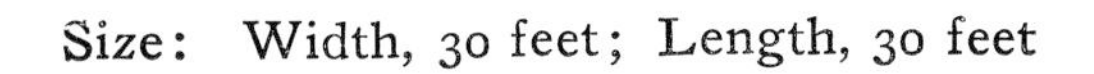

Size: Width, 30 feet; Length, 30 feet

Blue prints consist of basement plan; floor plan; front, rear, two side elevations; wall sections and all necessary interior details. Specifications consist of twenty-two pages of typewritten matter.

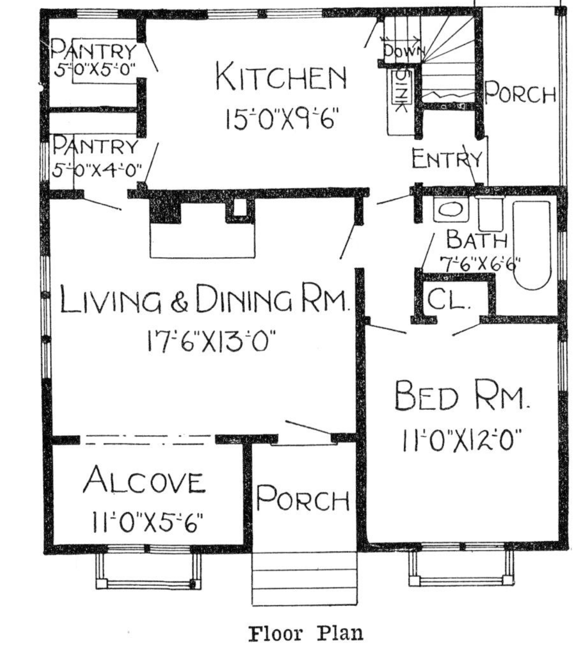

Floor Plan

PRICE

of Blue Prints, together with a complete set of typewritten specifications

ONLY

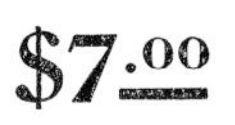

$7.00

We mail Plans and Specifications the same day order is received.

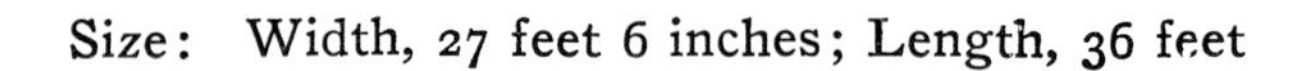

Design No. 5043

Size: Width, 27 feet 6 inches; Length, 36 feet

PRICE

of Blue Prints, together with a complete set of typewritten specifications

ONLY

$8.00

We mail Plans and Specifications the same day order is received.

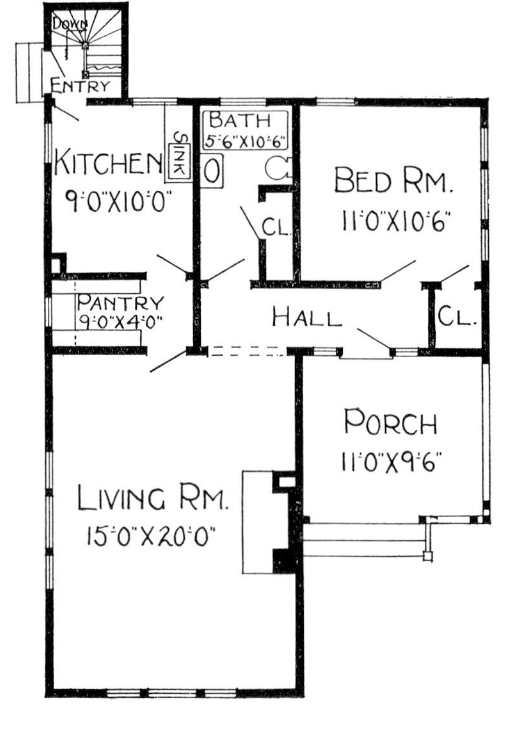

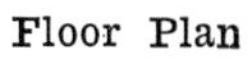

Floor Plan

Blue prints consist of foundation plan; roof plan; floor plan; front, rear, two side elevations; wall sections and all necessary interior details. Specifications consist of twenty-two pages of typewritten matter.

Design No. 7063=B

Size: Width, 30 feet; Length, 41 feet 6 inches

Blue prints consist of foundation plan; roof plan; floor plan; front, rear, two side elevations; wall sections and all necessary interior details. Specifications consist of twenty-two pages of typewritten matter.

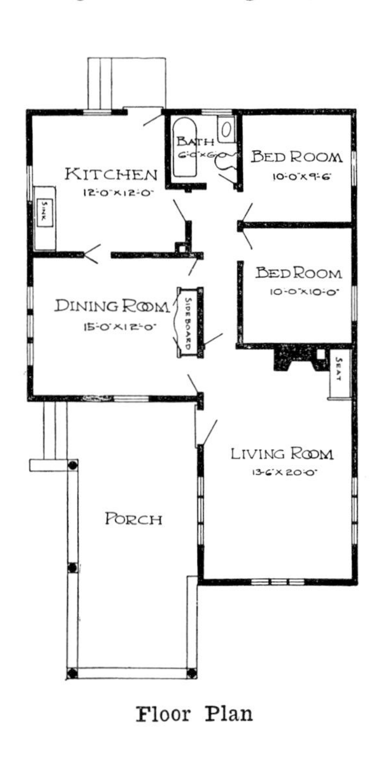

Floor Plan

PRICE

of Blue Prints, together with a complete set of typewritten specifications

ONLY

$10.00

We mail Plans and Specifications the same day order is received.

Design No. 2017=B

Size: Width, 27 feet; Length, 38 feet

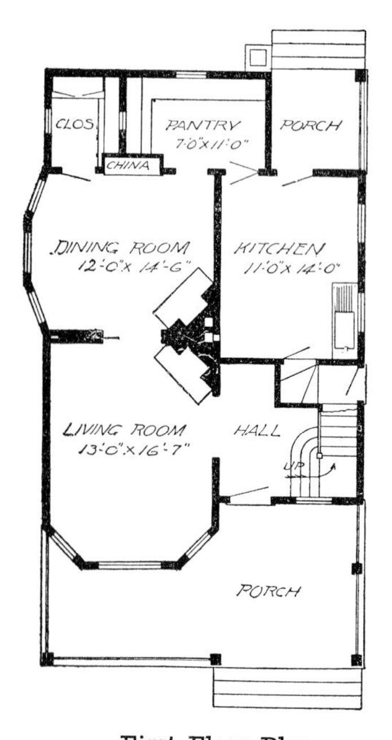

First Floor Plan

Blue prints consist of basement plan; roof plan; first and second floor plans; front, rear, two side elevations; wall sections and all necessary interior details. Specifications consist of twenty-two pages of typewritten matter.

PRICE

of Blue Prints, together with a complete set of typewritten specifications

ONLY

$12.00

We mail Plans and Specifications the same day order is received.

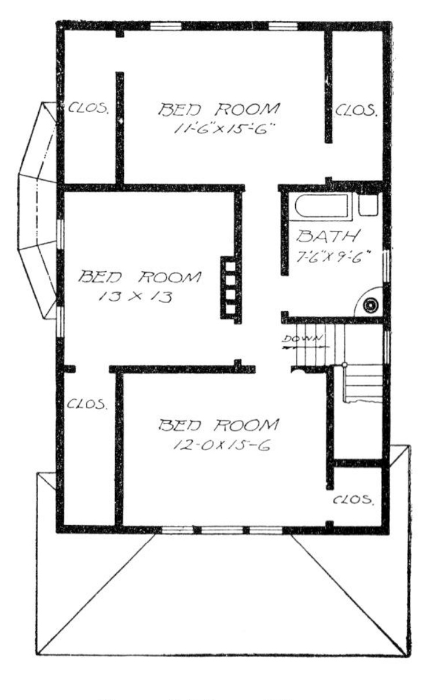

Second Floor Plan

Design No. 6056=B

Size: Width, 41 feet; Length, 23 feet

Blue prints consist of basement plan; roof plan; first and second floor plans; front, rear, two side elevations; wall sections and all necessary interior details. Specifications consist of twenty-two pages of typewritten matter.

PRICE

of Blue Prints, together with a complete set of typewritten specifications

ONLY

We mail Plans and Specifications the same day order is received.

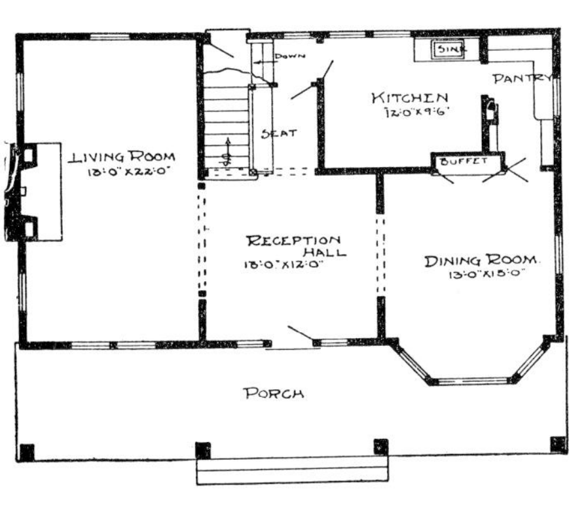

First Floor Plan

Second Floor Plan

Design No. 9085=B

Size: Width, 26 feet; Length, 44 feet

PRICE

of Blue Prints, together with a complete set of typewritten specifications

ONLY

$10.00

We mail Plans and Specifications the same day order is received.

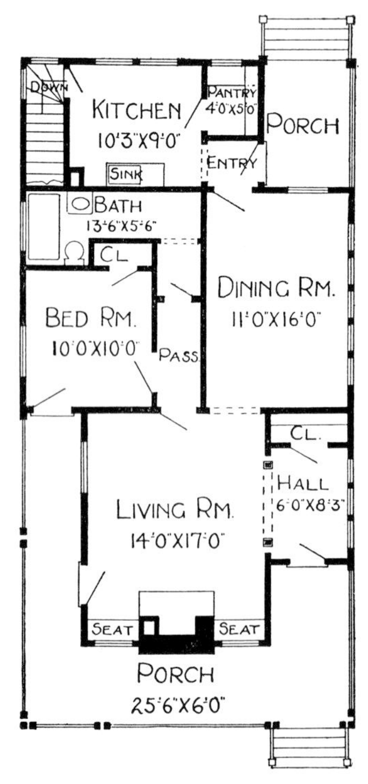

Floor Plan

Blue prints consist of basement plan; floor plan; front, rear, two side elevations; wall sections and all necessary interior details. Specifications consist of twenty-two pages of typewritten matter.

Design No. 5034

Size: Width, 27 feet; Length, 44 feet

Blue prints consist of basement plan; attic and roof plan; floor plan; front, rear, two side elevations; wall sections and all necessary interior details. Specifications consist of twenty-two pages of typewritten matter.

PORCH
DINING RM 14'6"X12'0"
KITCHEN 10'0"X12'0"
SINK
BUFFET
CL
BATH 10'4"X5'6"
PANTRY 7'6"X5'6"
CL
CLOS.
HALL
CLOS.
BED RM 10'0"X9'6"
BED RM 10'0"X9'6"
SEAT
BOOK CASE
LIVING ROOM 25'0"X12'0"
SEAT
SEAT
VEST
SEAT
PORCH 24'0"X9'0"

Floor Plan

PRICE

of Blue Prints, together with a complete set of typewritten specifications

ONLY

$10.00

We mail Plans and Specifications the same day order is received.

Design No. 5082

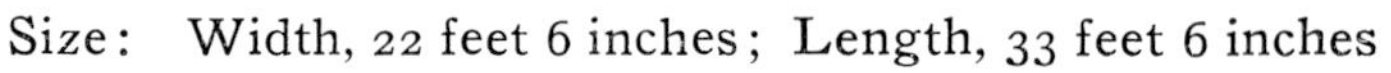

Size: Width, 22 feet 6 inches; Length, 33 feet 6 inches

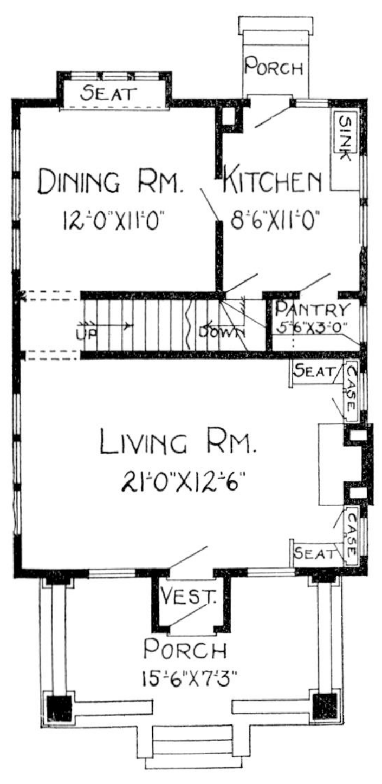

First Floor Plan

Blue prints consist of cellar and foundation plan; roof plan; first and second floor plans; front, rear, two side elevations; wall sections and all necessary interior details. Specifications consist of twenty-two pages of typewritten matter.

PRICE

of Blue Prints, together with a complete set of typewritten specifications

ONLY

$12.00

We mail Plans and Specifications the same day order is received.

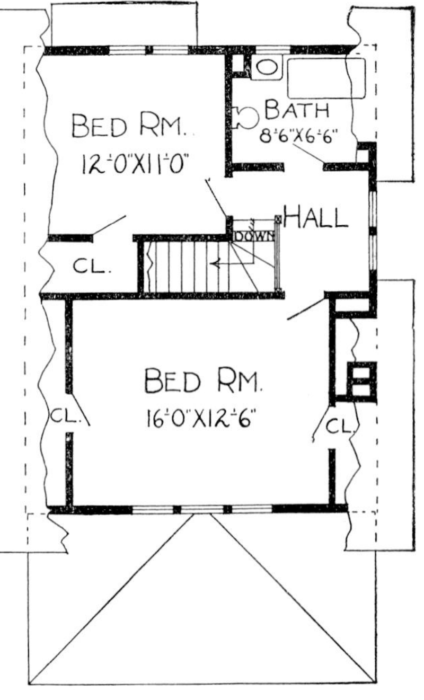

Second Floor Plan

Design No. 2115=B

Size: Width, 24 feet; Length, 31 feet

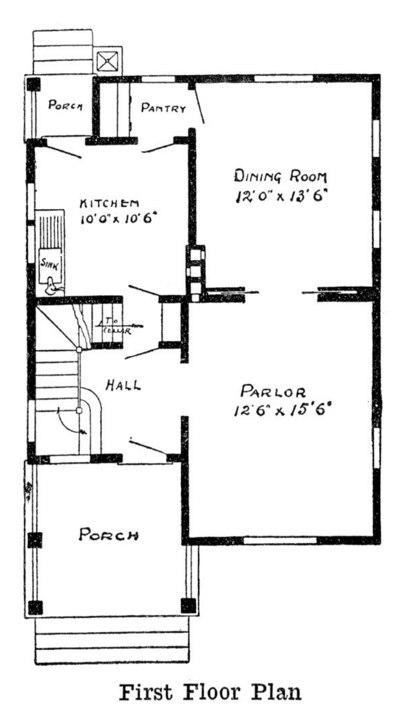

First Floor Plan

Blue prints consist of cellar and foundation plan; first and second floor plans; front, two side elevations; wall sections and all necessary interior details. Specifications consist of twenty-two pages of typewritten matter.

PRICE

of Blue Prints, together with a complete set of typewritten specifications

ONLY

We mail Plans and Specifications the same day order is received.

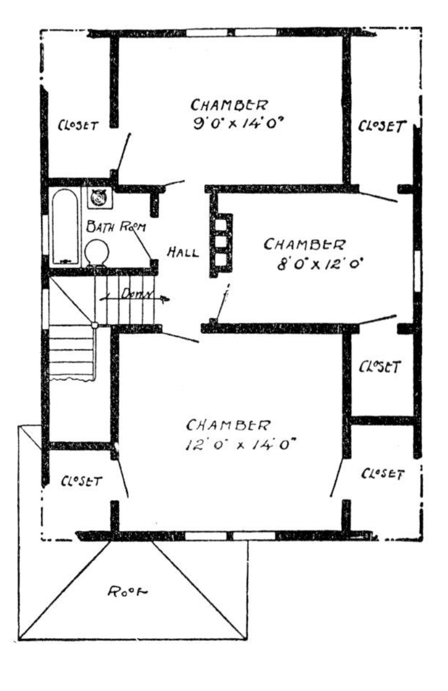

Second Floor Plan

Design No. 5011

Size: Width, 23 feet 6 inches; Length, 30 feet 6 inches

PRICE

of Blue Prints, together with a complete set of typewritten specifications

ONLY

$10.00

We mail Plans and Specifications the same day order is received.

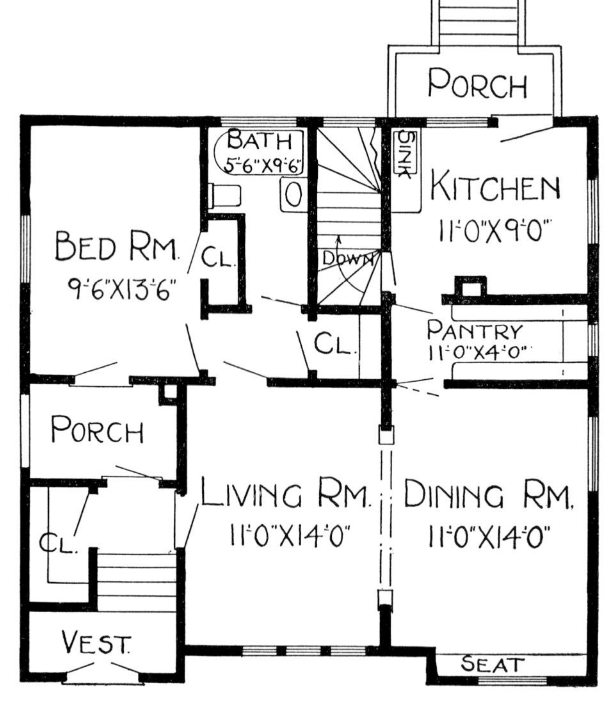

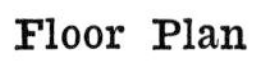

Floor Plan

Blue prints consist of basement plan; roof plan; floor plan; front, rear, two side elevations; wall sections and all necessary interior details. Specifications consist of twenty-two pages of tyepwritten matter.

Design No. 5045

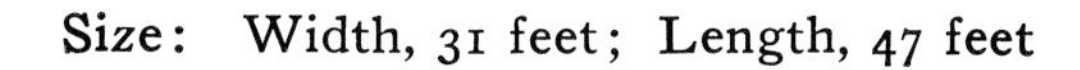

Size: Width, 31 feet; Length, 47 feet

Blue prints consist of foundation plan; attic and roof plans; floor plan; front, rear, two side elevations; wall sections and all necessary interior details. Specifications consist of twenty-two pages of typewritten matter.

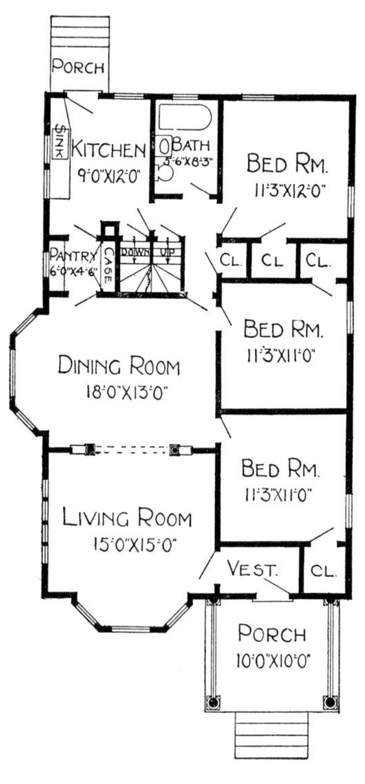

Floor Plan

PRICE

of Blue Prints, together with a complete set of typewritten specifications

ONLY

$10.00

We mail Plans and Specifications the same day order is received.

Design No. 7038=B

Size: Width, 26 feet 6 inches; Length, 29 feet 6 inches

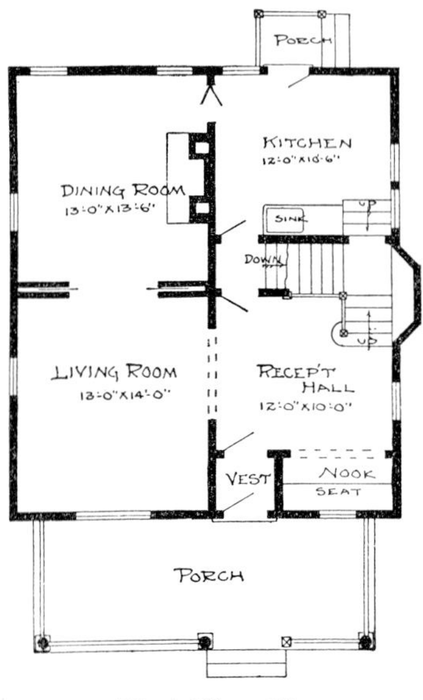

First Floor Plan

Blue prints consist of basement plan; roof plan; first and second floor plans; front, rear, two side elevations; wall sections and all necessary interior details. Specifications consist of twenty-two pages of typewritten matter.

PRICE

of Blue Prints, together with a complete set of typewritten specifications

ONLY

We mail Plans and Specifications the same day order is received.

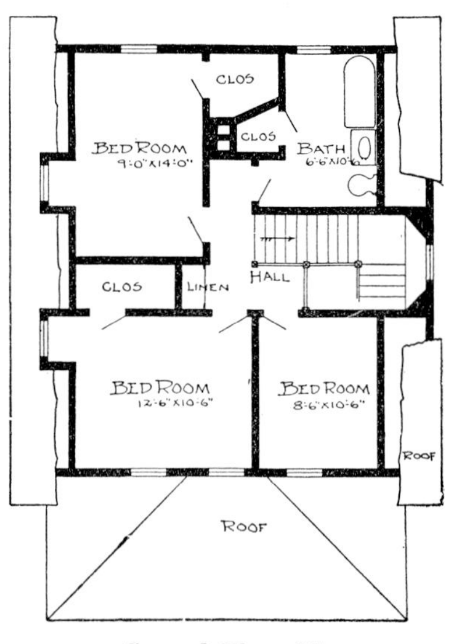

Second Floor Plan

Design No. 2546=B

Size: Width, 35 feet; Length, 61 feet

Blue prints consist of cellar and foundation plan; roof plan; floor plan; front, rear, two side elevations; wall sections and all necessary interior details. Specifications consist of twenty-two pages of typewritten matter.

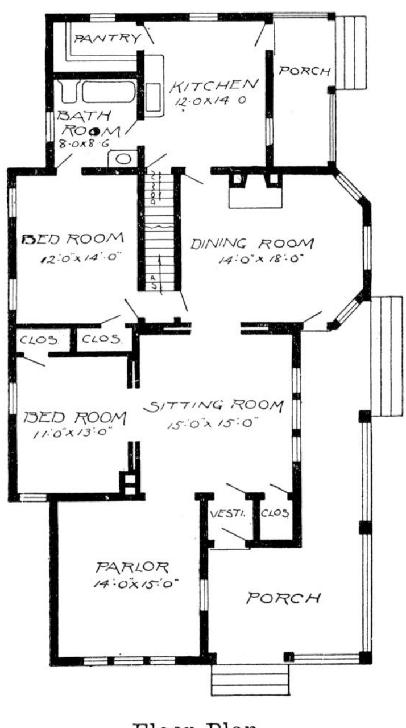

Floor Plan

PRICE

of Blue Prints, together with a complete set of typewritten specifications

ONLY

$10.00

We mail Plans and Specifications the same day order is received.

Design No. 9027=B

Size: Width, 36 feet; Length, 27 feet 6 inches

PRICE

of Blue Prints, together with a complete set of typewritten specifications

ONLY

$10.00

We mail Plans and Specifications the same day order is received.

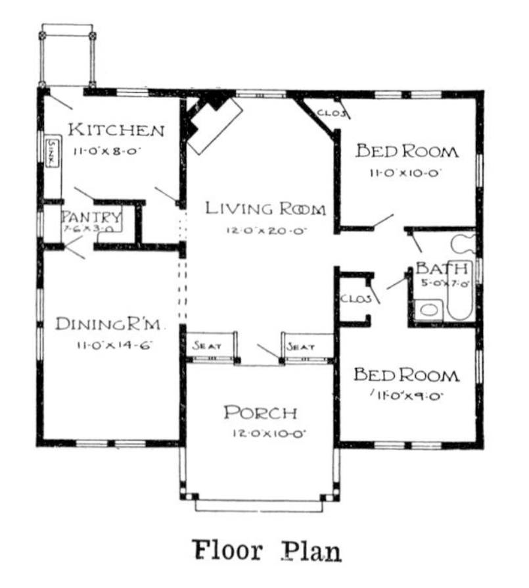

Floor Plan

Blue prints consist of floor plan; front, rear, two side elevations; wall sections and all necessary interior details. Specifications consist of twenty-two pages of typewritten matter.

Design No. 5118

Size: Width, 39 feet; Length, 26 feet 6 inches

Blue prints consist of foundation plan; floor plan; front, two side elevations; wall sections and all necessary interior details. Specifications consist of twenty-two pages of typewritten matter.

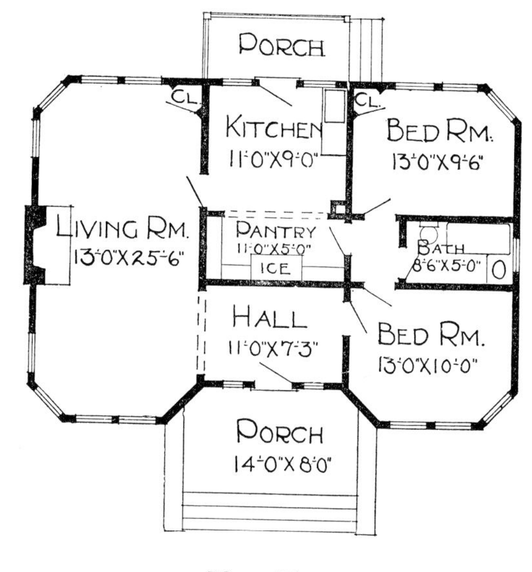

Floor Plan

PRICE

of Blue Prints, together with a complete set of typewritten specifications

ONLY

We mail Plans and Specifications the same day order is received.

Design No. 5150

Size: Width, 26 feet 6 inches; Length, 23 feet 6 inches

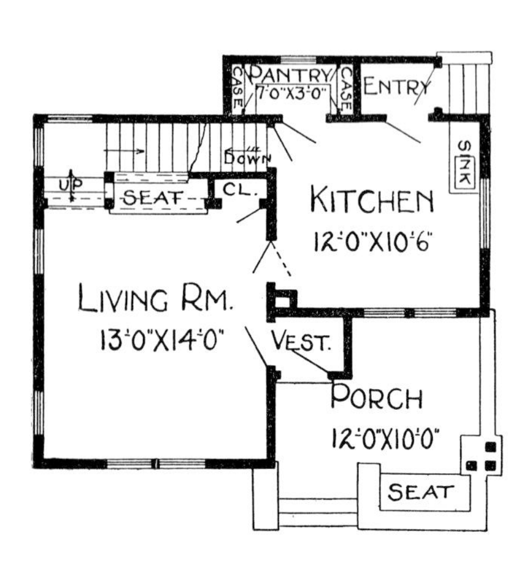

First Floor Plan

Blue prints consist of basement plan; first and second floor plans; front, two side elevations; wall sections and all necessary interior details. Specifications consist of twenty-two pages of typewritten matter.

PRICE

of Blue Prints, together with a complete set of typewritten specifications

ONLY

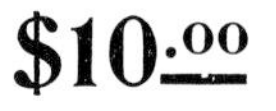

We mail Plans and Specifications the same day order is received.

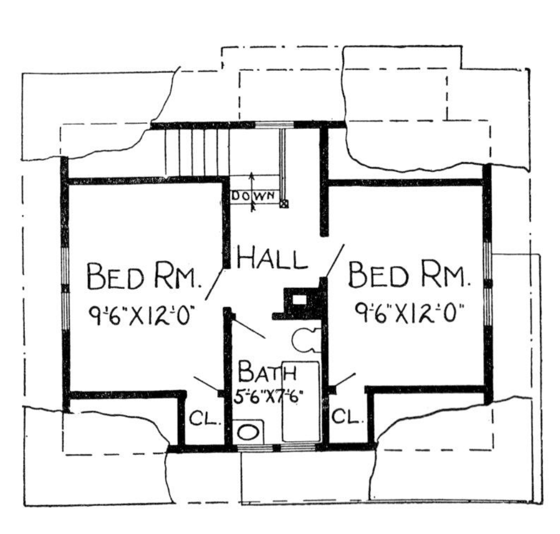

Second Floor Plan

Design No. 2560-B

Size: Width, 26 feet; Length, 38 feet

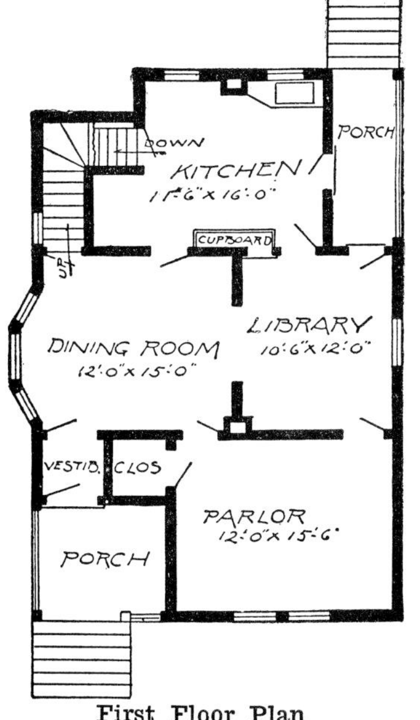

First Floor Plan

Blue prints consist of cellar and foundation plan; roof plan; first and second floor plans; front, rear, two side elevations; wall sections and all necessary interior details. Specifications consist of twenty-two pages of typewritten matter.

PRICE

of Blue Prints, together with a complete set of tyepwritten specifications

ONLY

$10.00

We mail Plans and Specifications the same day order is received.

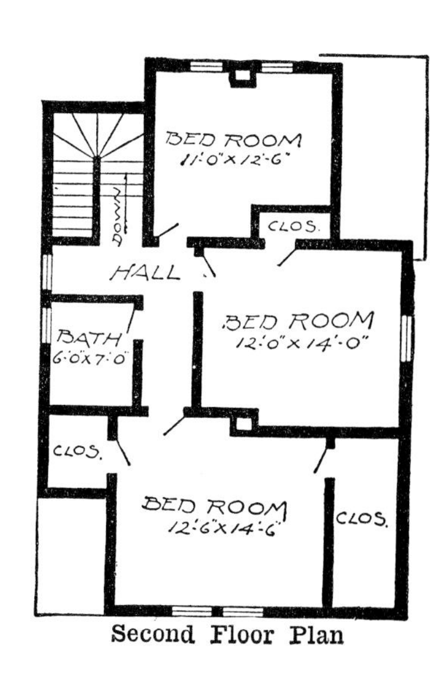

Second Floor Plan

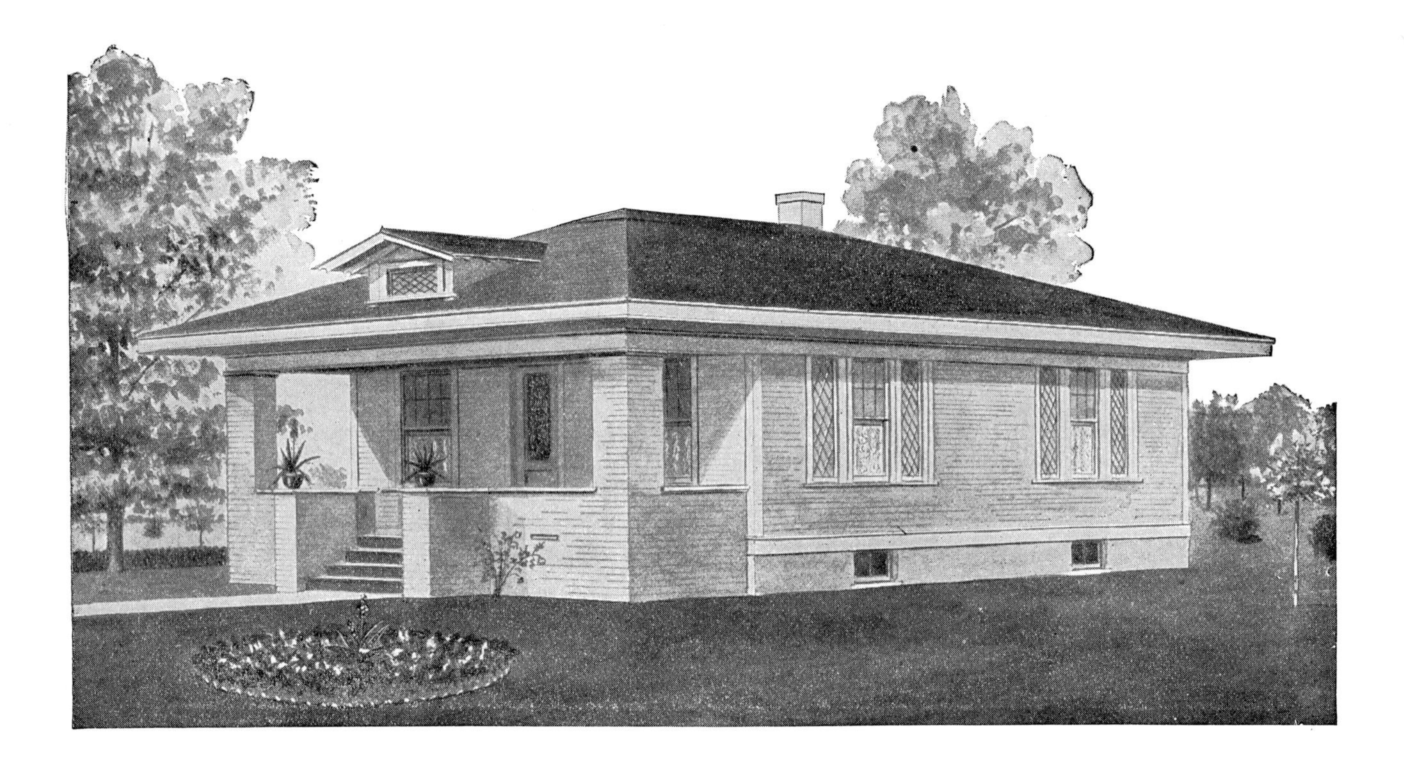

Size: Width, 26 feet; Length, 32 feet

PRICE

of Blue Prints, together with a complete set of typewritten specifications

ONLY

We mail Plans and Specifications the same day order is received.

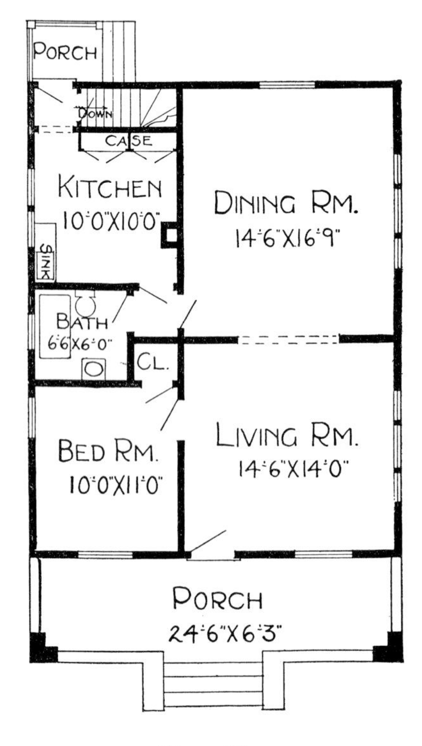

Floor Plan

Blue prints consist of basement plan; roof plan; floor plan; front, rear, two side elevations; wall sections and all necessary interior details. Specifications consist of twenty-two pages of typewritten matter.

Design No. 5112

Size: Width, 28 feet; Length, 30 feet

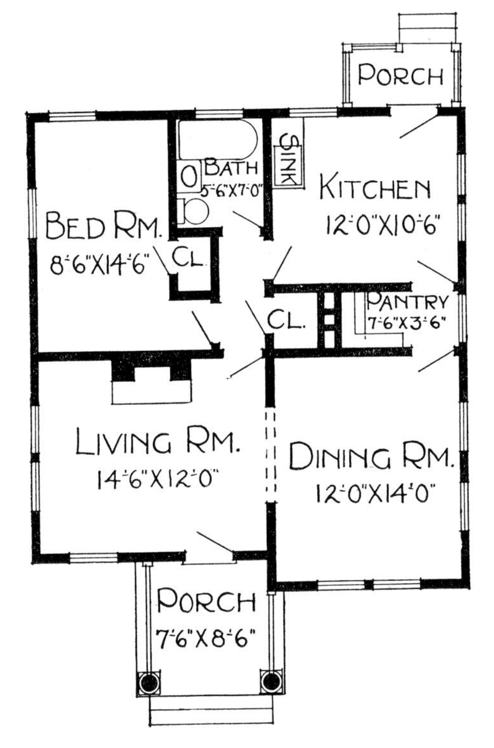

Floor Plan

Blue prints consist of foundation plan; floor plan; front, rear, two side elevations; wall sections and all necessary interior details. Specifications consist of twenty-two pages of typewritten matter.

PRICE

of Blue Prints, together with a complete set of typewritten specifications

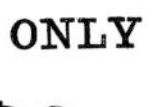
ONLY

$8.00

We mail Plans and Specifications the same day order is received.

Design No. 5132

Size: Width, 25 feet; Length, 28 feet 6 inches

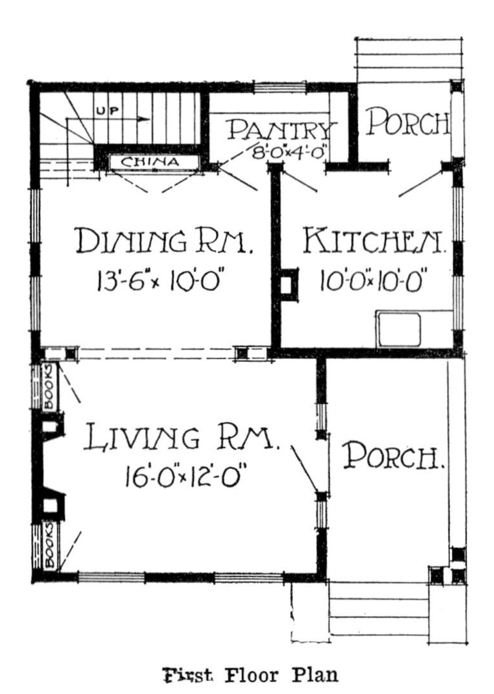

First Floor Plan

Blue prints consist of basement plan; roof plan; first and second floor plans; front, rear, and two side elevations; wall sections and all necessary interior details. Specifications consist of twenty-two pages of typewritten matter.

PRICE

of Blue Prints, together with a complete set of typewritten specifications.

ONLY

$12.00

We mail Plans and Specifications the same day order is received.

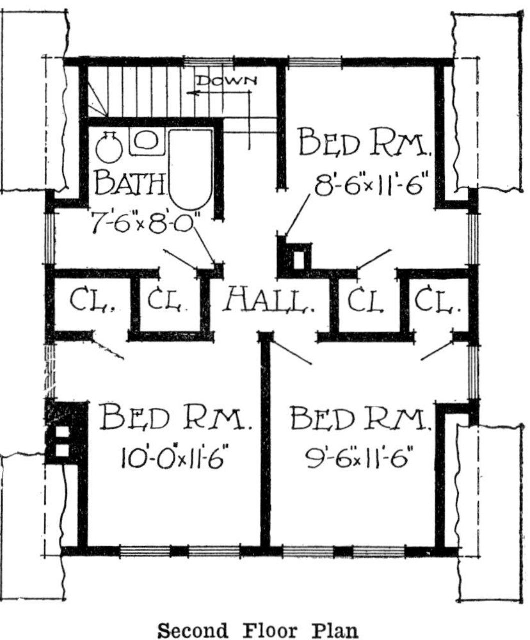

Second Floor Plan

Design No. 5116

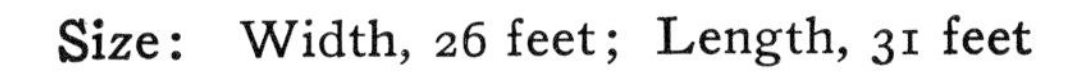

Size: Width, 26 feet; Length, 31 feet

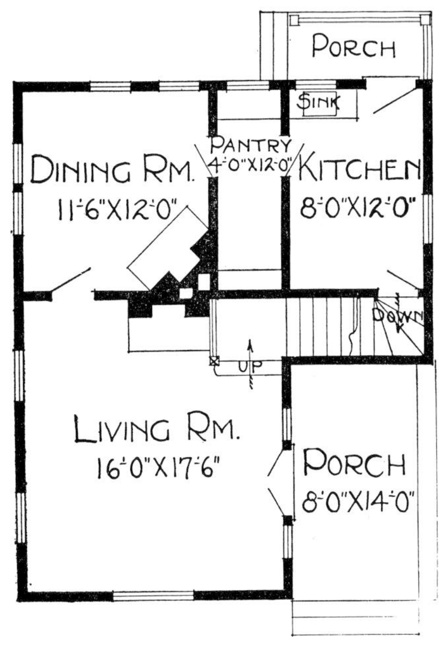

First Floor Plan

Blue prints consist of basement plan; first and second floor plans; front, rear, and two side elevations; wall sections and all necessary interior details. Specifications consist of twenty-two pages of typewritten matter.

PRICE

of Blue Prints, together with a complete set of typewritten specifications

ONLY

$10.00

We mail Plans and Specifications the same day order is received.

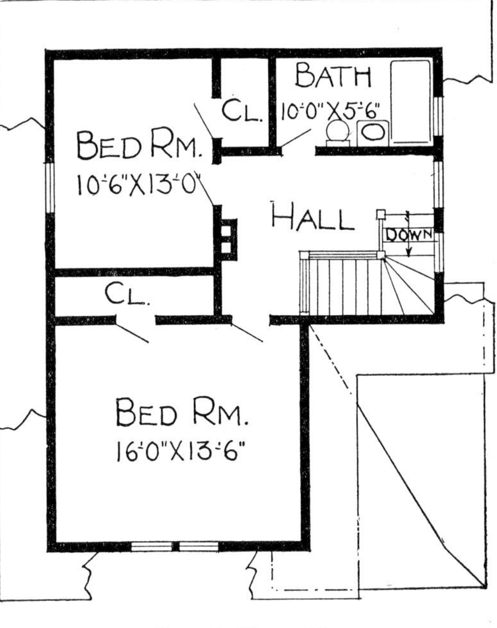

Second Floor Plan

Design No. 5067

Size: Width, 24 feet; Length, 31 feet

PRICE

of Blue Prints, together with a complete set of typewritten specifications

ONLY

$8.00

We mail Plans and Specifications the same day order is received.

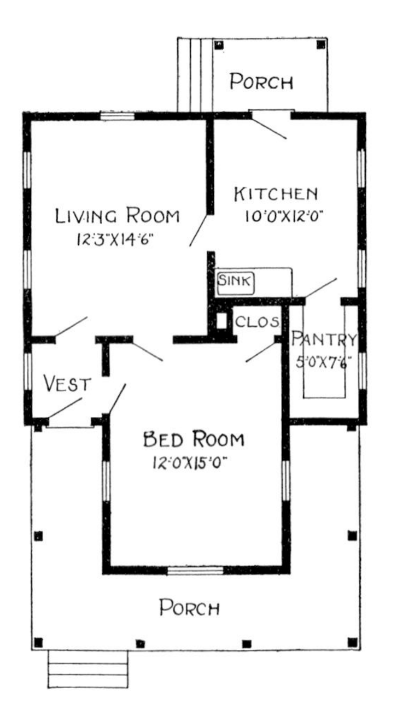

Floor Plan

Blue prints consist of foundation plan; attic plan; floor plan; front, rear, two side elevations; wall sections and all necessary interior details. Specifications consist of twenty-two pages of typewritten matter.

Design No. 7055=B

Size: Width, 35 feet; Length, 60 feet 6 inches

Blue prints consist of basement plan; roof plan; floor plan; front, rear, two side elevations; wall sections and all necessary interior details. Specifications consist of twenty-two pages of typewritten matter.

Floor Plan

PRICE

of Blue Prints, together with a complete set of typewritten specifications

ONLY

$12.00

We mail Plans and Specifications the same day order is received.

Design No. 5144

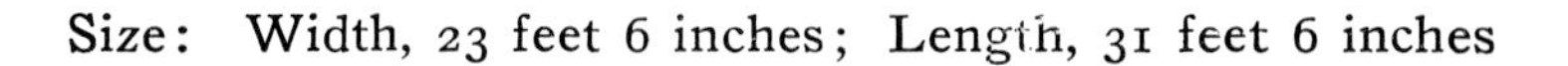

Size: Width, 23 feet 6 inches; Length, 31 feet 6 inches

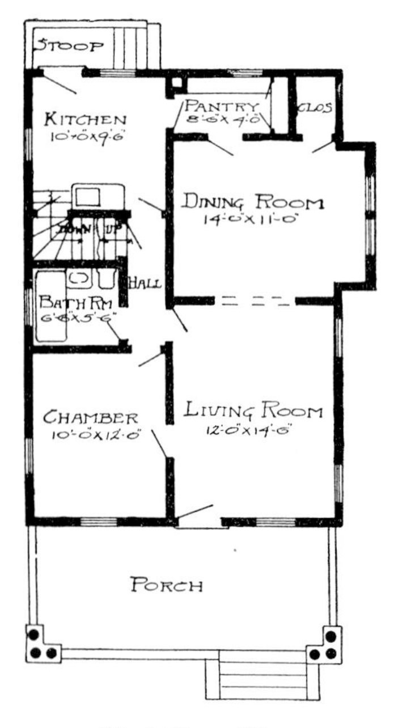

First Floor Plan

Blue prints consist of basement plan; first and second floor plans; front, rear, two side elevations; wall sections and all necessary interior details. Specifications consist of twenty-two pages of typewritten matter.

PRICE

of Blue Prints, together with a complete set of typewritten specifications

ONLY

$12.00

We mail Plans and Specifications the same day order is received.

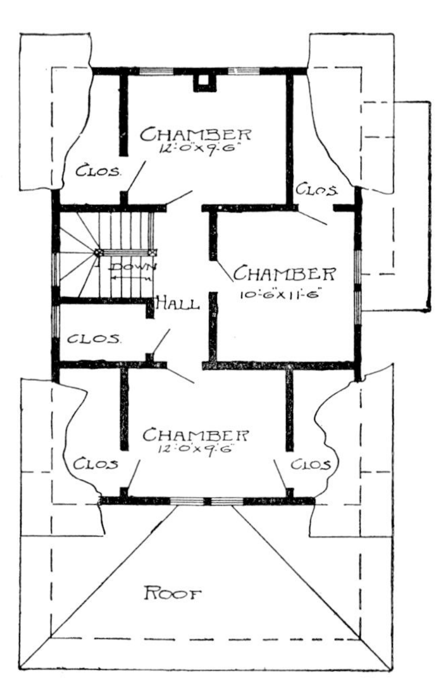

Second Floor Plan

Design No. 2005-B

Size: Width, 28 feet 6 inches; Length, 43 feet

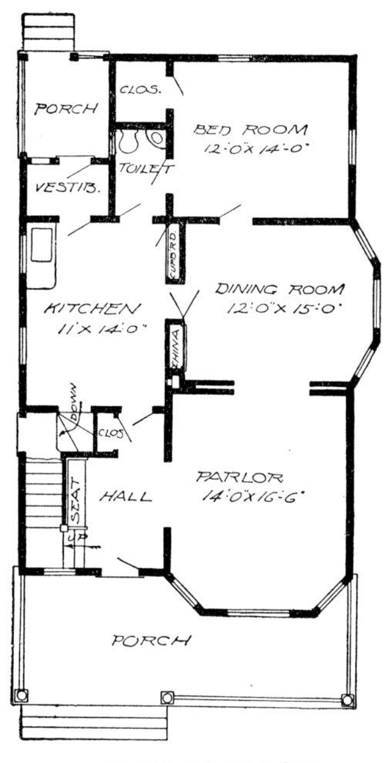

First Floor Plan

Blue prints consist of basement plan; first and second floor plans; front, rear, two side elevations; wall sections and all necessary interior details. Specifications consist of twenty-two pages of typewritten matter.

PRICE

of Blue Prints, together with a complete set of typewritten specifications

ONLY

$12.00

We mail Plans and Specifications the same day order is received.

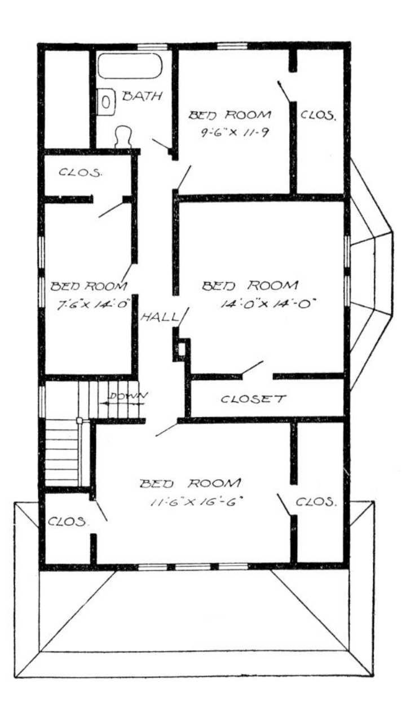

Second Floor Plan

Design No. 8255=B

Size: Width, 28 feet 8 inches; Length, 36 feet 8 inches

PRICE

of Blue Prints, together with a complete set of typewritten specifications

ONLY

$12.00

We mail Plans and Specifications the same day order is received.

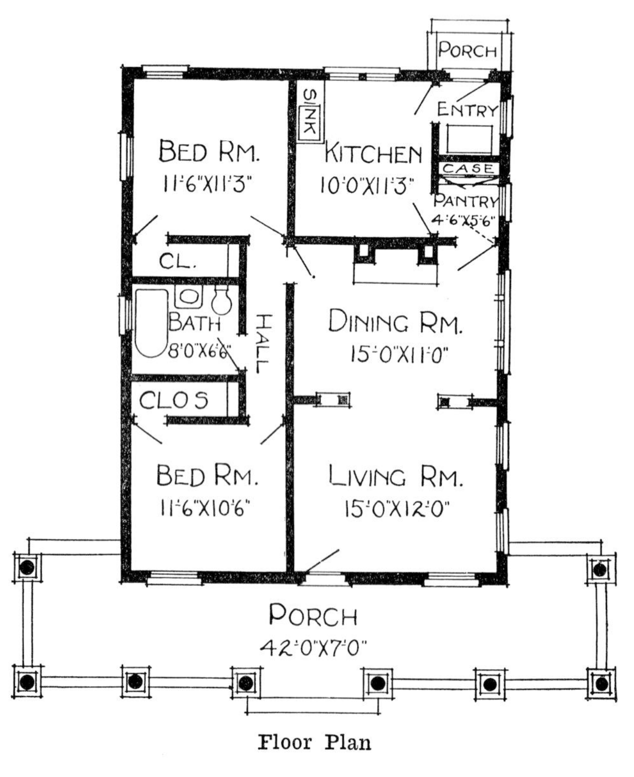

Floor Plan

Blue prints consist of foundation plan; roof plan; floor plan; front, rear, two side elevations; wall sections and all necessary interior details. Specifications consist of twenty-two pages of typewritten matter.

Design No. 5005

Size: Width, 37 feet 3 inches; Length, 22 feet

Blue prints consist of basement plan; floor plan; front, rear, two side elevations; wall sections and all necessary interior details. Specifications consist of twenty-two pages of typewritten matter.

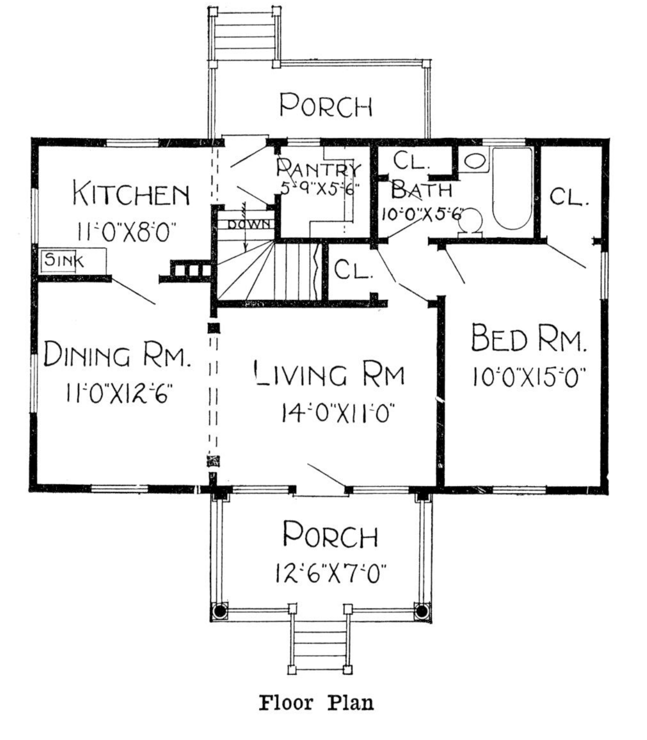

Floor Plan

PRICE

of Blue Prints, together with a complete set of typewritten specifications

ONLY

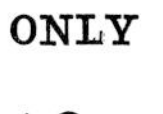

We mail Plans and Specifications the same day order is received.

Design No. 6073=B

Size: Width, 46 feet 6 inches; Length, 31 feet 6 inches

PRICE

of Blue Prints, together with a complete set of typewritten specifications

ONLY

$10.00

We mail Plans and Specifications the same day order is received.

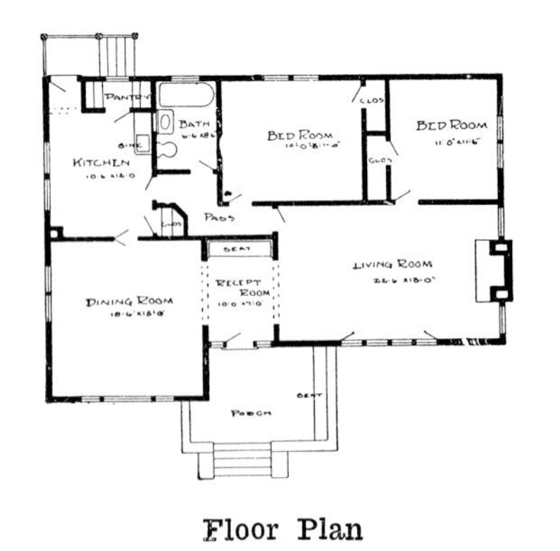

Floor Plan

Blue prints consist of foundation plan; roof plan; floor plan; front, rear, two side elevations; wall sections and all necessary interior details. Specifications consist of twenty-two pages of typewritten matter.

Design No. 9032=B

Size: Width, 36 feet; Length, 27 feet

Blue prints consist of roof plan; floor plan; front, rear, two side elevations; wall sections and all necessary interior details. Specifications consist of twenty-two pages of typewritten matter.

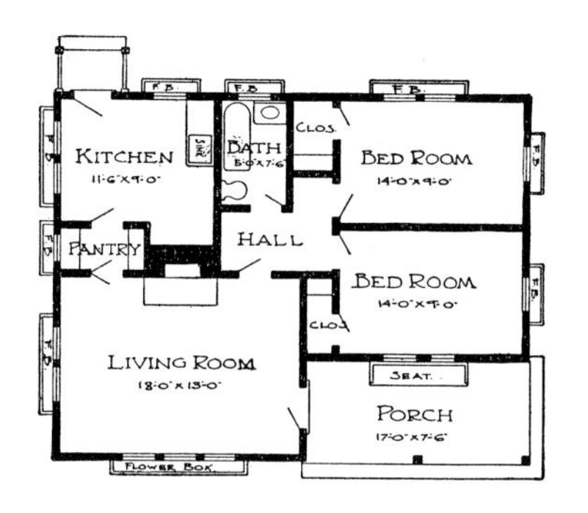

Floor Plan

PRICE

of Blue Prints, together with a complete set of typewritten specifications

ONLY

$10.00

We mail Plans and Specifications the same day order is received.

Design No. 5141

Size: Width, 22 feet; Length, 29 feet

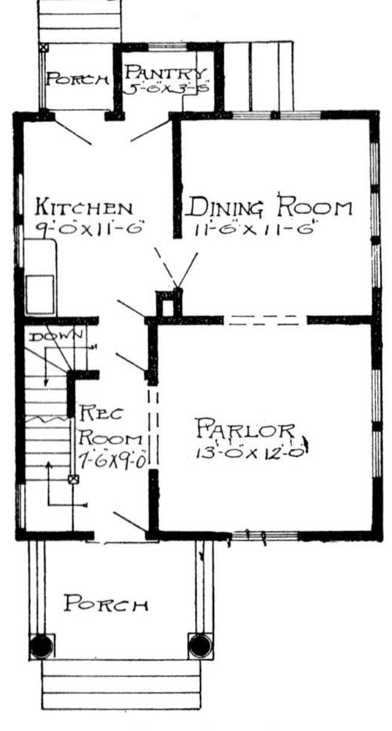

First Floor Plan

Blue prints consist of basement plan; first and second floor plans; front, rear, two side elevations; wall sections and all necessary interior details. Specifications consist of twenty-two pages of typewritten matter.

PRICE

of Blue Prints, together with a complete set of typewritten specifications

ONLY

We mail Plans and Specifications the same day order is received.

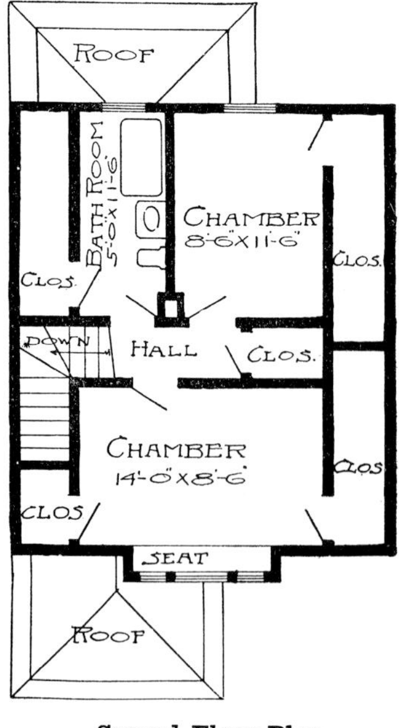

Second Floor Plan

Design No. 2046=B

Size: Width, 22 feet 6 inches; Length, 30 feet

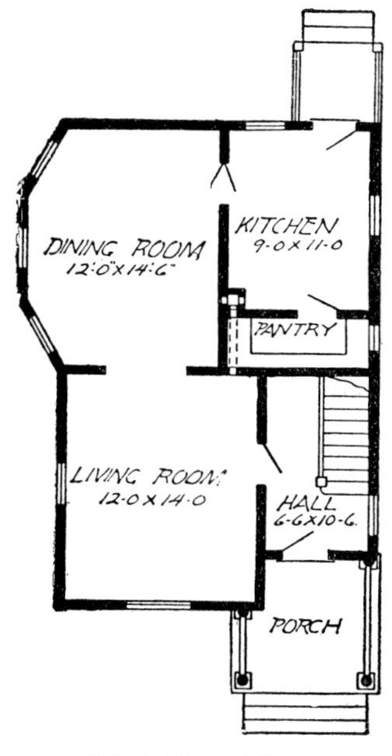

First Floor Plan

Blue prints consist of basement plan; roof plan; first and second floor plans; front, rear, two side elevations; wall sections and all necessary interior details. Specifications consist of twenty-two pages of typewritten matter.

PRICE

of Blue Prints, together with a complete set of typewritten specifications

ONLY

We mail Plans and Specifications the same day order is received.

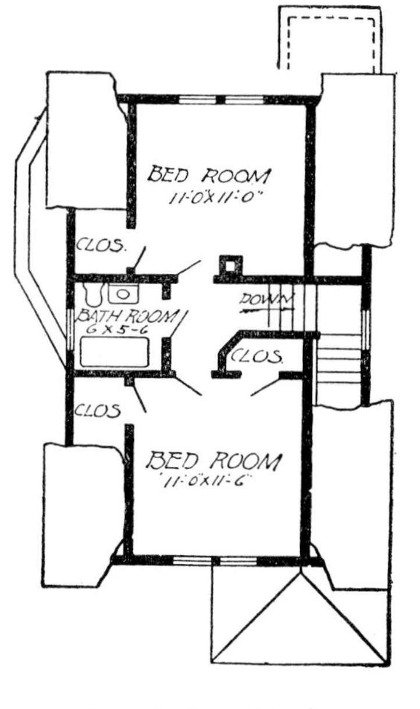

Second Floor Plan

Design No. 5122

Size: Width, 36 feet; Length, 31 feet 6 inches

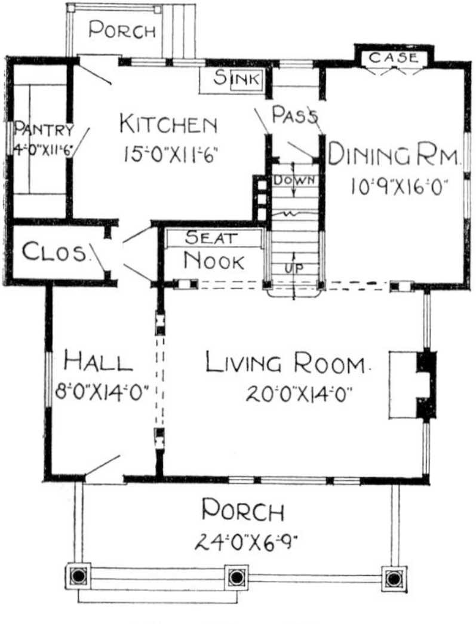

First Floor Plan

Blue prints consist of basement plan; floor plan; front, rear, two side elevations; wall sections and all necessary interior details. Specifications consist of twenty-two pages of typewritten matter.

PRICE

of Blue Prints, together with a complete set of typewritten specifications

ONLY

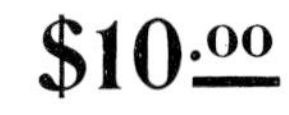

$10.00

We mail Plans and Specifications the same day order is received.

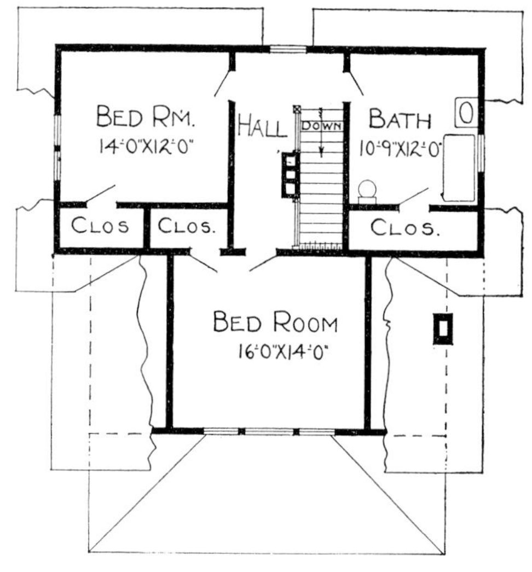

Second Floor Plan

Design No. 5070

Size: Width, 21 feet; Length, 39 feet 6 inches

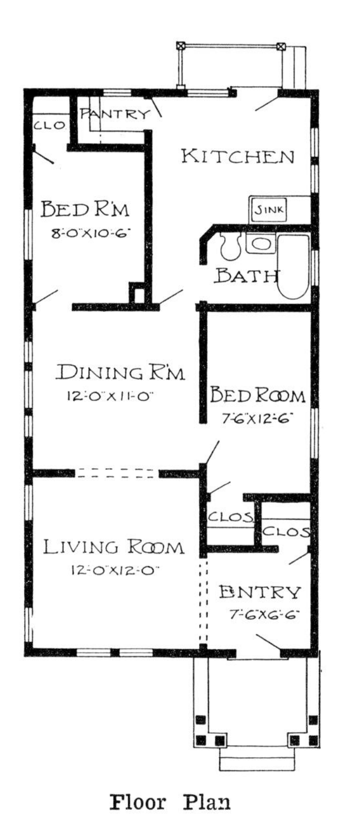

Floor Plan

Blue prints consist of foundation plan; roof plan; floor plan; front, rear, two side elevations; wall sections and all necessary interior details. Specifications consist of twenty-two pages of typewritten matter.

PRICE

of Blue Prints, together with a complete set of typewritten specifications

ONLY

$8.00

We mail Plans and Specifications the same day order is received.

Design No. 5099

Size: Width, 27 feet; Length, 36 feet

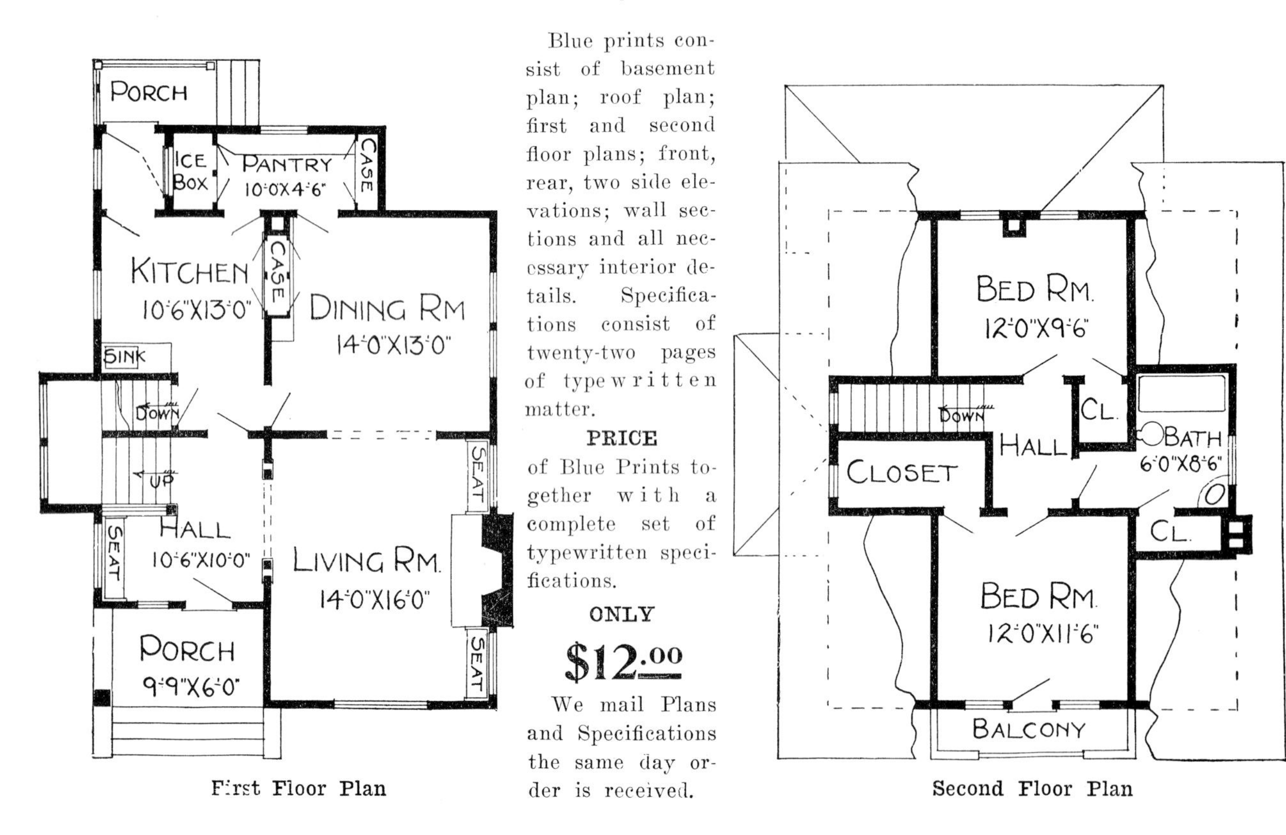

Blue prints consist of basement plan; roof plan; first and second floor plans; front, rear, two side elevations; wall sections and all necessary interior details. Specifications consist of twenty-two pages of typewritten matter.

PRICE

of Blue Prints together with a complete set of typewritten specifications.

ONLY

$12.00

We mail Plans and Specifications the same day order is received.

First Floor Plan

Second Floor Plan

Design No. 2131=B

Size: Width, 31 feet; Length, 60 feet

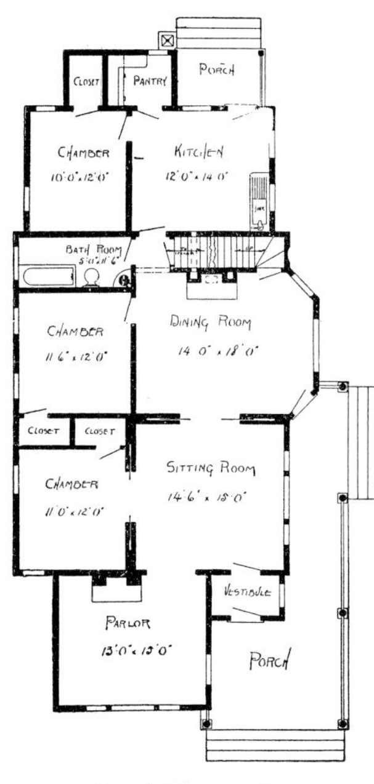

First Floor Plan

Blue prints consist of cellar and foundation plan; roof plan; first and second floor plans; front, rear, two side elevations; wall sections and all necessary interior details. Specifications consist of twenty-two pages of typewritten matter.

PRICE

of Blue Prints, together with a complete set of typewritten specifications

ONLY

We mail Plans and Specifications the same day order is received.

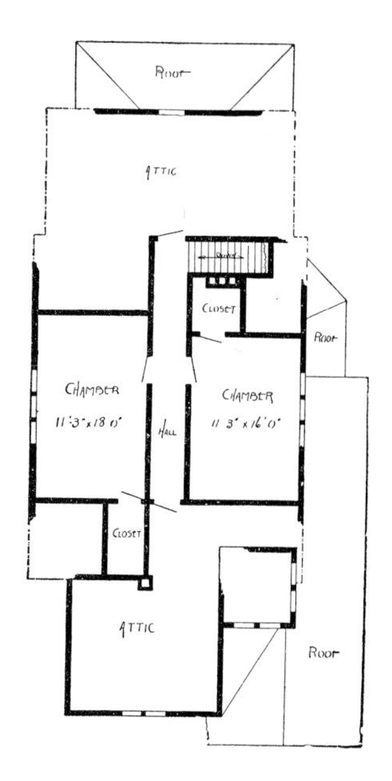

Second Floor Plan

Design No. 9042=B

Size: Width, 34 feet 6 inches; Length, 36 feet 6 inches

PRICE

of Blue Prints, together with a complete set of typewritten specifications

ONLY

$10.00

We mail Plans and Specifications the same day order is received.

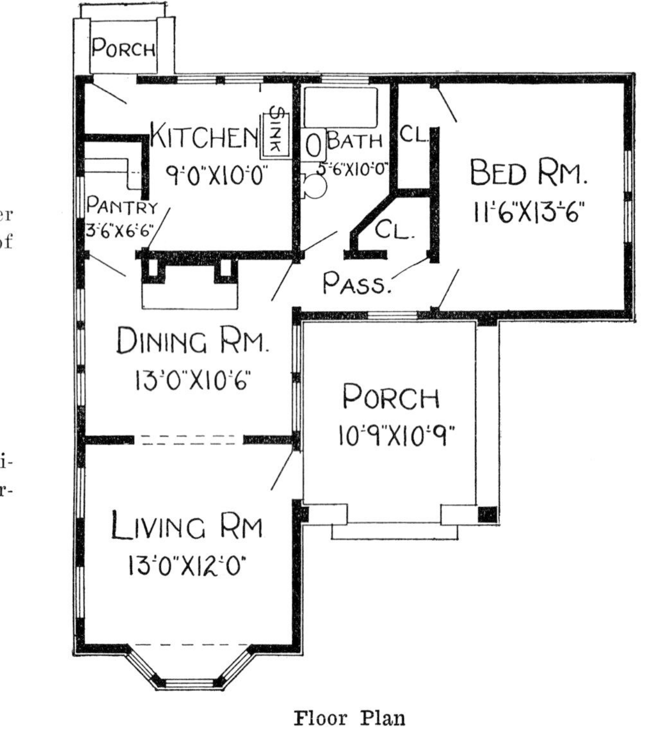

Floor Plan

Blue prints consist of foundation plan; floor plan; front, rear, two side elevations; wall sections and all necessary interior details. Specifications consist of twenty-two pages of typewritten matter.

Design No. 5142

Size: Width, 50 feet; Length, 28 feet 6 inches

Blue prints consist of cellar plan; roof plan; floor plan; front, rear, two side elevations; wall sections and all necessary interior details. Specifications consist of twenty-two pages of typewritten matter.

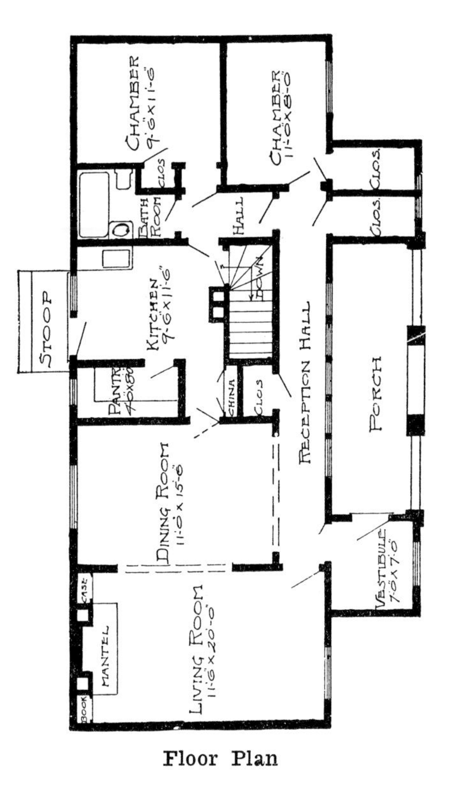

Floor Plan

PRICE

of Blue Prints, together with a complete set of typewritten specifications

ONLY

We mail Plans and Specifications the same day order is received.

Design No. 5014

Size: Width, 26 feet 6 inches; Length, 43 feet

PRICE

of Blue Prints, together with a complete set of typewritten specifications

ONLY

We mail Plans and Specifications the same day order is received.

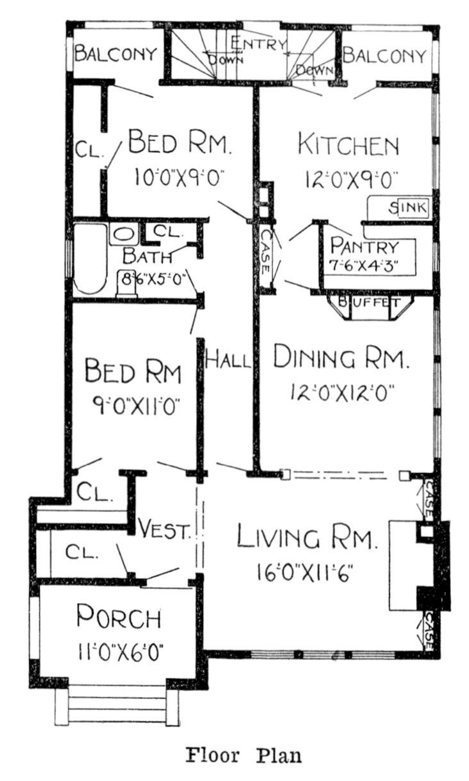

Floor Plan

Blue prints consist of basement plan; floor plan; front, rear, two side elevations; wall sections and all necessary interior details. Specifications consist of twenty-two pages of typewritten matter.

Design No. 5030

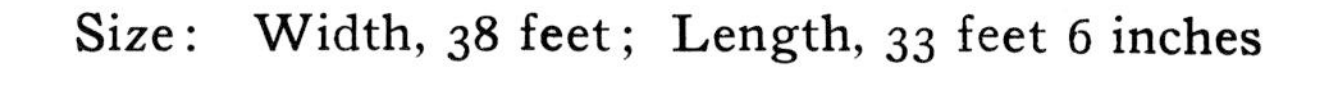

Size: Width, 38 feet; Length, 33 feet 6 inches

Blue prints consist of basement plan; floor plan; front, rear, two side elevations; wall sections and all necessary interior details. Specifications consist of twenty-two pages of typewritten matter.

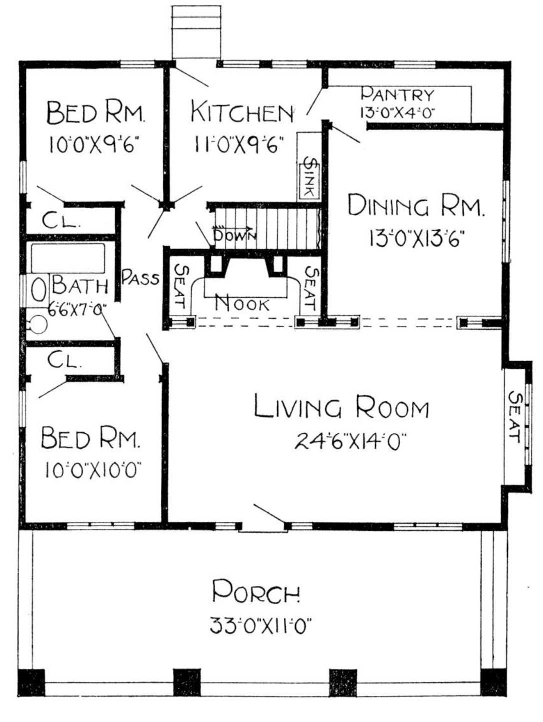

Floor Plan

PRICE

of Blue Prints, together with a complete set of typewritten specifications

ONLY

$10.00

We mail Plans and Specifications the same day order is received.

Design No. 5138

Size: Width, 25 feet 6 inches; Length, 26 feet

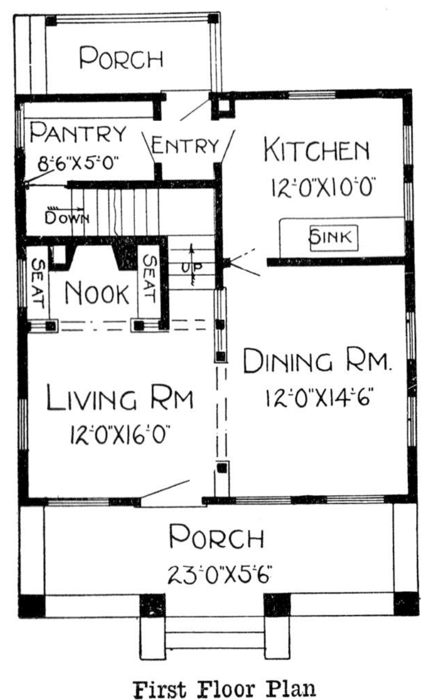

First Floor Plan

Blue prints consist of cellar and foundation plan; first and second floor plans; front, rear, two side elevations; wall sections and all necessary interior details. Specifications consist of twenty-two pages of typewritten matter.

PRICE

of Blue Prints, together with a complete set of typewritten specifications

ONLY

$10.00

We mail Plans and Specifications the same day order is received.

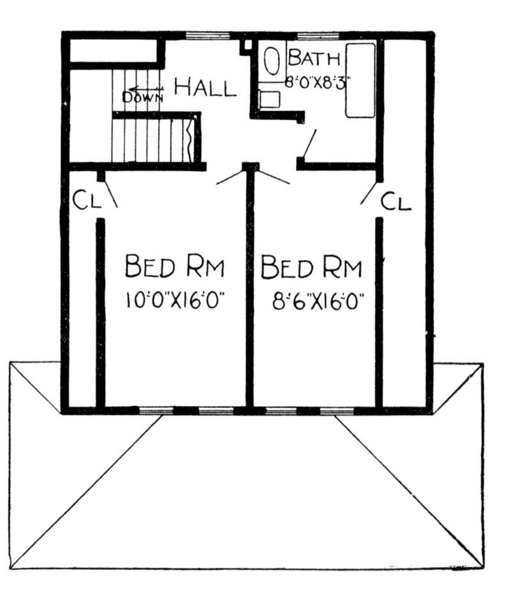

Second Floor Plan

Design No. 6065-B

Size: Width, 37 feet; Length, 28 feet 6 inches

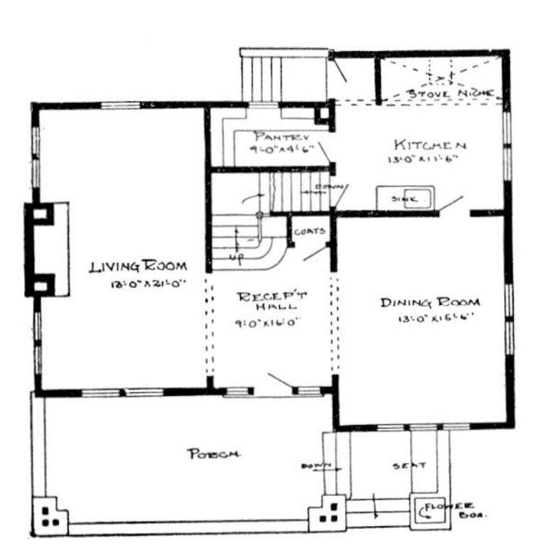

First Floor Plan

Blue prints consist of basement plan; roof plan; first and second floor plans; front, rear, two side elevations; wall sections and all necessary interior details. Specifications consist of twenty-two pages of typewritten matter.

PRICE

of Blue Prints, together with a complete set of typewritten specifications,

ONLY

$12.00

We mail Plans and Specifications the same day order is received.

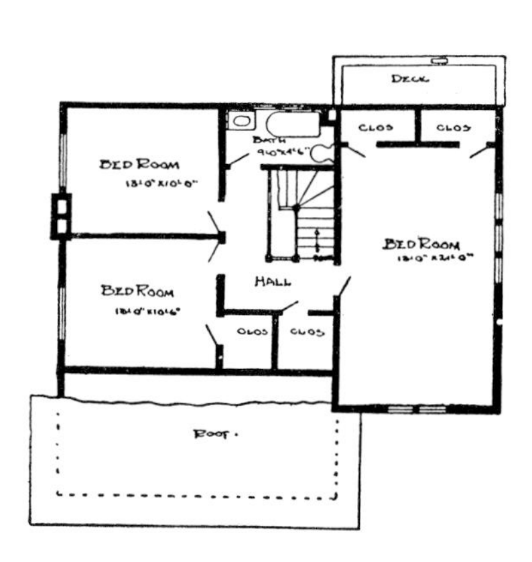

Second Floor Plan

Design No. 5147

Size: Width, 42 feet; Length, 27 feet 6 inches

PRICE

of Blue Prints, together with a complete set of typewritten specifications

ONLY

$8.00

We mail Plans and Specifications the same day order is received.

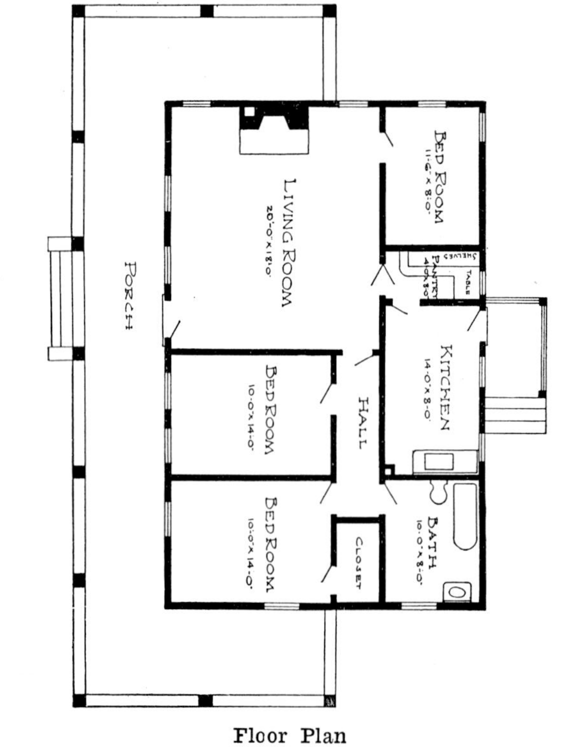

Floor Plan

Blue prints consist of foundation plan; roof plan; floor plan; front, rear, two side elevations; wall sections and all necessary interior details. Specifications consist of twenty-two pages of typewritten matter.

Design No. 5018

Size: Width, 37 feet; Length, 25 feet

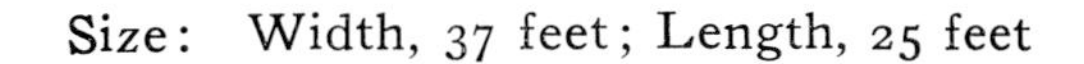

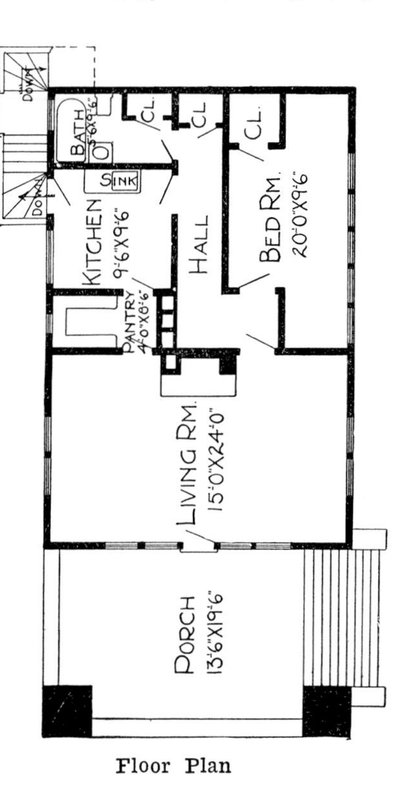

Floor Plan

Blue prints consist of basement plan; floor plan; front, rear, two side elevations; wall sections and all necessary interior details. Specifications consist of twenty-two pages of typewritten matter.

PRICE

of Blue Prints, together with a complete set of typewritten specifications

ONLY

$7.00

We mail Plans and Specifications the same day order is received.

Design No. 5033

Size: Width, 21 feet; Length, 26 feet

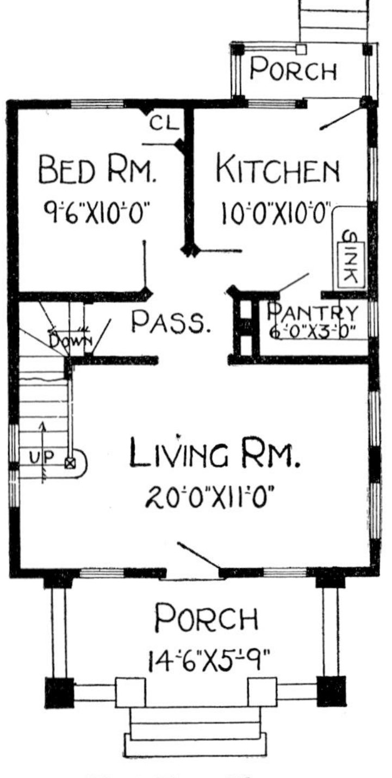

First Floor Plan

Blue prints consist of basement plan; roof plan; first and second floor plans; front, rear and two side elevations; wall sections and all necessary interior details. Specifications consist of twenty-two pages of typewritten matter.

PRICE

of Blue Prints, together with a complete set of typewritten specifications

ONLY

$10.00

We mail Plans and Specifications the same day order is received.

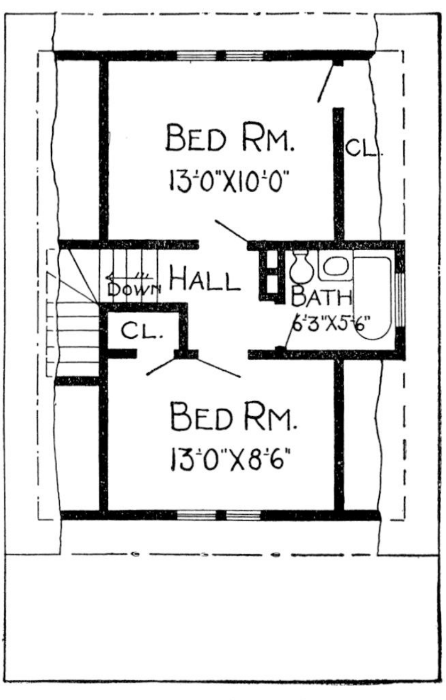

Second Floor Plan

Design No. 5073

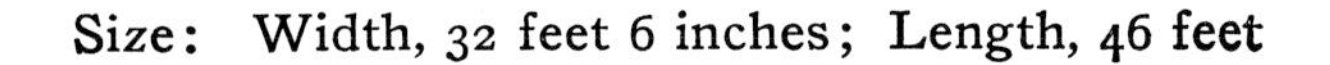

Size: Width, 32 feet 6 inches; Length, 46 feet

Blue prints consist of foundation plan; attic and roof plan; floor plan; front, rear, two side elevations; wall sections and all necessary interior details. Specifications consist of twenty-two pages of typewritten matter.

Floor Plan

PRICE

of Blue Prints, together with a complete set of typewritten specifications

ONLY

$10.00

We mail Plans and Specifications the same day order is received.

Design No. 5146

Size: Width, 27 feet; Length, 35 feet

PRICE

of Blue Prints, together with a complete set of typewritten specifications

ONLY

$8.00

We mail Plans and Specifications the same day order is received.

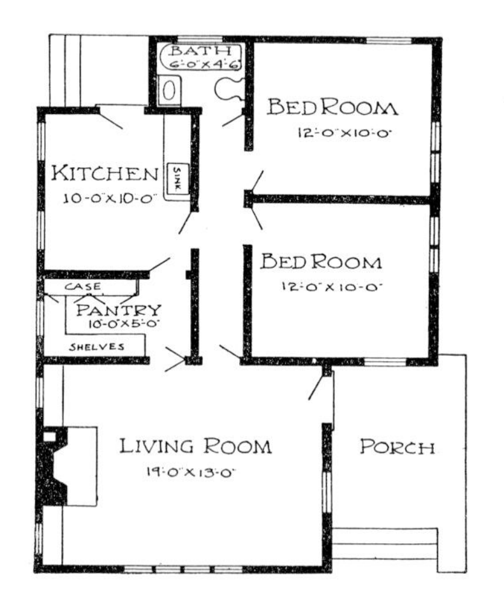

Floor Plan

Blue prints consist of floor plan; front, rear, two side elevations; wall sections and all necessary interior details. Specifications consist of twenty-two pages of typewritten matter.

Design No. 5143

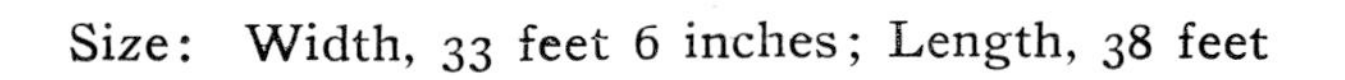
Size: Width, 33 feet 6 inches; Length, 38 feet

Blue prints consist of cellar plan; floor plan; front, rear, two side elevations; wall sections and all necessary interior details. Specifications consist of twenty-two pages of typewritten matter.

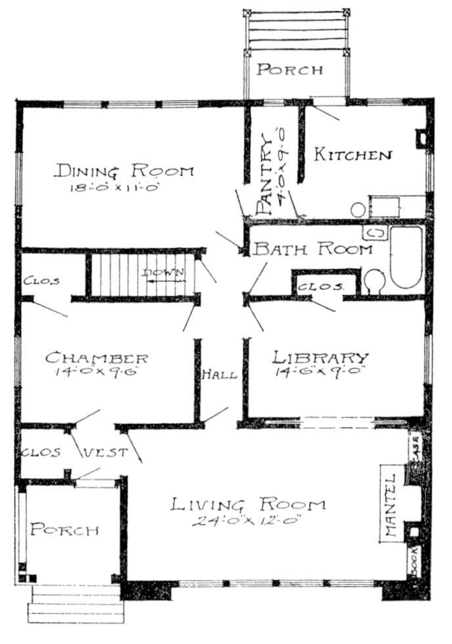

Floor Plan

PRICE

of Blue Prints, together with a complete set of typewritten specifications

ONLY

$8.00

We mail Plans and Specifications the same day order is received.

Design No. 5068

Size: Width, 16 feet 6 inches; Length, 24 feet

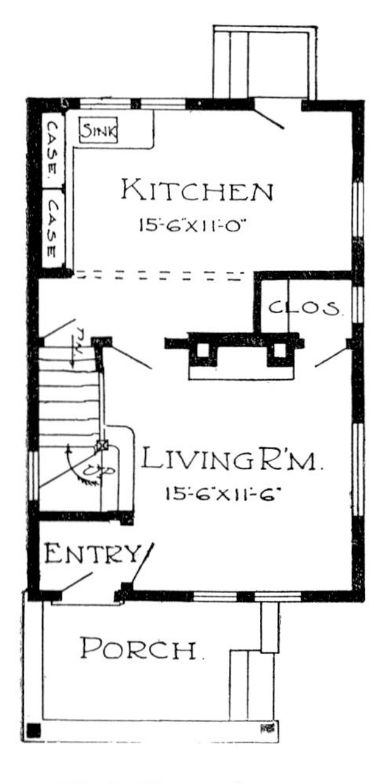

First Floor Plan

Blue prints consist of foundation plan; roof plan, first and second floor plans; front, rear, two side elevations; wall sections and all necessary interior details. Specifications consist of twenty-two pages of typewritten matter.

PRICE

of Blue Prints, together with a complete set of typewritten specifications

ONLY

$12.00

We mail Plans and Specifications the same day order is received.

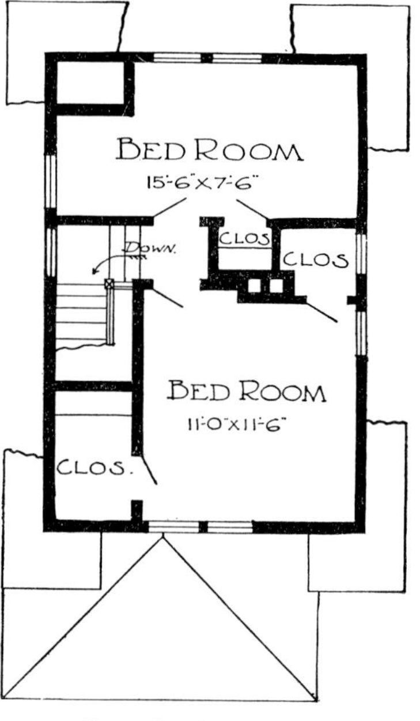

Second Floor Plan

Design No. 2003=B

Size: Width, 19 feet 10 inches; Length, 38 feet

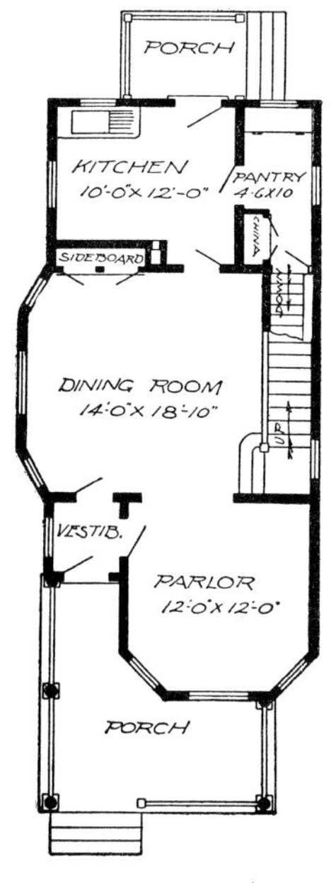

First Floor Plan

Blue prints consist of basement plan; first and second floor plans; front, two side elevations; wall sections and all necessary interior details. Specifications consist of twenty-two pages of typewritten matter.

PRICE

of Blue Prints, together with a complete set of typewritten specifications

ONLY

$10.00

We mail Plans and Specifications the same day order is received.

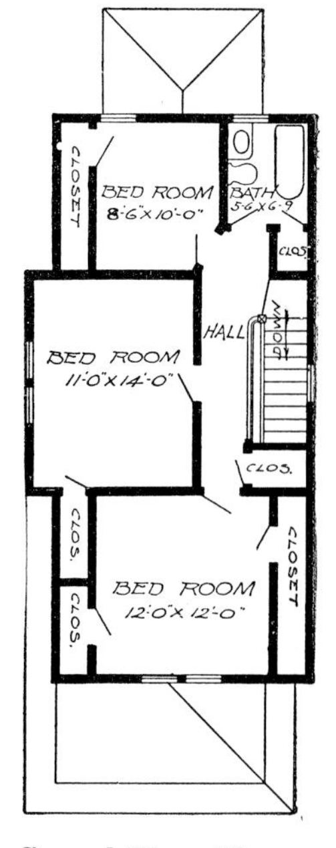

Second Floor Plan

Design No. 5053

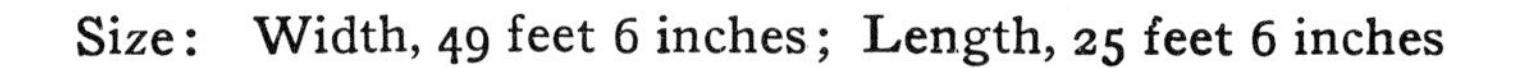

Size: Width, 49 feet 6 inches; Length, 25 feet 6 inches

PRICE

of Blue Prints, together with a complete set of typewritten specifications

ONLY

$8.00

We mail Plans and Specifications the same day order is received.

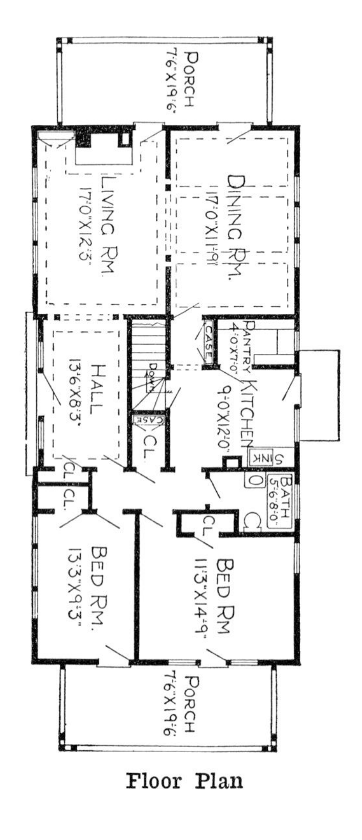

Floor Plan

Blue prints consist of basement plan; roof plan; floor plan; front, rear, two side elevations; wall sections and all necessary interior details. Specifications consist of twenty-two pages of typewritten matter.

Design No. 5017

Size: Width, 24 feet 6 inches; Length, 46 feet 6 inches

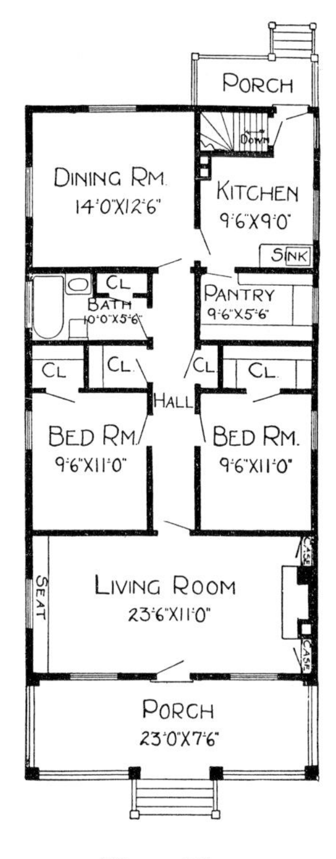

Floor Plan

Blue prints consist of basement plan; floor plan; front, rear, two side elevations; wall sections and all necessary interior details. Specifications consist of twenty-two pages of typewritten matter.

PRICE

of Blue Prints, together with a complete set of typewritten specifications

ONLY

$8.00

We mail Plans and Specifications the same day order is received.

Design No. 5083

Size: Width, 26 feet 6 inches; Length, 35 feet 6 inches

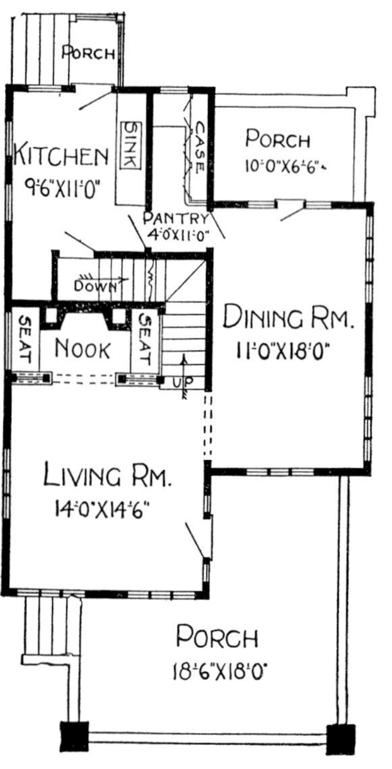

First Floor Plan

Blue prints consist of cellar and foundation plan; roof plan; first and second floor plans; front, two side elevations; wall sections and all necessary interior details. Specifications consist of twenty-two pages of typewritten matter.

PRICE

of Blue Prints, together with a complete set of typewritten specifications

ONLY

$12.00

We mail Plans and Specifications the same day order is received.

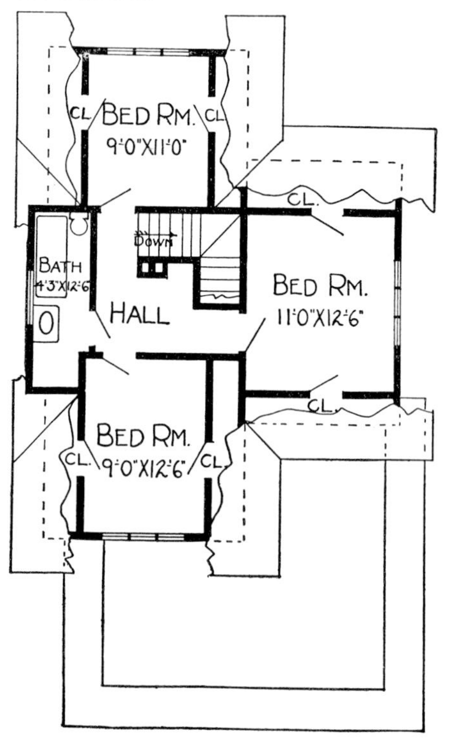

Second Floor Plan

Design No. 5086

Size: Width, 30 feet; Length, 28 feet

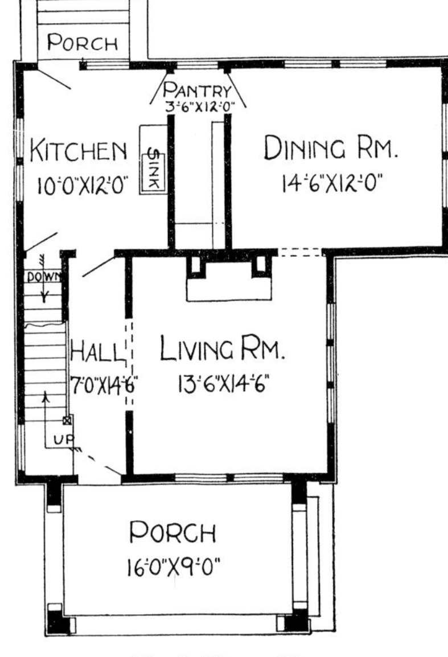

First Floor Plan

Blue prints consist of cellar and foundation plan; roof plan; first and second floor plans; front, rear, two side elevations; wall sections and all necessary interior details. Specifications consist of twenty-two pages of typewritten matter.

PRICE

of Blue Prints, together with a complete set of typewritten specifications

ONLY

We mail Plans and Specifications the same day order is received.

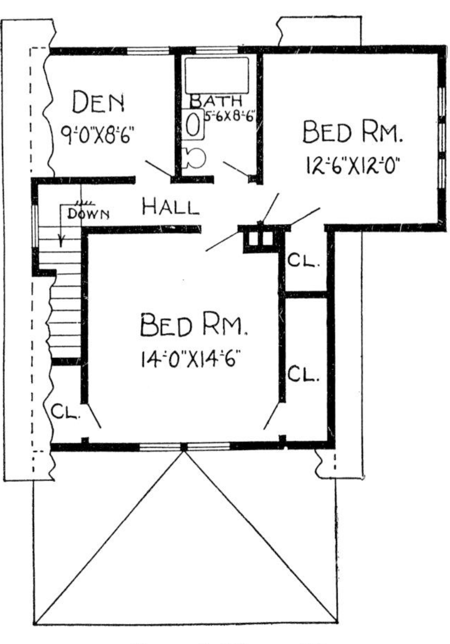

Second Floor Plan

Design No. 5115

Size: Width, 27 feet 6 inches;
Length, 23 feet 6 inches

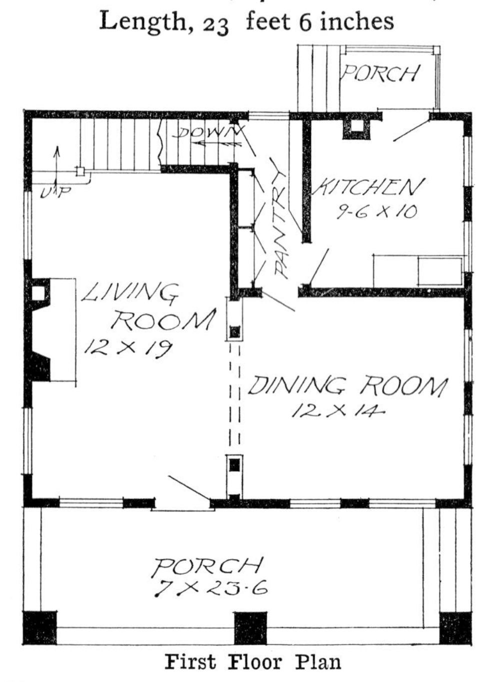

First Floor Plan

Blue prints consist of basement plan; first and second floor plans; front, two side elevations; wall sections and all necessary interior details. Specifications consist of twenty-two pages of typewritten matter.

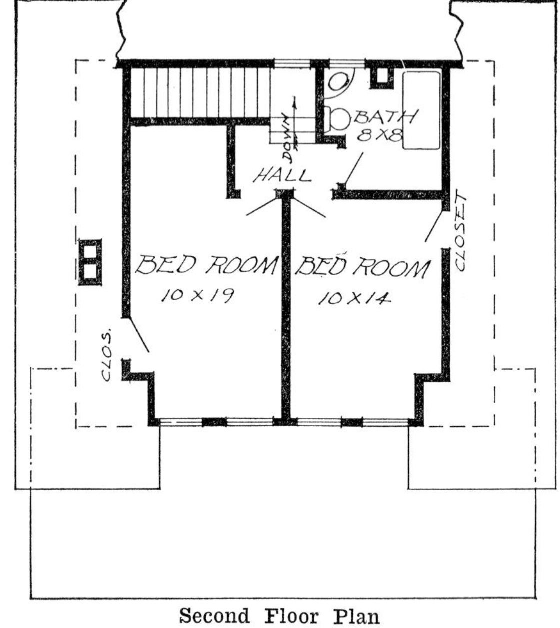

Second Floor Plan

PRICE

of Blue Prints, together with a complete set of typewritten specifications

ONLY

$12.00

We mail Plans and Specifications the same day order is received.

HOME

of the

Radford Publications

Radford Building

1827-29-31-33 Prairie Ave., Chicago, Ill.

INDEX

Design.	Page.	Estimated Cost. From About.	Estimated Cost. To About.	Price Plans and Specifi-cations.
5112	183	$1,375.00	$1,500.00	$ 8.00
5113	36	2,250.00	2,500.00	12.00
5114	96	1,650.00	1,825.00	10.00
5115	218	2,300.00	5,250.00	12.00
5116	185	1,550.00	1,700.00	10.00
5117	67	1,500.00	1,650.00	10.00
5118	179	1,575.00	1,725.00	8.00
5119	114	2,075.00	2,250.00	12.00
5120	52	2,750.00	3,000.00	12.00
5121	95	1,925.00	2,100.00	12.00
5122	196	2,650.00	2,850.00	10.00
5123	69	1,375.00	1,500.00	8.00
5124	92	2,150.00	2,325.00	12.00
5125	76	2,325.00	2,450.00	8.00
5126	158	1,150.00	1,300.00	8.00
5127	81	2,275.00	2,425.00	10.00
5128	145	1,400.00	1,550.00	8.00
5129	137	1,950.00	2,100.00	10.00
5130	80	1,475.00	1,650.00	8.00
5131	39	1,650.00	1,800.00	8.00
5132	184	1,875.00	2,075.00	12.00
5133	107	1,500.00	1,650.00	10.00
5134	109	1,650.00	1,800.00	10.00
5135	105	1,275.00	1,450.00	8.00
5136	61	1,350.00	1,500.00	10.00
5137	128	1,425.00	1,550.00	10.00
5138	204	1,450.00	1,575.00	10.00
5139	108	1,375.00	1,500.00	10.00
5140	104	1,350.00	1,525.00	8.00
5141	194	1,275.00	1,450.00	10.00
5142	201	2,275.00	2,450.00	8.00
5143	211	2,175.00	2,300.00	8.00
5144	188	1,850.00	2,000.00	12.00
5145	116	1,375.00	1,500.00	8.00
5146	210	1,125.00	1,250.00	8.00
5147	206	2,225.00	2,350.00	8.00
5149	117	2,425.00	2,600.00	10.00
5150	180	1,500.00	1,650.00	10.00
2003-B	213	2,550.00	2,800.00	10.00
2005-B	189	2,250.00	2,500.00	12.00
2008-B	154	2,000.00	2,250.00	12.00
2017-B	168	1,850.00	2,250.00	12.00
2046-B	195	950.00	1,100.00	10.00
2115-B	173	1,475.00	1,625.00	10.00
2121-B	143	1,675.00	1,850.00	10.00
2131-B	199	2,125.00	2.300.00	12.00
2138-B	126	1,625.00	1,775.00	10.00
2509-B	142	1,875.00	2,050.00	12.00
2525-B	149	2,125.00	2,300.00	12.00

Design.	Page.	Estimated Cost. From About.	Estimated Cost. To About.	Price Plans and Specifi-cations.
2544-B	135	$3,750.00	$4,000.00	$15.00
2545-B	134	4,250.00	4,500.00	15.00
2546-B	177	2,075.00	2,250.00	10.00
2560-B	181	1,250.00	1,400.00	10.00
6001-B	15	3,850.00	4,100.00	15.00
6039-B	25	3,950.00	4,100.00	12.00
6041-B	159	2,100.00	2,300.00	10.00
6042-B	31	2,400.00	2,550.00	10.00
6056-B	169	3,450.00	3,650.00	12.00
6061-B	30	2,150.00	2,300.00	10.00
6065-B	205	3,475.00	3,625.00	12.00
6073-B	192	2,900.00	3,100.00	10.00
6078-B	60	2,150.00	2,300.00	12.00
6086-B	136	2,250.00	2,400.00	12.00
7019-B	16	2,650.00	2,850.00	12.00
7021-B	97	2,550.00	2,700.00	12.00
7030-B	118	2,500.00	2,750.00	12.00
7038-B	176	2,825.00	3,000.00	12.00
7040-B	85	1,150.00	1,300.00	10.00
7044-B	119	3,000.00	3,250.00	12.00
7045-B	148	2,250.00	2,450.00	12.00
7047-B	57	1,850.00	2,000.00	12.00
7055-B	187	1,950.00	2,100.00	12.00
7063-B	167	1,600.00	1,750.00	10.00
7067-B	64	2,700.00	2,900.00	12.00
7081-B	62	1,000.00	1,150.00	10.00
7098-B	33	2,150.00	2,325.00	12.00
8199-B	28	1,975.00	2,200.00	15.00
8206-B	122	3,500.00	3,800.00	15.00
8209-B	87	2,200.00	2,450.00	10.00
8245-B	151	1,750.00	1,900.00	12.00
8254-B	153	1,675.00	1,825.00	10.00
8255-B	190	1,850.00	2,000.00	12.00
8295-B	70	2,150.00	2,300.00	10.00
8301-B	42	2,000.00	2,200.00	10.00
8302-B	19	2,275.00	2,500.00	12.00
8329-B	71	1,875.00	2,000.00	10.00
8334-B	23	3,200.00	3,400.00	12.00
9009-B	155	1,650.00	1,800.00	10.00
9027-B	178	1,400.00	1,600.00	10.00
9032-B	193	1,500.00	1,650.00	10.00
9039-B	56	2,650.00	2,800.00	12.00
9042-B	200	1,200.00	1,450.00	10.00
9046-B	34	1,500.00	1,750.00	12.00
9058-B	32	2,300.00	2,600.00	12.00
9065-B	147	900.00	1,050.00	10.00
9074-B	102	1,500.00	1,750.00	10.00
9085-B	170	1,350.00	1,500.00	10.00
9090-B	26	1,350.00	1,500.00	10.00
9515	121	6,475.00	6,875.00	26.00
9519	120	3,150.00	3,550.00	22.00